ISLAMIC MOVEMENTS
IMPACT ON POLITICAL STABILITY
IN THE ARAB WORLD

ISLAMIC MOVEMENTS
IMPACT ON POLITICAL STABILITY IN THE ARAB WORLD

THE EMIRATES CENTER FOR STRATEGIC STUDIES AND RESEARCH

THE EMIRATES CENTER FOR STRATEGIC STUDIES AND RESEARCH

The Emirates Center for Strategic Studies and Research (ECSSR) is an independent research institution dedicated to the promotion of professional studies and educational excellence in the UAE, the Gulf and the Arab world. Since its establishment in Abu Dhabi in 1994, ECSSR has served as a focal point for scholarship on political, economic and social matters. Indeed, ECSSR is at the forefront of analysis and commentary on Arab affairs.

The Center seeks to provide a forum for the scholarly exchange of ideas by hosting conferences and symposia, organizing workshops, sponsoring a lecture series and publishing original and translated books and research papers. ECSSR also has an active fellowship and grant program for the writing of scholarly books and for the translation into Arabic of work relevant to the Center's mission. Moreover, ECSSR has a large library including rare and specialized holdings, and a state-of-the-art technology center, which has developed an award-winning website that is a unique and comprehensive source of information on the Gulf.

Through these and other activities, ECSSR aspires to engage in mutually beneficial professional endeavors with comparable institutions worldwide, and to contribute to the general educational and scientific development of the UAE.

The views expressed in this book do not necessarily reflect those of the ECSSR.

First published in 2003 by
The Emirates Center for Strategic Studies and Research
PO Box 4567, Abu Dhabi, United Arab Emirates

E-mail: pubdis@ecssr.ac.ae
pubdis@ecssr.com

Website: http://www.ecssr.ac.ae
http://www.ecssr.com

Originally published in Arabic by
The Emirates Center for Strategic Studies and Research
Translated by Dr. Ahmad Moussalli

ISBN 9948-00-546-5 hardback edition

ISBN 9948-00-545-7 paperback edition

CONTENTS

Introduction

Contemporary Islamic movements were born out of the simultaneous convergence, both on the internal and external levels, of multiple, complex, diverse but interconnected factors impacting on or at play in the Islamic and Arab worlds. Externally, World War I and its outcomes resulted in an increase in the number of Arab and Islamic states under direct Western colonialist domination and the concomitant replacement of Islamic with Western values, which brought about a moral crisis within Islamic Arab society.

The collapse of the Ottoman Caliphate in 1924 was also a seminal event that heralded a new phase in the thinking of those intellectuals who contributed to the rise of Islamic movements. Renewed emphasis was placed on the Islamic state as a religious necessity that must be adhered to. Hence, politics overshadowed all the discourses of the Islamic movements, reflecting the belief that the rise of the state is essential for Islamic life and that its collapse leads to the disintegration of that life.

As these external factors exerted their influence, internal factors began to interact with them. The most important was the rise of the nation-state as an alternative to the comprehensive Islamic unity of Islamic and Arab states. The phenomenon of the nation-state ensued from a period of conflict waged by all indigenous forces against Western colonialism, ending in liberation and independence. The nation-states adopted different forms of liberal, secular or leftist thought instead of Islamic thinking. The means to effect a change in this way of thinking differed from one individual to the next and from one movement to another. It was attendant on the internal conditions of each state that predicated friction and confrontation or agreement and appeasement. Nonetheless, all these states used Islam, as well as some Islamic teachings relating to some aspect of life such as personal law, as an instrument to add legitimacy to their existence.

Many factors have shaped the relationship between Islamic movements and political regimes, manifest mainly through cautious appeasement or violent confrontation—the latter is rooted in a divergence of orientations and justifications, resulting in the rejection of the one group by the other. Some of the determining factors are the objectives of the Islamic movements, their particular contextual history and the various relations they formed with the diverse regimes, particularly in the Arab world. Also important in this respect are the different views and objectives of some of the movements' leaders and ideologists and their reading of the specific conditions of the Islamic movement and prevailing local factors. This is especially the case when it comes to their evaluation of regimes and the latter's objectives and characteristics, including proximity to Islam as well as the level of political freedom given to people or the exercise of tyranny and authoritarianism. Another factor is the position of the particular Arab and Islamic state within the regional and international contexts. Of note here are the experiences of the particular state in resisting colonialism and its participation in wars against Israel, the absence of democracy in many political regimes and the latter's inability to achieve progress on many fronts of political, economic and social life.

Furthermore, the Islamic movements have themselves fallen into many difficulties because of their ideologies and their inability to correctly understand the local and international social and political realities. They have been unable to provide realistic Islamic alternatives that take into consideration the challenges of the modern world, with its changes and contradictions, and to offer solutions to a variety of problems. The movements responded to the challenges presented by ruling secular regimes through the use of force and violence, be it to defend themselves or to achieve certain objectives, which has led movements and regimes in many Arab states into perennial conflict. Ironically, the result has been greater losses and more problems, and the further inability of the state to serve the people in all sectors of life. Moreover, these conflicts have not been limited to the regimes and the movements but have involved whole societies, which have paid heavily in terms of life, property and security. There are several examples of this in Arab countries.

This type of conflict – attack and counter-attack, suspicion, excommunication and charges of treason – has become important to a number of states for different reasons. In many instances there is an increase in the number of Islamic movements and the rise in popularity of some of them. This heightened popularity is grounded in the lack of a responsible reaction on the part of many Arab and Islamic states to the popular need for freedom, pluralism and political participation, and in the deterioration in many spheres that directly impact on the livelihood of people, such as unemployment and the high cost of living. These have been exacerbated by a restriction of freedoms and increasingly restrictive laws. There are other factors that impact on the Islamic nation as a whole, such as its weakening within Arab states that have experienced defeat in war or increasing foreign domination, both political and economic.

Other important aspects of regional and/or international significance witnessed in the last two decades of the twentieth century are the victory of the Islamic Revolution in Iran, the collapse of the Soviet Union and the socialist camp and the global hegemony of the United States.

During recent times, the convergence of all these factors has led the Islamic movements in general to direct their efforts not only against Arab political regimes, but also against the Western powers that back them. This, in turn, has increased the West's awareness of these movements and has resulted in attempts by some Western powers, especially after the collapse of the Soviet Union, to depict political Islam as the emerging threat, one that should be vigorously combated. Consequently, there is now a strong focus on studying this Islamic phenomenon and on the search for the reasons for its growth, expansion and strength, as well as the reasons why its proponents have resorted to force and violence. It is in

[3]

this context that The Emirates Center for Strategic Studies and Research in Abu Dhabi hosted a symposium to explore this phenomenon and its impact on stability in the Arab world. This book, which has emanated from the symposium, represents the views and analyses of a number of distinguished and specialist scholars on different aspects concerning Islamic movements.

The attempt to understand the Islamic movement phenomenon requires recognition of the causes and conditions that have led to its emergence and that have accompanied its growth. Chapter 1 by Abdulwahhab El-Affendi focuses on this aspect. He sheds light on the conditions of the emergence of Islamic movements and how these particular factors have affected the role each movement has played in the political and social life of Islamic states. He also discusses how the role of a movement may differ from its initial perception and the reason for this: Is it an aspect pertinent to the movement itself, to the Arab and Islamic states in which these movements find themselves or to their contextual and historical circumstances?

The concept of political Islam, in theory and practice, is not a new one but has old roots that Hasan Hanafi analyzes in Chapter 2. It is explored through a discussion of the Caliphate, belief and unbelief, and disobedience. Muslim sects have political origins, whether loyal to state powers, such as the Ash'arites, or opposed to them, such as the Mu'tazilites, Kharijites and Shi'ites. They include the modern roots of religious reform movements that started with Jamal Al-Din Al-Afghani and constituted the nucleus of Arab liberation movements against the modern colonialization of the Islamic world. The author also analyzes the contemporary roots of political Islam, especially after the confrontation of the Muslim Brotherhood in Egypt and Syria with the Free Officers and its subsequent exclusion from political life in the 1950s. The author is of the opinion that the slogans of political Islam reflect the psychological and social state of political Islamic movements, one that represents the rejection of human governance, secular ideologies and contemporary human laws which change according to political considerations. He discusses the dialectics of legitimacy and illegitimacy, the resort to political violence, and the ability of movements of political Islam to be

[4]

integrated into the political life of any society and to address the challenges of this age.

Some Islamic movements have characteristically employed force and violence to achieve their objectives, while others have not. Hence, it has become common to describe the movements as either moderate or radical, though moderation and radicalism are relative concepts and are subject to circumstances, causes and motives that differ from one place to another and from one age to another. Some causes are related to the nature of the movements and their understanding of their messages, others are external and relate to how societies and political regimes deal with them. These factors lead, in the final analysis, to diverse views and methods among Islamic movements. In Chapter 3, Emad Al-Din Shahin analyzes the themes of moderation and radicalism in an attempt to arrive at the consequences of moderation and radicalism and their impact on the future relationship between current regimes and Islamic movements and, thus, their impact on the Arab world.

Islamic movements have different views on democracy, political participation and pluralism emanating from diverse understandings of the legitimate sources of political governance and their legal underpinnings. Ahmad Moussalli explores the sources of these views in Chapter 4, and whether they are derived from categorical ideological and immutable positions or from tactical positions that allow the movements to participate in political systems and then to rise up against such systems. In other words, are the views of the Islamic movements also their objectives, or are they only means toward achieving their objectives, and how do these views impact on the nature of the relationship between the movements and the regimes?

In the final analysis, the Islamic movements represent one of the most important opposition forces in the Arab world. The relationship between the ruling regimes and opposition is generally characterized by confrontation. Fawaz Gerges discusses in Chapter 5 whether this kind of relationship will last or whether the regimes will initiate a positive engagement with the movements of political Islam, which can be used in a process of national renaissance. Are the regimes going to keep the door shut on political participation and therefore maintain the status quo of confrontation and instability?

The belligerence that characterizes certain Islamic movements in some Arab countries and their partial political participation in other countries poses many questions over the nature of the Islamic movements and especially their future within the context of local, regional and international realities. In Chapter 6, Ridwan Al-Sayyid analyzes the future of Islamic movements in light of their political participation in many Arab states and their discourses and practices, as well as the relationship between the particular discourse and the emanating practice. He also reviews the prospects of the movements at the political, organizational and intellectual levels.

The studies included in this book represent the views, perspectives and analyses of their authors who have expertise in a field that has become prominent in the world today, especially after the events of September 11, 2001 in the United States of America. The present scenario includes the fact that the United States has declared war against many Islamic movements in Afghanistan that have been linked to terrorism. In addition, strict laws and regulations over financing and supporting Islamic movements have been promulgated. In this context, it is important to note that the Islamic movements that seek change through political action in their respective countries have been confused with the Islamic movements that struggle to liberate their homelands.

1

Islamic Movements: Establishment, Significance and Contextual Realities

Abdulwahhab El-Affendi

Any discourse on the establishment of Islamic movements presupposes the existence of certain premises and assumptions that yield to the Islamic movements' self-description as being "Islamic," and draws the line between the Islamic nature of these movements and their non-Islamic nature. Therefore, before entering into a discussion on the topic of this paper, one must first explore the pertinent concepts and terminology and define them precisely, so as not to complicate the subject with unnecessary details.

The term "Islamic Movements" (some scholars prefer the term "fundamentalism" which is translated from English, while others tend to use "Islamism" which is derived from Islamist) is used to refer to those groups that are active in the political arena and call for the application of Islamic values and laws in the private and public sphere. Hence, they oppose their governments and other political and social movements, which they regard as either not following or opposing the teachings of Islam.

The term "Islamic movements" is mostly used for the movements that call themselves such and which are active in the domain of politics. It is rare to see this term applied to Sufi movements that are not politically active. Moreover, this description is not normally used for:

- Traditional movements with Islamic background, such as Hizb al-Istiqlal in Morocco or Hizb al-Umma in Sudan;

- Regimes and movements that traditionally rule by the *sharia*, as is the case in the Kingdom of Saudi Arabia, for example, while it is indeed used to describe the movements that oppose such regimes;

- Parties and movements in Iran, though the regime depends on Islamic legitimacy; terms such as "reformers" and "radicals" are mostly used to label the political trends there;

- Modern movements with partial or complete Islamic authority, such as Mujahidin Khalq in Iran, or the al-Hizb al-Jumhuri in Sudan that was set up by the late thinker Mahmud Muhammad Taha;

- Movements that call themselves Islamic, such as the Islamic League in Pakistan, notwithstanding its claim to be Islamic.

The above use of the terminology reflects the common or implicit theoretical assumptions about this phenomenon and the nature of its current understanding. These assumptions need to be noted and discussed in order to ascertain their soundness, which we will discuss later.

The Islamic movements seem to distinguish themselves from the general population by claiming Islam for themselves, as if they are entitled to issue judgments on society's inability to live by the values of Islam. They establish themselves as the authority in charge of reminding, calling and sometimes forcing people to address such inability. Some groups react to such claims by rejecting them, even though they may accept the characterization of society as negligent of Islam. They also reject the claim that the Islamic movements are the leaders of the hoped-for awakening. Another reaction completely rejects the bases and the meaning of the claims by saying that societies are really Islamic and do not need any group to remind them of their religion. Conversely, some secularists concur that the role of religion in social life has greatly weakened and that the Islamic movements try to revive it, although they believe that such an action is impossible or in principle undesirable.

We do not want, at this stage, to resolve these claims and counter claims or to decide conclusively on the definitions, until we have clarified some points concerning the theoretical basis for the dialogue, since the resolution of all these issues requires the adoption of a theoretical or moral position.

Theoretical Clarifications

There is an inherent contradiction when a treatment of religious affairs claims a scientific nature. Hugue Didier said that we publish studies about the history of religion because our culture, which we can call European, Western or secular, lacks a sacred physical or mental space. It also lacks all moral attachment to religion. The sacred that is subjected to analysis and jurisprudence loses its sacredness in the strict sense of the word and is transformed into that which is worldly or profane.[1] He adds that the only way that religious anthropology can speak of the sacred is by placing it in an external space, which renders it worldly.

This contradiction or harsh dichotomy may yet bear fruit.[2] The analysis here is based on certain assumptions about the existence of an absolute dichotomy between the worldly and the sacred, and it is an error that the above author falls into when he hastens to reject the common understanding of the relationship between religion and the world in Islam. He says that Islam, like other religions, distinguishes between the world and religion and the sacred and the ordinary. He argues that neither the religious and the worldly nor the sacred and the profane are necessarily connected in the same manner, yet this connection exists by necessity. The mere definition of the separating space or the perimeter delimiting the sacred or divine means drawing the borders and therefore defining what is outside it. The declaration of the sacred means the establishment of the foundations of the worldly system.[3]

Statements by Arab sociologists about the absence of religious sociology in the Arab world call to mind the views of Didier. This shortcoming is attributed to the general ideological environment, which makes the study of religion from a pure social and scientific perspective a

[9]

risk with dire consequences.[4] Such an opinion indirectly supports the perspective that Didier propagates and links the appearance of religious sociology in the West with secularism. The explanation for the lack of religious sociology in the Arab world is related to the continued influence of religion, while the explanation for having a religious sociology in the West rests on the dearth of religion.

This divergence in opinions indicates the existence of yet another crisis in dealing with the religious phenomenon. It is a crisis that some analysts maintain is proof of the failure of the analytical method, likened to a tunnel with no end in sight.[5] This failure is attributed to the core assumptions and premises that generally constitute the foundations of modern sociology and the social sciences. Many specific assumptions about the nature of the universe and the origin of man that underline these sciences make them reject the views of religion on fundamental issues. Furthermore, they fall into contradiction even at the level of basic concepts, as we have seen, when they speak of an absolute opposition between religion and the world, only to confirm that there is an unbreakable connection between what is within the sacred and what is outside of it. Thus, there is no religion outside the world or separate from man, who is the subject of religiosity and the essence of its meaning.

Notwithstanding the assurance of the sociologists that their subject is not the content of religious creed but its social impact, the truth of the matter indicates that the secular background of modern sociology, which opposes religion, cannot but affect how it views religion. The approach of sociology towards religion is amazement at religious fantasies and their dominance, as well as a clinical search for reasons for the continuance of adherence to religion, which is treated as a pathological phenomenon.

One of the most important interests of religious sociology in the West is the study of secularism in modern societies. It is a study that implicitly assumes that secularism is a natural phenomenon accompanying modernity. This is known as the "Secularization Thesis," which assumes that the modern age has witnessed the gradual weakening of the importance and influence of religion on both individual and social life. The role of religion has retracted in political life, social relations and, ultimately, in the life of the individual. Sociologists attribute this phenomenon to the impact of modernity on contemporary societies, starting with the modernization of the economy and the transformation of the economic domain to an independent space away from the impact of religion, then the spread of the impact of this domain to other domains, such as the political and scientific. All of this is reflected in the decrease in the popularity of religious creeds and their impact on society.[6]

According to this analysis, modern societies have lost their sacred center and have become composed of independent and interdependent spaces, each of which with its own special spaces isolated from the impact of religion.[7] The economic space deals with the logic of winning and losing, the political space with the logic of power and the scientific space with the logic of the search for truth. Therefore, generally there has been a near consensus that secularization is the twin of modernization. It is a one-way street, and when societies enter the world of modernization they naturally move toward and enter the world of secularization with no way back.[8] From this perspective, the phenomenon known as the Islamic revival confronts sociology with a problem that cannot be resolved. It contradicts and opposes the assumptions of secularism to a point that modernization seems to have had the opposite impact on Muslim societies, which reinforced religion while entering into the process of modernization.[9] This drove many researchers to conclude that Islam is incapable of secularization.[10]

Furthermore, Islam constituted a new problem for Western thought from the beginning of the latter's orientalist phase, which has added another question to the debate. The question that the specialists, most of whom were adherents to Christian and Jewish beliefs, attempted to answer about the Islamic world during the orientalist phase was: "How could religious innovation and error influence the minds of people in this way?" However, in the modern age, and after secularization became the dominant trend, the question has turned into the following: "Why does Islam stubbornly challenge modernization and secularization? What has happened to the Muslim people so that they continue to reject secularization and modernization? " At this point, we do not want to delve into a critique of orientalism, a mission that great scholars like Edward Said, Brian Turner and others have accomplished very well.[11] I have also discussed the subject elsewhere. It is sufficient here to emphasize an important observation, which is that the modern studies of Islam reproduce orientalism even when they criticize it.[12]

Some critics of the orientalist approach reject the view that Islam resisted secularism and emphasize that, from the early phase, Islam accepted secularization in practice while rejecting it in theory. Adherents to this view reject the common notion of the necessary concomitance between religion and the state in Islam. They insist, on the one hand, that the secular reality has affected Muslim society and that what is called the Islamic revival is a recognition of the reality of secularization, since some Islamic movements had to use repression and violence to impose their views on a society that they view as having disobeyed religious values. On the other hand, this revival is itself a reflection of the phenomenon of secularization and one of its manifestations.[13] Therefore, we are faced here with some basic theoretical dilemmas, starting with the tools and assumptions of the scientific method and ending with ideology and presumptions. All of these are problems that need attention in the study of the Islamic phenomenon. There are many platitudes about what has become known as the Islamic revival. These platitudes presume certain positions mostly without acknowledging, criticizing or proving them. However, the correct scientific study of this phenomenon must reject these positions if it cannot prove them. Hence, this study will follow a critical method towards such positions and assumptions, and draw attention to them when necessary.

Intellectual and Historical Background

The issues of renewal and religious resurgence are not intellectually and historically unexpected in the Islamic experience. The Islamic creed considers resurgence, renewal and revival to be an original part of its assumptions, starting with Islam itself which is regarded as a revival of Abrahamic monotheism, a renewal of that which was buried under the deviations that occurred to formerly divine religions and ending with an emphasis on the repeated Islamic texts regarding the need to protect religion from disintegration and deviation. Part of this necessity is the steps required for protection, including science and learning, worship, enjoining good and forbidding evil, *jihad*, self-criticism and everything that protects against deviation and negligence, as well as the ability to correct that when it happens.

Historically, the Islamic experience has witnessed continuous activity on all levels to achieve this objective. In Islam, many scientific and cultural movements have emerged, starting with the collection and writing down of the Qur'an, and then the establishment and development of Islamic sciences such as jurisprudence, *Hadith*, theology, the Arabic language, translation and transmission of sciences. There was also the rise of theological and juristic schools and intellectual and spiritual movements such as Sufism and philosophy. Politically, there have been many movements, confrontations and uprisings, starting with the wars of apostasy and the revolution against 'Uthman bin 'Affan and the al-Khawarij movement, then the revolution of Imam Al-Hussein, the movement of Al-Mukhtar Al-Thaqafi who established the first Shi'ite state in Iraq in the year 66 of the Hijra, the movement of 'Abd Allah Al-Zubayr, the revolution of 'Abd Al-Rahman bin Al-Ash'ath, then the movement of Al-Imam Zayd bin 'Ali and many others. Also included are the 'Abbasid revolution and the revolutions and uprisings that followed, as well as the states that they brought about such as the Buwaihids, Fatimids and Isma'ilis. All these movements and uprisings emerged in the name of combating deviations from the ideal model that the Prophet and his Caliphs established for the people, and were aimed at regaining the purity of that model. We should not forget, in this context, the continuous *jihad* to defend Islam against its enemies in the outside world, to expand the territories of its domain, or to defend it against any aggression, as well as to force out those who have succeeded in occupying the land of Islam. Thus, the phenomenon of revival and renewal and related claims are not new, and has not emerged only in this age.

Until recent times, history witnessed repeated calls where those in charge positioned themselves as the defenders of religion against any danger and deviation, while condemning the state or society for its deviation, which made rectification and reform necessary. This situation prevailed until the dawn of the modern age, where the domain of Islam went through many reforms aimed at the renovation of what had been destroyed in religion and the revival of what had been abolished. Included in such trends are the movement of Muhammad 'Abd Al-Wahhab in Najd (1703–1791), the Dalhawiyya in India (1702–1762), the al-Sanusiyya movement in North Africa (1859–1878), the al-Mahdiyya in Sudan (1881–1898), the movement of Dan Fodio in Nigeria (1754–1817) and others in many different lands of the Islamic world. The movements of mostly political nature were preceded and followed by many spiritual and social movements. Examples of the latter are the many Sufi orders that were established and spread, such as al-Khilwatiyya, al-Idrisiyya, al-Tijaniyya, al-Sumaniyya, and al-Khatmiyya in the eighteenth and the nineteenth centuries, as well as older Sufi orders, such as al-Naqshbindiyya, Shadhiliyya and al-Qadiriyya that were revived, and still others that spread widely.

Nevertheless, all of these movements that came before modernity are distinguished as being movements that made religion the basis of their work and their objectives. This also included the movements that tended towards politics, such as the al-Sanusiyya, al-Mahdiyya and al-Wahhabiyya. They were not concerned with playing a role in economic, political or social reform except when it was religiously mandated and was the fulfillment of some value or teaching. The reformers did not think that the objective of their reform was the improvement of livelihood, the increase of the welfare of Muslims or similar mundane interests. On the contrary, it is likely that they viewed the sacrifice of the ephemeral pleasures of the world as a means to get on the right track and to revive religion. In Sudan, Imam Muhammad Ahmad Al-Mahdi summarized this vision succinctly: "I came to you with the destruction of this world and the building of the next."[14] This meant that the ultimate authority for the Muslim nation was always internal and largely religious, for these movements were seeking to reform religious and worldly affairs from a purely religious perspective.

However, this characteristic started to change after the confrontation of the Muslim world with modernity, which included the military confrontation with rising European powers. That period witnessed the gradual transformation of the nation from a superpower, which ran its affairs and dominated its environment, to just one power among many great powers, as represented by the Ottoman Empire and, to a lesser extent, Egypt under the leadership Muhammad 'Ali. This status was quickly lost with the collapse of the Ottoman Empire and the fact that most of the Islamic states fell under the burden of colonialism.

Colonialism was a completely new experience for the Islamic nation, which had confronted many crises and trials before, including the invasion of the Moguls and the Crusaders, the loss of Spain and defeats in other wars, struggles, collapses, and the internal crumbling of its ideal system. However, none of these disasters affected the self-confidence of the nation as much as European domination. During the darkest periods of the Mogul Empire and the Crusaders' invasions, or in the calamity that followed the fall of Spain, the question "who was right?" was never entertained. The reasons were that the Moguls did not provide an alternative worldview of life and the universe, using only violent force to subjugate. For their part, the Crusaders in Palestine and Spain did not offer any thing new that was not known to the Muslims or any issue in theology that was not already resolved by the Muslims, even though the Crusader style did not differ much from that of the Moguls. Thus, the Muslim nation did not face an internal schism because of these confrontations and did not doubt its inevitable victory over its enemies. In fact, this victory would be massive and complete, militarily, politically, culturally and morally. This is why radical reconsideration of the experiences, ideas and practices was not seriously entertained, and the reaction was limited to repeating the well-established notion that the nation would not succeed in the future except by that which had made the nation succeed at its inception.

Nevertheless, something started to change gradually during the last three decades of the nineteenth century, and along with it came the change in the consciousness of the nation about the nature of the challenges that it was facing. In the beginning, the emphasis was on military challenges, where the focus was on reorganizing and modernizing armies and their armaments. In addition, attention was given to the acquisition of and training in the modern sciences, in fields such as engineering and medicine. This work was then extended to include the study of additional disciplines and the sending of research missions to the West, which led to more knowledge about what some regarded as the reasons for European superiority. Some then expressed the view that superiority was not related only to the military aspect. The initial infatuation with the Western political model, as was the case with Rifa'at Al-Tahtawi (1801–1873), changed to deep speculation about the secrets of its success – for example, Khayr Al-Din Al-Tunisi who died in 1890 – then to an ideological imitation as manifest in intellectual and political movements, which started with the national movement in Turkey and spread to the Arab world, then in the constitutional movements in Iran and the Ottoman Empire and finally in reform attempts in Egypt, Tunisia, Iran and the Ottoman state.

It was not long before the age of revolutions started, beginning with the revolution of Ahmad 'Urabi in Egypt in 1882, then the revolt of Harakat al-Itihad wa al-Taraqi in Turkey in 1908, the great Arab revolution in 1916, and then an unending chain of revolts and revolutions, the consequences of which still prevail. On the intellectual level many multi-dimensional issues were raised. The most profound and notable was raised by Jamal Al-Din Al-Afghani (1839–1897) who saw the dwindling of philosophical thought in the Islamic domain as the reason for the lack of scientific progress of the nation. He also raised some questions about understanding religion, repeated by many of his contemporaries and people after him, which emphasized the necessity of reconsidering the dominant religious concepts and the return to the pure origin of Islam, as was known by the pious ancestors. These questions included attempts to absorb new ideas and institutions, such as democracy, the parliament, modern economic institutions and others, and were met with admiration by Muslim thinkers.

What is noticeable is that the main concern for all reformist and intellectual movements, revolutions, revolts and upheavals was precisely the dire worldly situation, the backwardness, weakness and poverty of Muslims, and their decline in contrast with the progress of others. Shakib Arslan's book, *Limadha Ta'akhara al-Muslimun wa Taqaddama Ghayruhum?* translated as *Why Muslims Declined and Others Progressed*,[15] summarizes that concern. This approach constituted in itself an essential leap towards the objectives of the reformist orientations in the Islamic world.

One of the best examples of the distinctive characteristics of this prominent model was the marked difference between the theses and orientations of the Mahdi movement in Sudan, in 1881, and the 'Urabi revolution in Egypt in 1882. The two movements were launched about the same time and in one country, but the difference between them was great. The Mahdi movement almost never mentioned worldly concerns in its literature and theses, while the 'Urabi movement almost never mentioned religion. This was, in turn, an indication that the new world where the 'Urabi revolution took place was completely different in many of its characteristics, authorities and interests from the traditional world that the Muslims of pre-modernity had known.

Perhaps what really distinguished this new world was the Muslims' awareness of the existence of other worlds, dimensions and visions that were different from those known by their predecessors. In addition, they were affected by the new worlds and longed to participate in them. These were the worlds where the modern Islamic movements surfaced and began to take their form within new frameworks.

The Establishment of Islamic Movements

If we return to our previous discussion about the definition of modern Islamic movements, we can say that the most distinguishing characteristic of these movements is their modernity. They are movements that are established in the environment of modernity and as a response to it. They are also Islamic in the sense that they have selected an Islamic response to the challenges of modernity that is based on Islamic authority. They do not react, like other movements, out of the logic of mere effectiveness and do not depend on values, ideologies or authorities other than those of Islam. To a large extent, therefore, these movements are the child of the new world that regards the destruction of the traditional Islamic framework, in other words the modernity-secularization duality, as one of its most distinguishing characteristics. These movements have had to reflect the characteristics of this new world and largely shape themselves accordingly, as will be explained below.

There is a near consensus among analysts in this field on linking contemporary Islamic movements to the intellectual and reformist effort exerted by Jamal Al-Din Al-Afghani and his disciple Muhammad Abdu (1849–1905). Al-Afghani and Abdu brought to the fore the characteristics that would distinguish Islamic movements later on, particularly the way these movements are influenced by a modernity that they reject. Some critics of modern Islamic movements believe that linking these movements to Al-Afghani goes beyond intellectual heritage to include methods these critics object to. According to one of these critics, a well-known Israeli writer, Al-Afghani authorized the use of violence to these movements, as well as fickleness and *Taqiyya* (subterfuge).[16]

Attributing this to Al-Afghani requires correction. It is true that Al-Afghani was one of most distinguished reformers of the nineteenth century. He was a notable and inspired personality that combined intellectual depth, leadership abilities and awareness of the dangers that confronted the Muslim nation as well as the changes around it.[17] He also tried to combine in his approach the intellectual educational method with direct political activity. Thus, he was a scholar among politicians and a politician among scholars.[18]

Although Al-Afghani was the product of a traditional Islamic environment and immersed in its sciences, he was greatly aware of the spheres of traditional Islamic thought, for example, the philosophical and social thinking of Ibn Khaldun. This knowledge provided him with the elements that constituted his strength and ability to confront the challenge of the West. He was also open to learning from the outside world.

Al-Afghani influenced a whole generation of Muslims throughout the different regions of the Muslim world that he visited, beginning with Iran through Afghanistan, India, Egypt and then to Istanbul where he died. His influence spread through his journal *Al-'Urwa al-Wuthqa*, which he and Muhammad Abdu published for a year and half in Paris, starting in 1884. Although the two men announced the establishment of an international Islamic organization, also named "al-'Urwa al-Wuthqa," it seems that the organization was more wish than reality. Nevertheless, the impact of the journal was great. It inspired later generations that were moved by its ideas, as mentioned in the memoirs of many thinkers, of whom the most prominent is Sheikh Muhammad Rashid Rida (1865–1935), the disciple of Muhammad Abdu.

Al-Afghani's influence also spread through his disciples, such as Muhammad Abdu, who in turn influenced a whole generation of thinkers and intellectuals in Egypt and Syria, and contributed to the reforming of educational institutions, such as Al-Azhar, and state institutions like the courts. This influence spread through Muhammad Rashid Rida and his journal *Al-Manar*, whose influence reached the farthest corners of the Islamic world, from Morocco to Indonesia.

There is no doubt that the general legacy of this intellectual school, including its main principles and concerns – such as resisting colonialism and regaining the glory of the nation, establishing the basis of the *shura* and the reforming of government, religious reform and the renewal of religion – constituted the bases for the emergence of the modern Islamic movements.

Al-Afghani was keen to distinguish his intellectual and political position from other intellectual and political trends, especially those that tried to make peace with the West and accepted its political domination, or those that tried to give up or bend some Islamic teachings to suit modernity. He launched a strong attack against the modernist school propagated by the Indian reformer Ahmad Khan, criticized Egypt's policy of duplicity regarding the British, and attacked and even called for the killing of the Shah of Iran, Nasr Al-Din, because he gave some concessions to British companies. He also called for adherence to religion and for its revival through a return to its fundamentals and pure origins.

These principles and orientations that were followed by his disciples, for example Abdu and Rida, are considered to be the most distinguishing characteristics of the thinking of modern Islamic movements and their orientations. The theory of this continuity has been asserted by the leaders of the Islamic movements. Hasan Al-Banna did not hide his relationship with Muhammad Rashid Rida. Al-Banna even wanted to concretize his intellectual succession of Rida and his school through the continued publishing and editing of *Al-Manar*, but this was not realized.[19]

All these indications about continuity should not make us forget the different nature of the movement that Hasan Al-Banna established in Isma'iliyya in 1928. The movement was established while Muhammad Rashid Rida was still alive, and the direct factors that led to its establishment were derived from a specific vision of the crisis and the feeling that the existing Islamic institutions, including *Al-Manar* and its school, were not able to solve the crisis. As Al-Banna said, he was reacting to the period after World War I in Egypt, because of the emergence of trends that were very Western—intellectually, culturally, behaviorally and morally.

Al-Banna's perception of the threat moved him to mobilize scholars and the clergy of the religious institution in order to confront corruption and degeneration. However, their reaction was frustrating and drove Al-Banna to take a personal and individual approach to confront the crisis, including preaching in coffee houses and public streets. In Isma'iliyya, he soon faced the problem that his vision drew a following, and thus demanded action from his part to accommodate those who responded to his call. His response, in turn, also had unintended consequences, which began with answering some laborers' demand for help in studying the affairs of religion and the practice of rituals.[20] From this little nucleus the movement grew—from concerns about teaching, prayers, ablution and attendance in mosques to confronting larger issues, and then extending the group's membership and creating branches, until it spread all over the country and its membership reached tens if not hundreds of thousands.

Similar local and circumstantial issues were the decisive factor in the establishment of the Islamic group by Abu Al-A'la Al-Mawdudi, in 1941. Al-Mawdudi was a young man with a traditional religious education who, like Al-Banna, addressed public issues within the framework of the Muslim concerns in India, in the early phase of his life. He worked in journalism. Yet, unlike Al-Banna in Egypt, whose concerns were predominantly social, Al-Mawdudi's concerns were political in nature and revolved around the status of Muslims in India. Al-Mawdudi's contribution started on traditional grounds, where he defended Islam against its Hindu critics. However, he soon moved to criticize the orientations of the Islamic leadership in India, starting with decrying the call of the Indian National Congress to set up a democratic secular state that unified the Muslims with the Hindus, stressing that such a state would not be truly secular because it would favor the Hindu majority. He also rejected it on the grounds that the state would force Muslims to serve the national state and its principles, not Islam and its creed.[21]

Al-Mawdudi's strong feelings against the position of Muslims in the Indian state led him to agree with the call that the poet Muhammad Iqbal launched and which was carried by the Islamic League, namely, the establishment of a separate national state for the Muslims. However, Al-Mawdudi reserved his severest criticism for this national state, which was delivered in his famous lecture at Aligrah University, in 1940, under the title "The Method of Islamic Revolution," where he summarized the basic orientations of his thinking.[22] According to his vision, the call of the Islamic League to set up a national state for Muslims in India contradicted the teaching of Islam, and this could not lead to the establishment of an Islamic state in the long run, as its supporters claimed it would. The reason for this was that the national call essentially contradicted the Islamic ideal, and therefore it could not be a step towards Islam, but contrary to it. The principles of nationalism rested on unity in the interests of a specific group that controlled worldly goods only, while the Islamic state was based on an ideal and its Islamism was based on creed.[23]

The argument for Al-Mawdudi was that the Muslim nation would not succeed except by doing what earlier Muslims had done, and that the method that Prophet Muhammad had followed was to establish the Muslim nation first and then the Islamic state. This could happen when a nucleus of Muslims, who believed in the Islamic call, united people around it and persisted in maintaining its fundamentals without compromise, until it overcame difficulty and enmity and established the ideal of Islam. Through victory over difficulties, the group would earn the honor of carrying the banner of Islam. Thus, through overcoming difficulties and enemies, the Muslim nation and its state would be born, where governance would be for God only and this would manifest through obedience to the *sharia*.[24] Al-Mawdudi called this political model of the state a theodemocracy.[25] This implies that government is based on *shura* among people, but that ultimate authority is reserved for the rule of God and the *sharia* of Islam.

The two movements that were established by Al-Banna and Al-Mawdudi grew and spread outside their own countries. The Muslim Brotherhood became one of the most powerful political movements in Egypt to a point that some commentators even said that it might be the only real popular movement there.[26] It was exposed to conflict with political forces and the state, which twice led to its dissolution, in 1948 and 1955. After years of repression and the state's refusal to officially recognize it, it is still one of the stronger, if not the strongest, political movements in Egypt.

The Islamic group in India also acquired popular support, although it followed an elitist approach that was different from the popular method of the Muslim Brotherhood. The group intended to uphold an elitist discourse and to limit its membership, but worked to have an active presence on the Indian subcontinent (India, Pakistan and Bangladesh) and in emigrant countries. However, the intellectual influence of the group and its founder, Al-Mawdudi, extended to include the whole of the Islamic world. According to one analyst, Al-Mawdudi might be one of the most widely read Muslim thinkers in the world.[27] His influence reached the heart of the Muslim Brotherhood movement and, through it, the Arab world by way of the writings of Sayyid Qutb. Qutb derived an important part of his ideas from Al-Mawdudi, especially the concept of the *jahiliyya* of society and the role of the elite in establishing the foundations of Islamic society.

Many reasons have been given for the widespread existence of these movements in Islamic societies, especially after they gave rise to "the Islamic awakening" in the 1970s and 1980s. Some analysts saw in this success the surge of the petro-dollar and its impact.[28] Others concurred that the reason was a combination of pride after the October War of 1973, dismay because of the failure of secular governments and ideologies, and the crisis of identity and inferiority complex towards the West.[29] Still others justified this development by referring to different crises, from the global economic collapse and the recession of 1929, through to the economic and political crises that hit the Islamic world in the 1970s and 1980s.[30] These crises were accompanied by a tense class struggle and failure, and the bankruptcy of the secular opposition.

There are still other analysts who maintain that these movements are defensive reactions in the Islamic society, which was overrun by modernity and threatened with disintegration and collapse.[31] Similar interpretations ascribe the rise of the Islamic movements to the nature of Islamic religion itself and its inability to be rationalized and secularized. A number of them add that modernity strengthened the position of textual Islam as opposed to popular Islam, instead of leading to the decline of the influence of the text as happened with Christianity.[32] Some of the analyses that follow the same line of thinking refer the rise of fundamentalism to the failure of traditional concepts and modernist alternatives to attract the masses, for example, the analyses of Muhammad Abdu, 'Ali 'Abd Al-Raziq, Taha Hussein and others.[33]

What brings all these interpretations together is the logic that sees in the rise of the Islamic movements a symptom of dire crises that beset the land of Islam. This interpretation rests in turn on a presumption that sees in the rise of secularism and in the weakness of religion the natural development of contemporary societies, implying, therefore, that the course of Islamic societies goes in an opposite direction, that it is a pathological case, making it necessary to search for its causes and cure. Despite the fact that some of the analysts direct their criticism at the theory of modernization and its defective Western assumptions, and emphasize the concepts of the schools of post-modernism that criticized the theory of modernity in its Western context,[34] they nonetheless continue to interpret the Islamic phenomenon as an abnormal phenomenon that needs diagnosis and treatment at the same time.

Most of the dominant interpretations follow the method of social interpretation of secularization in their analyses and assessment of the Islamic phenomenon, but in reverse. Just as secularism tries to interpret the disintegration of religion in Western societies as a natural consequence of modernization, rationalization and enlightenment, the theorists of the emergence of Islamic movements question the causes that delayed this natural development in the Islamic world. This perspective has in turn influenced the questions of other analysts who considered it necessary to view the Islamic phenomenon in its natural framework and as a natural development of the reform and renewal movements in Islam.[35] Others believe that the diagnostic method that accompanies the secular assumption is incorrect, because it deals with it in an inverse manner. The question that must be asked is not "Why have the movements that call for adhering to Islam been established and flourish?" but rather "Why have the efforts and pressures to weaken adherence to Islamic teachings in Muslim societies failed?" The answer is that those individuals who wanted to offer alternatives to Islam did not provide Muslims with convincing arguments to turn them from their religion or with strong enough persuasion to give up their religion for immediate gain.

Contrary to what has been circulated by some analysts that the alternatives to Islam are secularism and enlightenment, the banner of rationalism did not disappear permanently from Islam and, in fact, human reason rejects all the alternatives that wanted to replace Islam. This has happened ever since Abu Hamid Al-Ghazali showed the incoherence and non-rationality of neo-Platonic philosophy and postulates. The opponents of Islam inside and outside the Islamic world resorted to violence and repression after failing to entice and persuade. When the Muslim masses overcame violence and repression, Islam returned to uphold its natural role in guiding societies.[36]

Other analysts criticize the conclusion that the return to Islam is a return to what is natural, and see it only as an ideological difference. This criticism is based on the perception that the concepts that the Islamic movements promote are not authentic concepts in Islam but invented. Examples of these are the term "Islamic state," which did not appear until the twentieth century, the formation of new parties with their organizations and new ideologies, as well as the Islamic movements' conceptualization of a golden age for the Islamic state, which is a mere ideological construction. Adherents to this view add that the fact that the leaders of the Islamic movements are mainly from the modern sector that is influenced by the West, and not from religious scholars and clergy, that their followers still constitute a minority, and that they adopt violence to achieve their objectives, is proof that what they have brought is an innovation and not, as they claim, a natural or authentic tendency in society.[37]

There is also a group of analysts who suggest that the main problem of the Islamic movements is reflected in a failure to realize their objectives. To some analysts, this problem in turn indicates a dislocation in the strategy and organizational structure of the movements. The Muslim Brotherhood, which was founded three quarters of a century ago, is still far from realizing its dream of establishing an Islamic state in Egypt or from concretizing its presence on the political arena. Similarly, almost all Islamic movements have failed to seize power in the countries of the Islamic world. In the few places where they came close to power,[38] either directly or through an alliance with other forces – as was the case in Iran, Afghanistan, Sudan, Yemen, Malaysia, Kuwait and Algeria – the crises were exacerbated and not resolved.

These analysts maintain that the crisis runs very deep and reaches the movements' internal intellectual and organizational structure, since these are protest movements in an environment characterized by rejection and hatred. The movements grow in this environment and embody many contradictions; for instance, they adhere proudly to Islam, claim that it is the solution to all problems and that it is a system superior to all others, while, at the same time, they embody the fear of losing Islam and the fear of the other. Furthermore, these movements claim to fight the West and its values, but assimilate some aspects of modernity in their thought and behavior, and the West's influence appears in all of their practices.

Adherents to this view state that the movements embody the bankruptcy of the trend that they represent, the shallowness of the thought on which that trend is based and the absence of modern solutions and programs to solve the problems of the people. Thus, they are no more than new sects drawing on heritage to escape from the world of modernity, which is regarded as evil from Satan. They aim at an impossible objective that constitutes a contradiction in itself. This is manifest in their aim to establish the Islamic state without which society cannot be virtuous, while, at the same time, they say that the Islamic state will not be established without the existence of a virtuous society. Thus, they are caught in a vicious circle of seeking the virtuous society without which the state will not be virtuous and vice versa.[39]

The problem of such analyses is that they move from condemnation of the thought and practices of the Islamic movements, which is everyone's right, to judging that they have failed and are on the way to disintegration, which has been said since the 1940s. For example, we find that the thesis of Olivier Roy on the intellectual bankruptcy of the movements of Islamic reform is close to a verbatim repetition of Hamilton Gibb's judgment on the movements of Islamic reform in the 1940s and draws similar conclusions to those of Malcolm Kerr in the 1960s.[40] Despite these forecasts concerning the end of Islam and the rise of secularism, significant events have in fact shown the opposite. For instance, one of the important American theoreticians published a book in 1983, where he emphasized that Algeria is the only Islamic country that transcended the phase of the domination of the *sharia* and entered the phase of an irreversible and complete secularization as opposed to all other Islamic countries—implying that Algeria is the future model for other Islamic countries.[41]

Statements and predictions of this nature are the reason why these analysts face surprises at every corner, when they discover the growing influence of these movements. Islamic parties, regardless of their

[26]

numerous defects and deficiencies, form today the strongest opposition movements in most Islamic countries, even though they are outlawed, as is the case in Egypt and Tunisia, or face severe enmity from the state, as in the case of Turkey. When they achieve victorious results in elections and the state-supported parties fail, despite the maneuvers, machinations and unlimited resources the state gives them, the talk about failure should be attributed to the losing parties and not to the Islamic movements. It is possible to say that the problem that the opponents of the Islamic movements, and maybe the movements themselves, face is that the movements have not started to disintegrate but that they are increasing their power, notwithstanding international and local attacks against them.

On the other hand, the failure of many Islamic movements is in fact an expression of the success of their message. In Egypt, Algeria and many other Islamic countries, we find that the thinking of the Islamic movement is socially dominant to a point that events have overtaken it. For example, the decisions to implement the *sharia* in Pakistan in 1977, in Sudan in 1983, and in Nigeria in 2000, and before that the decisions to consider the *sharia* to be a basic source for legislation in the Egyptian constitution, all occurred in the absence of contemporary Islamic movements. In fact, at times, this happened in an environment of strong opposition to them, as was the case in Pakistan, or in an atmosphere of doubt and suspicion against them, as was the case of Sudan in the 1980s and Nigeria today. The Islamic form of dress, for instance, and the religious rites are popular phenomena that extend beyond the membership of the Islamic movements and the circle under their direct influence.

Furthermore, many new Islamic movements exceeded the demands of the existing Islamic movements, accusing them of being soft regarding Islam. We frequently find that Islamic sentiments and demands explode in the form of popular uprisings that transcend even the Islamic movements, as has been the case with the implementation of the *sharia* in Nigeria lately, which surprised the Islamic movements more than anyone else. Thus, the Islamic movements are the most active forces in the political arena, whose impact on the political arena should be studied and analyzed as to whether they are a factor of stabilization or destabilization.

Ideas, Programs and Objectives

The conditions and circumstances of the establishment of the Islamic movements are the main factors that determine their objectives and the formation of their intellectual framework. Here too, analyses vary and depend on the perspective and understanding of the analyst concerning the motivations and conditions of their establishment. Those who say that the movements are natural products of partial modernization and immature secularization, perceive the movements' thought as an expression of the insecurity of their foundation, the wretchedness of their reality, and as reflecting "the thought of poverty and the poverty of thought," as one of their critics puts it. According to other analysts, they reflect the grievances and despair of the classes that have been transcended by modernity and marginalized by the class struggle.

There are also those who see these movements as a modern phenomenon, since relating their thought to an imagined Islamic heritage is somewhat like inventing a new heritage. It is no more than another innovation developed by the modernist movements that contest the Islamic heritage that is embodied in associations of Islam today. They only express the view of a minority that seeks to impose its new vision on contemporary Muslim societies. According to this analysis, the demands of the fundamentalist movements can be summarized in the following points:

- The call to regain the influence and authority of Islam in the world;
- Such an objective cannot be achieved except by returning to true Islam that the Muslims of this age have deserted. This return must be comprehensive and all aspects of Muslim life, starting with politics and ending with personal matters, should be subjected to the authority of Islamic law;
- Regaining the authority of the *sharia* is not possible without establishing a true Islamic state, where governance is for God alone; and
- The task of regaining the authority of Islam is a sacred mission that permits the use of any method, including violence and subterfuge.[42]

Other analysts view the emergence of the Islamic movements as a restoration of specific historical Islamic orientations, especially the Hanbali trend that was embodied in the ideas of Ibn Taymiyya and its restoration by the Wahhabi movement of the eighteenth century. This thought is characterized by its simplicity and Bedouin nature, which indicates why the main states that supported the Islamic awakening in the 1970s were Libya and Saudi Arabia, the states that were the scene of Hanbali revolutions in the eighteenth and nineteenth centuries — al-Wahhabiyya and al-Sanusiyya respectively.[43] These states were the scene for these revolutions precisely because they were marginal desert lands sustaining a Bedouin lifestyle, which made the Hanbali thinking dominant.

Those who maintain this opinion agree that this view contradicts the fact that modern Islamic movements were launched in Egypt and Pakistan, which are two largely urban countries regarded as the birthplace of the oldest civilizations. They try to overcome this contradiction by saying that the Kingdom of Saudi Arabia and Libya employed Egyptian and Pakistani thinkers to accord their campaign the intellectual dimension that was needed, especially since the two countries became a refuge for the Muslim Brothers who were persecuted in Egypt as well as for the expatriates from Pakistan. These countries also established direct relations with the leaderships of these Islamic movements.[44]

The problematic of the Bedouin orientation of the contemporary Islamic movements combines with other analyses, some of which go back to Arab thinkers, that link the rise of the contemporary Islamic tide to the continuity of, and increase in, Bedouin and rural influence in the Muslim world. These analysts think that one aspect of this influence is the negative transformation of Arab cities by the influx of poor villagers, including the Islamic movements, which are therefore considered to be an embodiment of a backward way of thinking with demands that are incompatible with the age.[45]

In this regard, there is an important observation made by Tariq Al-Bishri to the effect that the movements of Islamic reform during the age of modernity were launched from the periphery of the Islamic world. Examples are the Wahhabiyya in Saudi Arabia, Mahdiyya in Sudan,

Dalhawiyya in India, Sanusiyya in Libya and others.[46] The movements agreed to call for renewal, reform and the opening of the gate of *ijtihad*. The reason for the rise of movements in the periphery is that the central area of the Islamic world was difficult to renew or change because of the security, importance and conservative influence of traditional institutions and their connection to the government and the Sultan.[47] When reform was introduced in the center, it was introduced by state institutions. The institutions focused on reforming defense, education and the economy, and created parallel institutions to traditional ones. This, in turn, created a duality between the new and those regarded as authentic, the consequences of which still prevail.

The movements of Islamic reform, which were created in the center by people like Al-Afghani, faced this reality, which was dominated by attempts at partial reform that failed in confronting colonialism. A problem arose between reformers, which could be seen in the differences that came to the fore between Al-Afghani and his disciple Muhammad Abdu, where the former thought that the priority should be given to establishing a political movement that resisted colonialism, while the latter thought that the crisis was internal and could be treated by education and religious reform.[48]

The view of modern Islamic movements as a rebirth of the Hanbali thought sheds light on another angle that analysts have explored — the attempt to link the modern Islamic movements with the history of Islamic reform through generations. John Voll distinguishes between two trends of Islamic reform, one that depends on the centrality of the text, the other that depends on the centrality of the inspiring personality as being representative of the sacred authority. The first trend generally represents the traditional Sunni schools, in addition to the Khawarij, while the other trend is represented by Shi'ite schools and Sufi orders. In later periods, we can refer to the Wahhabiyya movement as representing the first trend, and the Mahdiyya and Sufi revivalism movements as representing the second.[49] This division is important because the theoreticians of secularism see that the transformation from the centrality of an inspired leadership in Catholic Christianity (like the infallible pope, saints, holy men, and intervention of the Virgin) to depending only on the authority of the text in Protestantism paved the way to secularism.[50] According to Marx Weber, this orientation has removed the sacred from the world and emptied it of any embodied spirituality, resulting in a way of life that discounts the existence of the spiritual world.[51]

In spite of continuing to depend, in varying degrees, on the inspired personalities of modern Islamic movements – especially Hasan Al-Banna and the movement of the Muslim Brotherhood, and Ayatollah Khomeini in Iran – the general attitude of the modern Islamic movements is to focus on the centrality of the text and a return to fundamentals. Some analysts attribute the modern Islamic phenomenon to the positioning of Islamic awareness, that is, to inventing objective criteria to measure the degree of Islamic commitment. These criteria were established by the spread of education, printed books and the tools of mass communication, which, in turn, led to the weakening of the religious intermediary, be it the clergy, the sheikhs of Sufi orders or the governing authority. Moreover, and from this perspective, the establishment of the Islamic movement is regarded as a herald for the collapse of the authority of both scholars and the state, particularly in cases where the leaders of the movements were mostly from outside the traditional circle, in addition to challenging the authority of the state.[52]

This explains the orientation of the Islamic movements and their demands, which center on the imposition of the authority of the *sharia* and a tendency to challenge at one and the same time the ruling authorities and the dominant social traditions. The latter are described as innovations, myths or deviations from true religion. The Islamic movements ask their governments to implement the *sharia* instead of secular systems, which those states adopted from non-Islamic sources. They call for Islamic unity against division and for independence from foreign influence instead of subordination. Socially, these movements direct their strongest criticism at the new habits such as food, relations between the sexes, arts and literature that resulted from Western influence. They call for the use of the authority of the state to stop such habits. On the level of international relations, they consider the call for Islamic unity to be pivotal, in addition

[31]

to fighting colonialism, foreign influence and Zionism and supporting Islamic states and minorities that are targeted by strong enemies.

We notice that there are differences between the priorities of one movement and another. The movement of the Muslim Brotherhood, for instance, was established from its founders' awareness of the people moving away from Islam, either intentionally, as is the case of the rich classes that are affected by the West, or unintentionally, as is the case of the majority of people that lack awareness and education. Early on, the leader of the movement warned against the British political, military and economic influence, and prioritized the fight against it. The priority of Islamizing society and fighting colonialism led to a focus on the role of the state and political action. The issue of Palestine played a decisive role in the orientation of the movement, especially with regard to political mobilization and the use of military action, which had an impact on the future of the Islamic movements.[53]

Hasan Al-Banna summarized the essence of the Muslim Brotherhood's call in the following points: freeing the Islamic homeland from every foreign power and establishing in that homeland a free Islamic state that works according to the rules of Islam, implements its social system, upholds its principles and spreads its wise call to people.[54] The road to all of that is a spiritual reawakening and a true revival of the consciousness and sentiments of those who believe in this call and gradually spread it in society. In this way, the existence of the Muslim individual, Muslim family and Muslim society can be realized. This in turn leads to achieving the goal, which is to establish an Islamic state in Egypt that espouses the Islamic call and unites the voice of the Arab world. It also works for the good of the people, protecting Muslims in all Islamic lands from every aggression and spreading God's word while propagating His message, so that there is no strife and religion can spread all over the world.[55]

In India, however, the question raised was about the fate of Muslims in it: Would they integrate themselves into the Indian national movement or call for a national state for Muslims? The Islamic movement there was set up in the framework of rejecting both positions. Hence, Al-Mawdudi focused his writings on detailing the ideal Islamic state and the work that was needed for its establishment. In practice, the Islamic group in India finally participated in the politics of a national state, although its principles rejected this orientation. Contrary to Al-Banna who accepted the centrality of nationhood in Egypt and saw no contradiction between the call to Arab nationalism and the Islamic call, Al-Mawdudi brought together the complete rejection of secularism and nationalism, as well as democracy. Nationalism is the deification of national interests, while democracy is the deification of man and making the desires of the majority the governing principle of the state. These principles contradict the Islamic *sharia* that upholds the universalism of the call of Islam and the principle of divine governance. This means that the freedom of the majority is restricted to what God has revealed and to the principle of submission to the authority of Almighty God over people's life, both private and public. Thus, the objective of the Islamic nation must be the establishment of the divine caliphate based on the worship of God in every aspect and domain.[56]

The ideas of the Islamic movements and their demands in other countries were also affected by their conditions. For instance, in the Arab Gulf countries that accept the principle of implementing the *sharia*, the Islamic movements there turned to into lobbying groups, some with close relations to the ruling regimes, and limited their demands mostly to the social and cultural side. However, in countries where secularism is deeply rooted, like Turkey and Tunisia, the demands of the movements were limited to democracy and the freedom of political action. In Sudan, where the traditional religious sects with Sufi origins have dominated the political and social domain, the Islamic movement started to focus on combating the communist danger, because of the increasing communist influence in the modern sector. The Islamic movement moved toward making people aware of innovations and deviations from traditional Islam. With the passage of time, the movement turned to a pressure movement, demanding the implementation of an Islamic constitution, a call that was welcomed by traditional parties. Then the movement became a political party that allied itself with traditional parties against the rule of Ja'far Al-Numayri, then with Al-Numayri against these parties. Finally, the movement monopolized power after the coup of 1989, which it sponsored and supported.[57]

It is possible here to shed more light on the essential difference between the orientation of some Islamic movements that call for participation in political activities, like the movements of the Muslim Brotherhood in Egypt and Sudan, and others that reject it at least intellectually, as is the case of the Islamic group in Pakistan. This difference in methodology reflects, to a large extent, the old difference between Al-Afghani and Abdu over the priority of political action or the priority of education and teaching. Al-Mawdudi and later Sayyid Qutb maintained that the establishment of an Islamic group should precede the establishment of the Islamic state and consequently every political action. The establishment of the state, even if it is like Pakistan that has the name of an Islamic republic, without a prior existence of a group of believers committed to Islam is like putting the cart before the horse and would not lead to an Islamic status. The state does not create an Islamic nation, rather the opposite is true.

Sayyid Qutb maintained that it was an erroneous position for Islamic movements to enter into any debate about their programs and objectives with their opponents or to think about solutions for the problems of contemporary societies, since the latter relate to pre-Islamic societies and most of them will disappear with the establishment of the Muslim society. This is why Sayyid Qutb refused the principle of requesting Islam to find solutions to the problems of contemporary societies by saying that Muslims should adopt Islam in its entirety or leave it altogether.[58] The method that Al-Banna followed, and Al-Afghani before him, is based on the notion that the Islamic nation exists and that society is fine, but that the problem lies in the leadership and the state. The priority is then to reform the leadership, that is, reforming the state and public institutions, although this requires the establishment of the Muslim society, as Al-Banna emphasized.

Most writings and analyses about Islamic movements attribute the responsibility for the establishment and the increase in violent Islamic movements to an antagonistic intellectual orientation to politics in its traditional meaning, and especially the manifestation of this orientation in the views of Sayyid Qutb.[59] However, this attribution is not correct, because Qutb's thought is derived mainly from Al-Mawdudi who invented the concepts of contemporary *jahiliyya*, God's governance and other idioms. Qutb depended on these for a sharp distinction between the selected vanguard, that is, the real Islamic movement and the *jahiliyya* that surrounds it, which includes the Islamic movements that deal pragmatically with conditions of the *jahiliyya*.

Nevertheless, Al-Mawdudi's thought did not produce, on the Indian subcontinent, the violent movements of the kind that emerged in Egypt and around it. In fact, the logical conclusion of Al-Mawdudi and Qutb's thought is to give up politics altogether and every interaction with the world, including violence, until the Islamic group is established. The basis of this orientation is that Muslims today are in a period similar to that of the Meccan period in the Prophet's life. This means that the conditions for *jihad* and the ingredients of the state do not exist. This explains why the groups that followed the teachings of Sayyid Qutb opted for isolation from society and the establishing of counter societies.[60] These were attempts that were destined to fail, either through internal disintegration and collapse or through the confrontation with the respective authority that did not allow this isolation.

It is possible to say that the Islamic movements have acquired certain characteristics from the circumstances of their establishment that have governed, to a large extent, their intellectual orientations and political objectives. These movements position themselves to compete and challenge the existing political authorities due to reasons of principle and circumstance. However, the fundamental reason is that the Islamic movements were established to fill the vacuum created by the collapse of the central Islamic religious authority as represented by the Caliphate. This explains Tariq Al-Bishri's statement that the Islamic reform movements were not raised in the center before the deterioration and collapse of the Caliphate. Given the existence of an Islamic authority whose legitimacy was recognized, there was no justification for the emergence of movements to lead the course of reform, their presence was mostly to provide advice to the Caliph. Hence, the reform movements that were set up in the peripheries in the phase before the collapse of the Caliphate were considered to be either a challenge to the Caliphate, offering opposing religious views like Al-Wahhabiyya and Al-Mahdiyya, or were established outside the area that was under the authority of the Caliphate like Al-Dalhawiyya in India, and the movement of Dan Fodio in Nigeria (which named itself a caliphate), or those that arose in a vacuum and in the peripheries of the authority, without challenging it directly, like al-Sanusiyya in Libya.

The awareness of the collapse of the Caliphate was an important factor in the institutional thinking of the founders of these movements. In his youth, Al-Mawdudi joined the movement of the caliphate that was set up in India and represented, to a large extent, the first modern Islamic movement of a popular international nature with a unifying agenda. Al-Banna was greatly agitated by the collapse of the Caliphate as he mentions in his memoirs. Without the collapse, the emergence of movements – which claim for themselves the legitimacy to speak in the name of Islam and position themselves for the political and spiritual leadership of the nation – was not conceivable.

However, the circumstantial reasons for opposition to the state are explained by the need to reject the colonialist domination of the country and, in the case of Pakistan, the rejection of both the need to establish a national state for Muslims as well as of the secular nature of the state. There are also objections to specific policies, whether in the social and economic domain or in international relations. This challenge is also linked to the fact that the state refused to take on religious leadership, or its failure in this sphere. Confronting the authority is also linked to challenging traditional religious leaders, such as the scholars, sheikhs of Sufi orders and traditional institutions, such as Al-Azhar and the Mufti.

The emergence of the modern Islamic movements is in itself a condemnation of these leaderships and institutions. The rationale being that had they fulfilled their role there would have been no justification for the movements to begin with. It is known that, at the beginning, Al-Banna and Al-Mawdudi tried to seek support from and ally themselves with traditional religious leaders and institutions and did not turn to an independent course except after the failure of such attempts. Al-Banna mentions in his memoirs how he first resorted to the scholars and sheikhs, urging them to perform their role of confronting moral laxity and the waves of sexual permissiveness and atheism, but the response had been weak and dismaying.[61] Al-Mawdudi, however, worked in the movement of the caliphate in his youth, and shouldered some responsibilities in the traditional institutions with a reformist orientation, such as Aligrah University.

The practical condemnation of the traditional institutions by the Islamic movements is two fold: one is moral, accusing the scholars of weakness in performing their duties, and the other is practical, which embodies a judgment that these institutions are intellectually and structurally incapable of shouldering this task. There is an irony in revealing that the movements represent, to a large extent, the completion of the modernization of the Islamic world and that the movements have reached the domain of religion.

When the leaders of the Islamic states initially confronted reform, they tried to modernize institutions, beginning with the army, educational institutions and then the institutions of the state itself. However, their inability to modernize specifically the educational institutions forced the leaders to create parallel institutions, while allowing the religious educational institutions to maintain their status quo. This created dislocation and duality in society between the old and the new and the traditional and the modern.[62] The religious institutions remained as the last strongholds of the traditional and the old. This is why the modern Islamic movements are regarded as a direct blow aimed at the strongholds of traditionalism and perhaps the last nail in the coffin of the old status quo. Some analysts consider that the establishment of the Islamic movements under these conditions is the logical step to eradicate duality and then to achieve the comprehensive reconciliation within and the reunification of Islamic societies.

The Islamic movements are undoubtedly the product of modernity and the reality of secularization. However, simply because these movements

[37]

exist within the framework of modernity does not mean that there is no truth to the prevalent view that the Islamic movements are antagonistic to modernity. Nevertheless, although antagonism to secularism is a prominent feature of the Islamic movements, there are many indications that they experience tremendous difficulties in transcending the secular framework that rules the international community and its states.

This adjustment to secularization has taken many forms, starting with the dialogue that the governments with Islamic orientation, such as in Sudan and Iran, have with international bodies. It also goes further. Many Islamic governments have, to a large extent, adjusted to secularism, especially the Refah party in Turkey, the movement of Islamic renaissance in Tunisia and Hizbullah in Lebanon. These movements play by the secular rules in their countries and have repeatedly stressed that they do not intend to change them in the near future. To a lesser extent, we find that the movement of the Muslim Brotherhood in Egypt, Jordan and Syria, the Islamic movements of Kuwait, Yemen and of other countries also accept being contained within the secular framework.

Such a framework makes it difficult to distinguish between the Islamic and the secular movements. In addition, we find that governments with Islamic orientation also show attitudes that bring them closer to their secular counterparts. In January 1988, the late Iranian leader Ayatollah Khomeini elevated this circumstantial closeness to the degree of closeness in principle when he declared the doctrine of the absolute *velayat al-faqih* (the rule of the jurist). For him it meant that the jurist can transcend the whole Islamic law in the interests of the state. According to a *fatwa* (legal opinion) by Khomeini, the protection of the Islamic state and its power is the supreme principle of the Islamic *sharia* and precedes all other principles that depend on it. This is why the ruler can suspend all or some legal rules, if it is necessary for the preservation of the Islamic state. Khomeini gave this legal opinion an institutional dimension by establishing "The Expediency Council," which is the council that defines the interest of the state and is the final judge over the Islamic *sharia*, and not the other way around.[63]

[38]

Similarly, we find other governments that declare adherence to Islam, like the Sudanese government, but do not shy away from actions that oppose the Islamic *sharia* and justify that by necessity. *Fatwas* might be sought to add legitimacy to these positions. All of this means that transcending the period of secularization to the supposedly Islamic state constitutes a multidimensional dilemma, and that there are essential, if not logical, problems that transcend the boundary between the two areas.

The Role of the Islamic Movements

It is now possible to go back to some points that were raised earlier, starting with the issue of definitions. However, it remains necessary to emphasize the centrality of the concept of crisis in interpreting the resurgence of the Islamic phenomenon. This should not imply agreement with the views that try to picture this phenomenon as a pathological or unnatural expression of an irrational reaction toward economic, social or political crises. Furthermore, even from the perspective of the Islamic movements themselves, this emergence is a response to the crises of the deviation of Muslim societies from the obligation of true religiosity and the increase in external dangers that threaten the existence and independence of the nation, in addition to the negligence of the traditional scholarly and political leadership in confronting the crises.

Up to that point, it was possible to regard these movements as a normal phenomenon in line with the organizations of civil society, including the associations of human rights and voluntary and philanthropic associations, anti-abortion groups and others. These organizations emerge from a common sentiment of their members and the groups that they represent in the face of a crisis. The same happens when there is negligence in some aspects of government and the inability of the legal apparatuses to secure human rights, or the society's inability to curb undesired phenomena, such as abortion or to support the poor, the old, orphans and others.

However, there are important and even essential differences between the two phenomena. Although the above-mentioned organizations of civil society may at times object to the values of the majority and put the moral value system up for questioning, as is the case of the anti-abortion groups, these organizations function within the dominant values and focus only on deviations. The concerned organizations do not argue for preserving human rights or helping the poor or improving the social services. However, organizations should question dominant values to strengthen the bases of society, as well as maintain its value structure and its social fabric. Since these organizations have a ceiling beyond which they cannot go, they do not aim at transforming the system of societies or at challenging the values and customs that they depend upon.

This is the difference with the radical parties and movements of Marxism, anarchism, Faschism and others that do not aim only at a partial reform of their societies, but rather to destroy their structures from the very foundations and reframe them in a new system. The Islamic movements, especially those that are classified as moderate, were at times described as being part of the organizations of civil society. The Muslim Brotherhood in Egypt, in its early years, and Islamic movements in countries like Jordan, most of the Arabian Gulf states and even Palestine in 1987 saw their role as reformation, not revolution. They often focused on individual and social reforms and social services, and accepted the recognized frameworks in their countries.

There are also those Islamic movements mentioned before, such as Hizbullah in Lebanon, Welfare in Turkey and Al-Nahda in Tunisia that accepted clearly the secular ceiling that their states impose. However, the common description of "Islamic movement" is not often used for those movements that have partial interest, as we said. Sufi orders and reform associations like the Muslim Youth Association in Egypt, the International Conference of Islamic Youth and others are not classified as fundamentalist movements. Also included in this category are philanthropic and voluntary organizations of Islamic nature.

The common usage of the "Islamic movement" description refers precisely to those groups that see a need for radical changes in society. This may be applied to most jihadist movements and to those that have been affected by the ideas of Al-Mawdudi and Sayyid Qutb. However, even the moderate movements that see their mission as reform accept no ceiling and call for the subordination of all aspects of social life to the teachings of Islam as they perceive it. The emphasis on the comprehensiveness of Islam is one of the most significant characteristics and features of contemporary Islamic movements. This is why they refuse, in principle, concepts that view the role of religion in society as partial reform, and believe that their objective cannot be realized unless there is a comprehensive change in society.

This does not mean that movements that publicly accepted a ceiling below total reform are practicing a dual discourse, as some of their opponents accuse them of doing, because such acceptance does not imply that they have given up their ultimate ambitions in the long run. Muslims that have migrated to Ethiopia, for instance, and the Christians that accepted to live under the Roman Empire according to the principle of giving all temporal power to Caesar were not seeking power, in the short or long term, in those countries. They had no plan to destroy the power of the Negus or Caesar. However, this did not mean that they did not dream that later generations could fulfill the task of establishing their dream society and God's kingdom in that place or somewhere else. In fact, the theories of Al-Mawdudi and Qutb did not have a revolutionary orientation either, notwithstanding the sharp revolutionary idioms flowing from their writings — the focus of their radical campaign did not deviate from the Islamic call, but sought to make their ideas clear allowing them to mature from one generation to another.

To summarize, the Islamic movements can be defined as those movements that believe in the comprehensiveness of Islam in all aspects of life and posit themselves as the leadership for what they regard as the necessary effort to re-emphasize the totality of Islam against the background of the laxity of society and the shortcomings of its leadership, negative influences and the intrigue of enemies. By doing so, they claim for themselves the role of the moral leadership of society, thereby challenging both the traditional political and religious leaderships. The movements have been able to play this role because of the circumstances surrounding their establishment, including the vacuum in this domain and thus the opportunity for change. Nevertheless, a mere claim to moral and religious leadership is not sufficient; what gives the role of leadership its strength is the response that it receives. This response depends on the credibility of the call and the caller, as well as the prevailing conditions and circumstances.

Equally important, the fact that the Islamic movements carry this responsibility and attempt to monopolize the Islamic description does not necessarily imply that they deny these attributes to others, in the same way that a movement that describes itself as democratic or socialist does not preclude it from seeing others as democratic or socialist. This should be viewed as part of the competition over common symbols and meanings of society as well as a quest to distinguish themselves from each other with some key indicators. For example, the Mu'tazalites called themselves the people of justice and *tawhid*, and the Shi'ites call themselves the members of the Prophet's family, even though no Muslim disputes the importance of God's *tawhid* or justice, or disregards the members of the Prophet's family and the need to esteem them.

The role that the Islamic movements perform and their magnitude in the social domain are not defined by their claims and hopes but by many complex factors, from the potency of the discourse of the group, the qualifications of their leaders and their ability to best use the circumstances, through to the response that they receive from the masses, and the reactions of their competitors, whether governments, antagonists or foreign parties. It is possible to estimate the attraction and vitality of the Islamic phenomenon by its increase in popular influence or its decrease vis-à-vis those factors that aim at its neutralization and the elimination of its influence. The more the influence of the Islamic movements increases in unfavorable circumstances and in the face of ferocious resistance, the greater the indication of their vitality and effectiveness. Conversely, the more these movements retract the more this indicates the reverse.

It is possible to view this role from the perspective of the main problematic of the Islamic world today, which could be summarized as living in secularization, while holding to the teachings of Islam in theory. With the exception of a radical secular minority, which has lately become more vocal without any indication that its popular base is increasing, what we hear from the majority of political leaders and main political movements is the emphasis on adhering to the teachings of Islam as both a creed and a law. From this, it might be said that the establishment of the Islamic movements was a natural result of this situation, where discussion had to consider how to bridge the gap between real secularization and theoretical Islamism, and how a group might undertake this mission. This role had to lead to a struggle over the qualification of those in charge and to competition over religious and moral authority. The logic in nature maintains that if there is a vacuum it will be filled, and the logic of social life dictates that if there is a function, someone must carry it out. The Islamic groups confronted the issue of harmony between the teachings of Islam and social life and provided theoretical and practical reasons for it. Other scholars and thinkers from diverse specializations also confronted the matter. The continuous dialogue about this issue is further proof of its primary importance in contemporary Muslim society.

Aspects of Success and Failure

Most of the Islamic movements started as marginal in their societies but then their situation changed. The movement of the Muslim Brotherhood in Egypt was initially a small group established outside the capital. Most of its members were workers, junior employees and some students. However, it quickly grew to include hundreds of thousands of members and sympathizers and an important segment of the educated elite. Only two decades after its inception, the movement found itself at the heart of the political domain in Egypt and came close to participating in the government of Jamal 'Abd Al-Nasir. Soon after, it suffered its greatest blow in 1954, which was followed by a judicial decision to dissolve it, and then it suffered its second blow in 1965. The government only distanced itself partly from its activities, but it was still banned. Nonetheless, since the latest Egyptian elections in 2000, the movement has become the largest opposition party, notwithstanding the ban and the government's intervention in the electoral process. There is no doubt that the government's decision to continue the ban on the organization expresses the belief that lifting the ban may lead to the rapid transformation of the movement into a popular party that seizes power from the current regime. Even if the fear is exaggerated, the facts confirm that the movement still has influence and magnitude.

On the other hand, it is noticeable that the center of power of the movement has moved from the poor classes and provincial groups, in its early stage, to a strongly middle class membership, including professionals and intellectuals. It is also noticeable that the movement did not gain any segment of the higher classes, senior landowners or businessmen. The course of the movement in Egypt was repeated in most other countries, where the movements normally started out with few individuals that might be students, as is the case of Sudan and Malaysia, or students and junior employees, as is the case in Tunisia and Algeria, or a coalition of junior employees, teachers and scholars, as is the case in Syria, Jordan, Lebanon and Palestine, or all of these in addition to traders, as is the case in Kuwait. However, development soon followed a similar course, where the movement rapidly flourished and became the main opposition movement, for example, in Tunisia, Egypt, Syria and Palestine, or became the strongest political force even if it did not come into power, as is the case of Algeria, Jordan and Kuwait. In all of these countries, it seems that the major support for these movements came from the intellectual and middle class, the petite bourgeoisie and city dwellers in general.

The movement that was established on the Indian subcontinent originally arose within the middle class and took an elitist orientation. This orientation was maintained, which limited its popular influence. In the late 1970s and early 1980s, it had the chance to participate in the power structure of Pakistan during the presidency of the late Zia Al-Haq, and it did initially do so. However, it later withdrew because of differences over the program of Islamization that Zia Al-Haq followed.

It is noticeable that the Islamic movements, with few exceptions, could not come into power in any Arab or Islamic country, notwithstanding their wide popularity. Some Islamic movements have succeeded in participating in government as in the case of Jordan, Yemen, Kuwait,

Malaysia and Pakistan, as well as Sudan in the 1970s and 1980s, or entered into parliament as in the case of Egypt, Lebanon, Algeria and Turkey, as well as Syria in the 1950s and 1960s. However, this participation did not develop into a more effective role in government. On the contrary, we find that it has, in many cases, led to the weakening of popular support for the movement.

Even in countries where Islamic rule has been realized such as Iran and Afghanistan, we find that the modern Islamic movements have lost the battle for government and have either become one of the staunchest critics of the regimes or their opponents. This is the situation with the Freedom Movement in Iran and its founder Mahdi Bazarkan, the first prime minister of Iran after the Islamic Revolution, and with the Islamic parties in Afghanistan. In both cases, the parties lost the battle to the traditional forces as represented by traditional scholars on whose ruin the modern Islamic movements have ascended. For this reason, even many contemporary Islamists regard this situation as a step backward.

The only case where an Islamic movement has come to power is the Sudan, but that was done through a coup and without a popular base. As was the case in Iran and Afghanistan, the practices of the Islamists in Sudan lessened their popularity. These countries faced a civil war or a deteriorating economic situation, for example, in Afghanistan and Sudan, which forced their Islamic governments to take repressive measures that in fact lessened their ability to resolve the problems of the country and its citizens. As a result of such developments, the attractiveness of Islamism dwindled somewhat and its luster weakened, especially in light of splintering and infighting between the Islamists in Sudan and Afghanistan, and hindering the course of reform in Iran.

Many analysts, like Olivier Roy, speak now of the failure of political Islam or as Ibrahim Karawan put it, the Islamists have reached a dead-end. Such a judgment may be premature, and it is based on a tendency to exaggerate in much the same way as saying that the fundamentalist danger is about to overcome the world. However, there is no doubt that the Islamic phenomenon is now at a crossroads. What the movement in general achieved through attempts to reform and revive Islam and the popular support for the revival, which is expressed in near or actual participation in government, has placed the movements of contemporary Islamic revival squarely in the face of difficult questions and practical choices that have to be resolved. This has, in turn, revealed many problems in the theoretical, intellectual and moral assumptions on which the movements were founded and has necessitated a comprehensive review of their thinking.[64]

These movements and Islamic intellectual leaders have begun to confront these problems through what has been described as "the new Islamic movements" or "Islamic liberalism." This has been embodied in the setting of Islamic movements that believe in democracy and pluralism, such as the Islamic movement in Tunisia and some Islamic movements in Malaysia and Turkey, in addition to some wings of the movements in Egypt, Jordan, Lebanon and elsewhere. Furthermore, the voices from within the movements that call for self-criticism have become louder. A lot has also been written on the subject.[65] Within this framework, we can classify the reform movement that is led by President Muhammad Khatami in Iran. While these attempts are important, the movements are still incapable of confronting the existing problems and achieving the required reform.

Concluding Remarks

It is possible to say that the Islamic movements emerged as a reaction to a crisis that they wanted to get out of, yet they were unable to succeed and ended by adding to the problem. However, if the crisis that the contemporary Muslim societies face is a structural crisis, as we said earlier, and if the efforts of the movements failed in solving the crisis, the responsibility for this failure does not fall on the Islamic movements alone but on the entire nation. If the activities of the Islamic movements have created a state of instability in their societies, this is because the state of instability lies in the structure of these societies and because of the problems mentioned earlier.

If the religious calls in the Western industrial societies do not create a similar state of instability in them, it is because religious matters there are largely decided by the active social elements and groups. On the other hand, we find that racial and fascist calls have created a storm in the industrial societies and still constitute a real threat to their stability. This means that the potential for these societies to be agitated by racial calls is greater than by religious calls. Perhaps the reason is that secularism penetrated the fabric of society and became part of it more than religious thought or the approach of religious institutions themselves. However, secularism destroyed the defenses of these societies against racism or made religious fanaticism take a new form—the racist. This does not mean that we equate religious calls with racist tendencies or even religious fanaticism with racial discrimination, but there are some similarities in the manner each affects the stability of societies.

Therefore, resolving the problem of instability should not mean launching a war on the movements that call for the respect of Islamic values, but to resolve the questions, issues and functions that the movements stir. War expresses the old policy of putting one's head in the sand, which goes back to the Umayyad dynasty. This is embodied by the saying of 'Abd Al-Malik Bin Mawran when he performed the pilgrimage as the Caliph for the first time in the year 75 of *hijra* after the defeat of 'Abd Allah Bin Al-Zubayr: "You put on us the duty to be like the predecessors but you do not do their doing. I swear, if any man tells me to fear God, I will chop his head off." The significance of this saying is that the moral burden that the nation has shouldered in the realization of the ideal is a tradition inherited from the pious ancestors. It is, according to the above statement of the Caliph, a burden that cannot be shouldered. Furthermore, continuous efforts to attain the ideal will shake the stability of society. The rulers and other leaders of society perceive the burden that is placed on the leaders as unjust, since the citizens should also adhere to the high standards that they demand of their leaders. Regardless of the truth of this claim, chopping people's head is not exactly the best way to resolve the intricate issues.

Another problem is the intellectual attempts to defeat the thinking of the Islamic movements or the attempts to explain them away through misinterpretations that conceive of their concerns as mere social, political and economic issues, and thus deprive them of their true foundation. Such interpretations seek to deny the reality of these movements rather than attempt to understand the phenomenon.

There is no doubt that the political, psychological, economic, and social complexity that surrounded the Islamic phenomenon and contributed to its spread is worthy of consideration, for this helps to understand the reality and circumstances, and sometimes sheds light on how to deal with the phenomenon. However, the analysis of the spread of a specific idea does not replace the need for an in-depth discussion of its connotation or for understanding its content and the reason why it has become a choice among many. This might happen if the analyst starts from presupposed assumptions, like the Marxist view that religion is the opium of the people and aims then to discuss the spread of the phenomenon as pathological, similar to a sociologist or psychologist who seeks the reason for the spread of drug taking among youth or the spread of violent crimes in a poor neighborhood. However, even at the theoretical level, this analytical methodology is insufficient.

We find in Algeria, for instance, five major Islamic organizations, of which three are legitimate. They are Harakat al-Silm headed by Mahfouz Nahnah, Jama'at al-Nahda al-Islamiyya that was headed by 'Abd Allah Jab Allah, and the party that is headed by former President Ahmad Bin Billa. The two banned parties are al-Jabhat al-Islamiyya li al-Inqadh and al-Jama'a al-Islamiyya al-Musallaha, which in turn split into groups, of which the most important is al-Jama'a al-Salafiyya li al-Da'wa wa al-Qital. However, the analyses that used the crisis as the pivot to interpret the Islamic phenomenon do not provide an explanation for the sweeping success of al-Jabhat al-Islamiyya li al-Inqadh rather than other Islamic organizations, especially given the fact that all of the reasons mentioned for interpreting the rise of the Islamic phenomenon, such as organizational skills, using the mosques, the weakness of competing trends and financial resources can be applied to all other organizations that had little success. For example, Jama'at al-Nahda al-Islamiyya and Harakat Mujtama' al-Silm enjoy stronger organizational structures and have external connections and long histories. Nevertheless, al-Jabhat al-Islamiyya sprang up overnight and experienced rapid growth in the early 1990s, even though almost no one had heard of it or its leaders before its appearance. Its organizational structure was chaotic and it had no relations with Islamic organizations elsewhere or financial resources from outside Algeria. Thus, we need to go back to the origin and reformulate the questions and the tools of analysis so that ignorance does not inform our deliberations.

In order for the study of the contemporary Islamic phenomenon to increase our knowledge, there must be an exploration of the inherited assumptions from contemporary sociologists about the nature of religion and its role in society and freedom from ambiguous concepts. For instance, the attempt to build on an assumed separation between state and religion and the worldly and the divine forgets that every religion is in the final instance a worldly matter, which means that religion has no existence outside of life in the world and cannot survive separate from human life. Similarly, there is no proper life without religion, if we look at the functional definition of religion by Thomas Luckman and others who say that religion is by definition the ultimate concern of people.[66] Every individual and every society has a system of values that defines the ultimate concern and sets limits that cannot be crossed.

Confusion also exists among the Islamic movements that take practical and, sometimes, theoretical 'secular' positions, because of an assumed separation between what is sacred or imposed by the *sharia* and what is worldly demanded by reason, correction, perception and worldly necessities. In this context, we find that the most radical Islamic movements often take many steps that are contrary to the *sharia* in the name of interest and necessity. Thus, the theoretical framework of this discussion needs a comprehensive rethinking, because the real comparison is not in fact between a religious perspective, on the one hand, and a worldly one, on the other, but is the sum of complicated, diverse and multi-dimensional comparisons.

This leads us to the issue of the modernizing role of the contemporary Islamic movements. It is a complex role that emerges from the fact that the movements are the product of modernity, on the one hand, and a

[49]

reaction against other trends, orientations and real consequences of modernity, on the other. The comparison here between the assumed modernity represented by the opposition trends and a call to pre-modernity by the Islamic movements is incorrect. This view does not understand modernity, on the one hand, and the Islamic phenomenon, on the other. This can only be true if we perceive modernity as an assumed value and a prescribed ideal, not as a realistic phenomenon. What has been called modernity is no more than a reiteration of a heritage on which it depends, and what is called heritage is not separate from contemporary frameworks used to interpret it in the most "modern" way.[67]

We might say that the establishment of the Islamic movements reflects the reality of their societies in being, first, the product of the influence of modernity, and second, an expression of the structure of these societies in terms of the function that they perform. The movements have historical and intellectual roots that depend on concepts of faith in Islam – resurrection and renewal, and enjoining the good and forbidding evil – and belong to the heritage of historical and intellectual movements that still have influence and enjoy acceptance. These movements reflect the nature of religious authority in Islam and express the crisis in the traditional centers of this authority, especially the regress of the leading role of religious scholars in the cultural and moral fields. The importance of these movements and the influence that they enjoy have become functional, for they perform a vital role imposed by the nature of these societies and their social and cultural structures.

The Islamic movements are considered to be a new phenomenon in Muslim societies, notwithstanding the fact that they express values and orientations that have roots and precedents in Islamic heritage. They are attributed to a group of reformist leaders, of whom the most important are Jamal Al-Din Al-Afghani and his disciples. Their history goes back to a foundational phase that only began in the third decade of the twentieth century. The movements started as a marginal phenomenon in their societies and then gained an increasing influence without succeeding in dominating their societies. Many analysts attribute their increasing influence and even their foundation to intellectual, moral and social crises within Muslim societies.

However, such analyses are insufficient, as we mentioned earlier. The movements were established out of a crisis, but it is a crisis of functional dislocation in Muslim societies and their moral, political and intellectual structures. It is a crisis related to the structure and existence of these societies and is not transitional in one aspect of their life, whether economic, demographic, structural or other. The Islamic phenomenon is an expression in societies that differ widely in their social structures and economic conditions, including the Western industrial societies where Islamic communities live. Thus, the issue revolves around the influence of the Islamic faith over societies and not because they are suffering from a transitional crisis.

This emphasizes the point that the deep crisis that the Islamic movements are undergoing and the failures that they have suffered have not been enough to end their existence or to transcend the crisis that has led to their emergence and co-existed with them. We have seen, for instance, how the fall of fascist or communist movements in the societies that they dominated did not leave any important impact on these societies, which quickly left these movements behind. However, even in Islamic countries with the weakest Islamic movements, like Tunisia and Turkey, the governments and the governing bodies behave as if these movements are dominant, while the governments are the opposition that struggles to be freed from the grip of the Islamic movements.

Thus, the current crisis is not the crisis of the Islamic movements alone, but is a general crisis facing the Muslim world and secular regimes, as well as those regimes that claim to be adhering to Islamic *sharia* and yet are confronted by these movements, which we have called here, or call themselves, Islamic. The other opposition movements also face the same problem. What is true is that the Islamic movements constitute the pivot of the crisis because of their influential role. The double failure – the failure of the movements to resolve the conflict in their interest and the failure of their opponents to neutralize the movements and to terminate their influence – is what has made societies reach a dead-end. The movements are unable to proceed or retract.

Political Islam: Between Thought and Practice

Hasan Hanafi

Religion is not only a theoretical change in worldview, from one that maintains that this world was created out of nothing and ends in the same way, to one that perceives man as a passer-by who works and is finally judged by his works; one which maintains that beyond this visible world there is another that is invisible but manifests itself in the visible one and rules over it. Religion is not only a set of practices – relating to individual and social rituals and rites of symbolic significance – which protects man from the dangers of the environment, the power of nature and ferocious animals, so that man can have tranquility in his life and live in peace and security.

Furthermore, religion is not a set of authoritarian institutions of the clergy who rule over it and decide its laws and rituals, and who work as intermediaries between the world of humans and the world of the gods, having both human and divine abilities at the same time. They are closer to the sacred rather than the worldly and some of them have even used the titles of sons, spirits and words of God. Religion is not isolation in caves, sitting before the fire, the smoke of scents and the fragrance of perfumes, the singing of hymns, invoking good spirits and exorcising bad spirits, treating the sick and converting the spiritual word into the material one.

The Old Roots of Political Islam

Religion has always been a tool of cultural, political and social change, and a social movement that represents marginal or persecuted elements of society against authoritarian and tyrannical forces, such as Namrud, Haman, Abi Jahl, Abi Lahab and the elders of Mecca, who accused the Prophet of turning slaves against them.

Religion was the tool of liberation of entire peoples, like the liberation of the Jews from the grip of the Pharaoh under the leadership of Moses and the migration of the Prophet Abraham and his people from the North of Iraq to Hijaz to avoid the worship of idols and to build the foundation of a new house for God, in which to worship God and not idols. It was also the instrument to unite fragmented and conflicting tribes, like the Arab tribes, and to bring people together, like the brotherhood between the al-'Aws and al-Khazraj and between al-Ansar and al-Muhajirin. "If thou hadst spent all that is in the earth thou couldst not have attuned their hearts, but Allah hath attuned."[1] It also brought the tribes together to carry the Black Stone that the Prophet put on his gown, where one individual from each tribe held to the edge of the gown, an action which later came to represent a togetherness, through "a firm handhold which will never break."[2]

Religion was the instrument to unite homelands and unify cultures. This was the case in the Arabian Peninsula, by uniting the theists – Judaism, Christianity – and enhancing the culture of poetry, especially the verses of priests, the poetry of the Christians and al-Sa'aliq. The culture of poetry was also the culture of Arab popular proverbs that carried Arab values, which in turn were connected to the values of Islam, such as generosity to the guest, helping the oppressed, protecting the stranger and fulfilling promises. The same applies to the political culture represented by the alliance of Fudul and the peace treaty of Hudaybiyya that recognized all people, "And have made you nations and tribes that ye may know one another."[3] "For each We have appointed a divine law and a traced-out way."[4]

Religion is also the instrument of cultural liberation, the liberation of Adam from temptation, and the liberation of the son of Noah from judging natural phenomena according only to natural law – such as the mountain that was not covered by water during the flood – and the liberation of the Prophet Jesus of the Israelites from the tyranny of the clergy, who blindly adhered to the law, as well as the liberation of the temple from being used as a market place. It is also the instrument for the foundation of a new contract based on love and obedience instead of the Old Testament that depended on choice and selection, and the liberation of the Roman from relying on physical strength in order to uphold the intellect, and from attention of the body to care of the soul.

Every claim that there is no religion in politics and no politics in religion is meant to isolate religion from politics so that the authoritarian can secure himself against any opposition in the name of religion that may destroy him. Furthermore, isolating politics from religion means that the political regimes do what they want, according to the interests of the political elites and with no regard to any law or rule. It is also a negative political message expressed against the natural relationship between religion and politics, since religion is an instrument of liberation for humankind and politics is an instrument of executing its laws. The separation of religion from politics and politics from religion, as modern secularism demands, is thus both a negative political and a negative religious act—the political entity wants to rule alone without competing with the religious, as is the case in contemporary Arab regimes. Conversely, the religious entity that wants to exclude the political wants to claim ownership of religion, and wants to create a closed world or kingdom without competition from politicians.

The Islamic sciences have all been founded along political and social lines, in a political environment where the tribe is transformed into a state, the prophethood into a caliphate, and the caliphate into a kingdom. The Prophetic Tradition says that the Caliphate was to last for thirty years after the Prophet was gone and then it was to become a strict kingship. The Islamic sciences accompanied this political and social transformation and expressed it.

Theology was founded on a political basis and was related to the Caliphate after the death of the Prophet, whether it was based on a text and an oath of allegiance, on an appointment or a choice, on a pact or a contract.

Political difference and theorizing about it started between the different opposition forces, like the Shi'ites, and those who were in power like the Umayyads, who brought their political theorization from the Ash'arites. In addition, the secret political opposition brought forward its belief in the Imamate. The Mu'tazilites, with their public intellectual political opposition, theorized on the five fundamentals—*tawhid*, justice, promise and threat, the status between belief and disbelief, and enjoining the good and forbidding evil. The Kharijites upheld armed opposition on the fringes of the cities, which followed the theorization of the Mu'tazilites about *tawhid* and justice and that the Imamate was not necessarily for the tribe of Quraysh. The Kharijites also rejected the notion of the status between belief and disbelief and claimed that people were either believers or unbelievers, that belief could not be viewed in isolation from work and that there was no middle ground for hypocrisy or heresy. They also turned enjoining the good and forbidding evil from advice into opposition by force against the unjust ruler.[5]

Sufism started as a counter-political approach and as a reaction to the excessive competition over the world, the life of luxury and extravagance, and the difficulty of actually resisting this worldly trend after the martyrdom of the Imams of the Prophet's family— resistance became difficult and the scholars were caught in the power and enticement of Mu'awiyya. A group decided to save their souls if they were unable to rectify the wrongs of the world, and to ensure that their conscience was clear and their heart pure even if the body had to yield to the needs of worldly life and the essentials of survival. After the Great Turmoil (*Fitna Al Kubra*)[6] there was the birth of a generation of monks and mystics who yearned for earlier days and especially the days of the Prophet and the Caliphs. The Ahl al-Saffah lived their life in pity for others. From this environment, the first Sufi movement emerged without any foreign influence and by a purely internal momentum.

The foundation of the science of the fundamentals of jurisprudence is also purely social, for every new fact needed a judgment. It was natural that analogical deduction was invented, as was expressed by 'Umar Bin Al-Khattab, "Deduce things from similarities and different things from differences," and the Prophet's saying to Mu'adh Bin Jabal who said that he would rule by the Qur'an, then the Prophetic Tradition, and then by analogical deduction without fear or awe. In the Qur'an there is mention of deduction and reasoning, "he would have taught him that thing that they deduce from."[7]

The sciences of wisdom were established by the state. Al-Ma'mun dreamed of Aristotle and dialogued with him over the issue of the rational and religious good and evil. He also worked for the establishment of the House of Wisdom (*Bait Al Hikma*) and appointed its translators, headed by Hunayn Bin Ishaq who bought manuscripts from the country of the Romans with gold. The goal was to know the cultures of the conquered peoples, the West and the Romans, and not to destroy and terminate them as modern colonialism has done. Greek political thought, especially Plato's *Republic* and Persian Political thought, especially *Jawida Dakhard*, stood side by side with Islamic political thought as inherited in *Al-Ahkam al-Sultaniyya*.

In addition to the four traditional rational sciences – theology, philosophy, Sufism and the fundamentals of jurisprudence – the other traditional sciences, that is the Qur'an, *Hadith*, Exegesis, the Prophet's biography and jurisprudence, all emerged out of social and political motivations. The Qur'an was collected and checked over during the reign of 'Uthman out of fear and for the purpose of fixing the text, an act which was equal to fixing political authority. The collection of *Hadith*, two centuries later, was motivated by the same cause, that is, to fix the Prophetic sayings after opposition groups invented unauthentic Prophetic sayings in order to support their views. The sciences of exegesis were subject to same concern, especially against the exoteric and rational interpretations of the opposition. The theological school was also propped up in order to argue that the creed of political power is included within the sciences of exegesis over destiny, predestination and the Imamate.

[57]

The sciences of the Prophetic biography were founded as the People of the Book formed their biographies of their prophets, which was done in order to show their miracles. The sciences of the Prophet's biography represented a movement away from the real and implicit social and political role of the Prophet, in order to boost the morale of the Muslims, so that they did not feel that they were inferior to the Christians who had written the biography of Christ.[8] The political biography is obvious in the contemporary biographies of the Prophet; the liberal biography in two books by Muhammad Husayn Haykal, *Hayat Muhammad* and *Fi Munzal al-Wahy*, and in Taha Husayn's book *'Ala Hamish al-Sira*, the socialist biography in 'Abd Al-Rahman Al-Shirqawi's *Muhammad Rasul Allah*, and the political biography in *Fatrat al-Takwin fi Hayat al-Sadiq al-Amin* by Khalil 'Abd al-Karim. Finally, the sciences of jurisprudence were formed according to the priorities of the classical age and its circumstances, that is the priority of the jurisprudence of worship over the jurisprudence of human interactions. The political order monopolized transaction in society, especially those matters pertaining to political organizations and turning against the unjust ruler.[9]

The Modern Roots of Political Islam

Political Islam is both an old and a modern phenomenon. It has existed since Salah Al-Din and has continued up to the emergence of the current Islamic groups. Islamic reform was established out of political motives, emanating from the weakness of the Ottoman Caliphate, the occupation and partition of the nation's lands, the nation's backwardness in terms of modern civilization, repression of the people notwithstanding the creed system (*Millat*) and its characteristic hyper-centrality, the emergence of the ambition of the East and West over the territory of the Sick Man of Europe, and the desire of countries like Egypt in the period of Muhammad 'Ali to inherit the Caliphate after its collapse in 1924.

The greatest representative of political Islam and the pioneer of modern Islamic movements is Jamal Al-Din Al-Afghani who developed political Islam—that is, Islam in confronting external colonialism and internal repression, and Islam working for the liberation of the Muslim land, for Muslim freedom, for the poor, for identity, progress and mobilization. The 'Urabi revolution rose from these teachings—Ahmad 'Urabi stood in 'Abidin Palace before King Tawfiq saying, "God has created us free and did not bequeath us any property, by God we will not bequeath things after today." The nation's speakers and scholars, like 'Abd Allah Al-Nadim, continued both openly and secretly to resist and fight the British occupation of Egypt.[10]

Most of the national movements sprang from religious reform. Al-Afghani introduced the motto, "Egypt is for the Egyptian." Although Muhammad Abdu refused any relation with the 'Urabi revolution, he was the author of the national party program. The Egyptian national movement continued, from Mustapha Kamel to Fathi Ridwan, and from the national party to Misr al-Fatat. It was connected to both the reform movements and political Islam. It was also Al-Afghani who called for the unity of the Nile valley – Egypt and Sudan – as well as for Arab unity starting with Egypt and Syria, the unity of Egypt and the Arab West, and the renaissance of Egypt with the renaissance of the East. Although Muhammad Abdu diluted the revolutionary spirit of Al-Afghani's work, the revolution of 1919 was still influenced by the latter. Sa'd Zaghlul was one of his disciples, as were the second generation of the renaissance pioneers, like Qasim Amin, Mustapha 'Abd al-Raziq and Taha Husayn. The Pact of 1963 recognized them in the chapter on the 'roots of national struggle.'[11]

In the Arab West, like in Egypt, the national movement was connected to religious reform and sprang from it. In Morocco, 'Allal Al-Fasi founded Hizb al-Istiqlal and the scholars of the Qarawiyyin with the royal court established the national movement; the royal court represented by Muhammad V, embodied the tie between the homeland and Islam. *Jihad* took on the new meaning of independence, and the king in Morocco took the title of the "Emir of the Believers" because of his genealogical ties to the Hashimite family, as in the case of Jordan.

In Algeria, the national movement also emerged from the Association of the Scholars of Algeria and developed with its scholars — 'Abd al-Hamid Bin Badis, 'Abd Al-Qadir Al-Mughrabi, 'Abd Al-Karim Al-

Khattabi and Malik Bin Nabiy. With the weakening of the national movement after independence and the return of the francophone elite, Islam once again became the vehicle for the anger of the masses and the voice for their social aspirations to eliminate poverty and unemployment. When the social Islamic movement did return, it won the majority in the legislative councils. Its success brought the army up against it and armed conflict erupted, resulting in more than seventy thousand martyrs.

In Tunisia too, the national movement crystallized around the scholars of al-Zaytuna, such as Al-Tahir and Al-Fadil Bin 'Ashur. People were resisting the French occupation as part of Islamic *jihad*, irrespective of their orientation and whether it relates to trade unions, liberal ideals or spontaneous nationalism. This is clearly evident in the literature on resistance and in popular poems, in the methods of exegesis of al-Zaytuna scholars, in religious speeches, afternoon lessons and popular demonstrations.

In Libya, the al-Sanusiyya movement carried the *jihad* against Italian occupation and continued through 'Umar al-Mukhtar. The resistance was launched from the mosques and religious places and depended on belief in God and the *jihad* against the infidels. Occupation represented unbelief, and resistance was directed against the infidels from Al-Kufrah in the south of the desert. The revolution of 1969 sprang from a nationalist sentiment as a reaction to the defeat in the Six-Day War of 1967. After a quarter of a century of diluting the revolutionary trend and continuing the same political discourse without visible results in the transformation of the cultural, social and political reality, armed Islam once again sprang in the mountains around Benghazi, as the representative of the movements of social protest and political opposition.

The Arab East did not differ from the Arab West on this issue. In Syria, 'Abd Al-Rahman Al-Kawakibi theorized about Muslim freedom in his book, *Tabai' al-Istibdad wa Masari' al-Isti'bad*, and in another one of his books, *Um al-Qura*, he analyzed the phenomenon of indifference or apathy in the nation, which he said led to its submission and occupation. He constructed nationalism on the basis of Islam and applied the culture of freedom in the West to the reality and conditions of the Muslims.

[60]

In Lebanon, the resistance movement in the south emerged from the Shi'ites and their parties and organizations, and succeeded in liberating the south of Lebanon. It became a model that was followed in Palestine, Kashmir and all occupied territories. Both the Shi'ites and the Sunnis contributed to the resistance movements and theorized about the modern Islamic revolution, especially in the writings of Muhammad Mahdi Shams Al-Din and Muhammad Husayn Fadlallah, perhaps transcending the ideology of Islamic revolution in Iran and "the rule of the jurist."

In Yemen, the free imams led the struggle against the rule of the tyrant imams and became martyrs, like Ziad Al-Mushki, for the freedom of the homeland. The Brothers participated in many revolutions against the imams until the success of the Free Officers, when 'Abd Allah Al-Sallal and his company finally succeeded in bringing to an end the rule of darkness. Yemeni poets and literary figures expressed the conditions of repression and the call for independence, and worked with the nationalists in Egypt to make the revolution successful. After unity was achieved, the Islamic movement participated in national life, although relationships with the political regimes went through ups and downs, as was the case of the societies that moved from authoritarianism to freedom.

In the Sudan, the al-Mahdiyya movement led the struggle against British occupation under the leadership of Muhammad Ahmad Al-Mahdi, using all of the traditional weapons against the modern British army, with Lord Jordan being killed by one of the fighters of al-Mahdiyya. In the modern history of Sudan, al-Mahdiyya became synonymous with fighting for the cause of God, and Sufism was transformed into a revolution, notwithstanding the spread of al-Wahhabiyya and the dropping of the duty of *jihad* by the Republican Brothers.

In Palestine, the movements of Islamic Hamas and Islamic Jihad led the Islamic resistance in conjunction with other Palestinian resistance movements. In its initial formation, the movement of Fatah consisted of the Muslim Brothers who fought side by side in Palestine with the Arab armies in 1948. The 'Iz al-Din al-Qassam revolution in 1935 was the model for the first Islamic resistance against British occupation. Two uprisings took place, the first in the period of 1987–1993 and the second that started at the end of September 2000 under the slogan of the al-Aqsa Mosque, whose defamation and occupation has inflamed Muslim sentiment from the farthest lands of Asia to West Africa.

Muhammad Abdu had turned against his master Al-Afghani's political revolution and politics of revolt against the rulers, after the failure of the 'Urabi revolution and the British occupation of Egypt. Similarly, Rashid Rida turned against Muhammad Abdu, moving away from reform to Salafiyya after the Kamelist revolution in Turkey in 1923, the abrogation of the Caliphate and the success of the Jam'iyyat Turkiyya al-Fatat and Hizb al-Itihad wa al-Taraqi in seizing power. There were three choices: reform, which had led to the occupation of Egypt; secularism that led to the destruction of the Caliphate in Turkey; and Salafiyya with which Rida was left and to which he resorted in his new defense of the Caliphate in his book, *Al-Khilapha aw al-Imama al-'Uzma*.

He rediscovered Muhammad Bin 'Abd Al-Wahhab, the founder of the Wahhabi movement in Najd, who had in turn discovered Ibn Taymiyya, the leader of both old and modern Salafiyyin. The roots of the latter go back to Ahmad Bin Hanbal, the founder of the first Salafi movement, who established it in reaction to Abu Hanifa and the Mu'atizilites' absolute use of reason. Moreover, this was a reaction to the Malikites' heavy emphasis on the use of the concept of interest, to the view that what the Muslims found good was divinely good, and that interest was the basis for legislation, as Al-Tufi said in Andalusia. It is better to return to the pure text and to obey divine orders and prohibitions without the interference of human thought through understanding, interpretation, analysis or reasoning. In this probably lies the beginning of the spread of Wahhabi Islam and its influence in the rest of the contemporary Islamic movements.

Hasan Al-Banna, the disciple of Rashid Rida, was immersed in the Salafi spirit. He wanted to fulfill Al-Afghani's dream of establishing an Islamic revolutionary party capable of carrying the revolutionary Islamic ideology and achieving the Islamic project of liberation. He established the movement of the Muslim Brothers on the banks of the canal in Isma'iliyya in 1928, and in less than a quarter of a century it became the strongest and most dynamic Islamic movement in Egypt, Syria, Yemen and Jordan. Al-Banna was able to formulate a clear and simple theoretical and practical Islam that had an activist concept of the Brothers as fighters during the day and monks during the night. In the forties, the Brothers entered into the fervor of the Egyptian national movement, fought in Palestine in 1948 and opposed the tyrannical feudal system of the British, the Palace and minority parties. They represented, along with the Wafd party and the communists, the main opposition to the existing policies in the 1940s, notwithstanding their own ideological differences.

Hasan Al-Banna was assassinated in February 1949 after giving a lecture to the Association of Muslim Youth. The Palace, the British and some minority parties were behind the assassination. Then a series of reciprocal assassinations took place, resulting in the death of Al-Nuqrashi and Ahmad Maher, which were followed by the arrest and torture of the members of the Brotherhood. The Palace established the Iron Guards, which included Anwar Al-Sadat in its membership. The communists had their own secret apparatuses and the Brothers also set up their secret apparatus to prepare for essential changes and to overcome the regime by force.

The Brothers did not only lose the founder of the Brotherhood through the assassination of the martyr Hasan Al-Banna, but also its guide, theoretician and spiritual father. No one, be it lawyers, judges, jurists, preachers, officers, politicians or businessmen could succeed him. His post remained open for two years till one member of the Guidance Bureau suggested the name of Sayyid Qutb. However, other members objected because this new name was associated with the secularists, the communists, the socialists and literary figures, and because Qutb was not one of the founding members, as were 'Umar Al-Tilmisani and others. He also did not have the legal weight of 'Abd Al-Hakim 'Abdin or 'Abd Al-Qadir 'Awda, or the juristic knowledge of Sayyid Sabiq, the oratory skills of Muhammad Al-Ghazali or the political skill of Hasan Al-'Ishmawi. Nonetheless, he was appointed as the general secretary of the Propagation (Da'wa) and Thought Section and as a member of the Guidance Bureau.

In fact, Sayyid Qutb was a unique personality in the history of Egypt and the relationship between the Free Officers and the Muslim Brothers.

This was obvious in the last phase of his life, which is the political phase. He went through four phases: the first is the literary phase of the 1930s, when he was a romantic poet composing national romantic poetry, such as *Al-Shati' al-Majhul* in 1934. Then in the 1940s, he wrote in the literary genre for children, with books such as *Ashwak*, *Al-Atyaf al-Araba'a* and *Al-Madina al-Mashura*, and also autobiographies such as *Tifl fi al-Qarya*, much as Tawfiq Al-Hakim had done in *Yomiyat Na'ib fi al Aryaf*. He was also the author of literary innovations through his literary criticism, starting with *Muhimmat al-Sha'ir fi al-Hayat*, which was introduced by Mahdi 'Allam, Dean of Arts at the Alexandria University. In the mid-1940s, he published *Al-Naqd al-Adabi...Usulih wa Manahijih* where he used Qur'anic verses as literary examples. He then applied his theory in existential impressionist criticisms, which depended on the music of language, in his book *Al-Taswir al-Fanni fi al-Qur'an al-Karim wa Mashahid Yawm al-Qiyama fi al-Qur'an*, two decades before the book *Al-Juwaniyya* by 'Uthman Amin was published.

This happened at a time when Khalaf Allah Muhammad Khalaf Allah wrote his Master's thesis *"Fan al-Qasas fi al-Qur'an"* under the supervision of Amin Al-Khawli, which was turned down by the university authorities, who claimed that the thesis rejected the historical events in the stories of the prophets. It was the same charge that had been brought earlier against Taha Husayn in his book, *Fi al-Shi'r al-Jahili* and later against Hamid Nasr Abu Zayd in his book, *Mafum al-Nas*. Sayyid Qutb was in the camp of the new against the old and with 'Abbas Mahmud Al-'Aqqad against Taha Husayn, and it was he who introduced the trilogy of Najib Mahfouz to the world.

The second phase is the social phase, when Sayyid Qutb discovered the social aspect of Islam after having discovered the literary aspect of the Qur'an. He wrote his book, *Social Justice in Islam*, first in the form of an article, reflecting the spirit of the social conflict in the 1940s. It was then published in book form in 1949. In the book, he linked the issue of social justice – then a recurrent theme in cinema, poetry, novels, political thought and parties of the time like the Wafd vanguard – to the concept of *tawhid*. *Tawhid* is composed of three principles: human freedom, human equality and social solidarity. In 1947, he gave historical examples from the sayings of the Prophet's companions and the imams on Islamic socialism. Then Qutb wrote *Ma'rakat al-Islam wa al-Ra'simaliyya* as if it were a communist declaration authenticating Marxism, in which he showed the contradiction between Marxism and Islamic socialism. After this, he wrote the book *Al-Salam al-'Alami wa al-Islam*, where he set the responsibility for peace on the conscience, that is, man's satisfaction with himself, then his move to peace in the family and harmony among its members, to peace in society that worked for dissolving the difference between classes. For this reason, the Egyptian revolution appointed him head of the Liberation Rally, which was its first political organization, and as the supervisor of its magazine and publications.

The third phase is the philosophical one, where he delved into the theoretical side of Islam through the foundation of an Islamic ideology in his book *Khasa'is al-Tasawwur al-Islami wa Muqawwimatih*, which depended on divine oneness, idealism, equality, balance, mobility and sentimentality. He was closer to Muhammad Iqbal than to the Muslim Brothers. Since the book was a response to Alexis Carrel's book, *Man the Unknown*, there were comparisons between the self and the other, and Islam and the West. This became more focused after his visit to the United States of America on an educational mission, where he suffered from cultural shock caused by the contradictions between the two societies. Then, in his *Al-Mustaqbal li Hadha al-Din*, he wrote the future of the self and the end of the other. Finally, he collected a few articles on religion, politics, literature, sociology and history in his *Dirasat Islamiyya*. It was the last of his theoretical works and contained the highest level of Islamic ideology during the early phase of the Egyptian revolution.

The fourth phase is the political phase. When the revolution of the Free Officers took place in 1952, Qutb had already been a member of the Muslim Brotherhood for two years. Because he was known for his socialist writings, he was asked to give talks on the radio about nationalism, socialism and revolution. When the revolution dissolved parties, it exempted the Brotherhood because of its relations to the revolution. Sayyid Qutb wrote the program of the Brothers because the revolution asked the parties to write their political programs.

[65]

After the schism between the Free Officers themselves, that is, between Jamal 'Abd Al-Nasir and Muhammad Najib, which became know as the crisis of March 1954, the Muslim Brothers joined Muhammad Najib because he seemed to unite the two halves of the Nile valley, since his father was Egyptian and his mother was Sudanese. When Najib lost, the conflict between the Brothers and the revolution took place and reached its apex in July 1954, when a member of the Muslim Brotherhood fired at 'Abd Al-Nasir at the Manshiyya Square in Alexandria in an attempted assassination. This gave 'Abd Al-Nasir and his comrades the opportunity to dissolve the Brotherhood and to arrest the members of the Guidance Bureau. 'Abd Al-Qadir 'Awda and other members of the organization were executed and Qutb was jailed.

Out of the terrible torture and the darkness of the prison, and because of his intense pain, Sayyid Qutb wrote *Ma'alim fi al-Tariq*, adopting some its chapters from *Fi Zilal al-Qur'an*. Some of the chapters express the agonies of the innocent who have been jailed. In this book, the contrast between Islam and *jahiliyya*, between belief and unbelief, and between God and tyranny is sharpened. This contrast cannot be reconciled and one party will eliminate the other. Because there is no victor but God, Islam will overcome *jahiliyya*, God will overcome tyranny, belief will overcome unbelief. This will happen through the rise of a unique Qur'anic generation, the elite of the elites, who will spread justice throughout the world as it is now full of injustice.

When the book was published in the 1960s, no one knew its importance but 'Abd Al-Nasir read it, after a visit to Moscow to which he went to convalesce. His own organizational experience led him to suspect that there must be a secret organization behind the book. He asked his minister of Interior, Shi'rawi Jum'a, to uncover this organization. Qutb was arrested again two years after his release and was accused of conspiring to overthrow the regime. After a mockery trial, he was condemned and was sentenced to death in the summer of 1965, notwithstanding that many Arab and Muslim rulers interceded on his behalf.

The Free Officers revolution was then on the defensive after their promulgation of the socialist law of 1962–1963, enacted in the aftermath of the Egyptian–Syrian separation. The revolution stood side-by-side with the revolution in Yemen, and could not allow any challenge, external or internal. Nonetheless, the defeat of June 1967, two years after the hanging of Sayyid Qutb, was the beginning of the end of the first republic, which finally collapsed after the death of Jamal 'Abd Al-Nasir, in September 1970.

The book, *Fi Zilal al-Qur'an*, is considered to be the latest of what has been published in the sciences of exegesis in modern Islamic thought, which followed the exegesis of *Al-Manar* by Muhammad Abdu and Muhammad Rashid Rida. In it, the four phases of Sayyid Qutb's life are interwoven: he brings together the literary, social and philosophical interpretations. Contemporary Islamic groups read *Ma'alim fi al-Tariq* and forget his books, *Al-Taswir al-Fani fi al-Qur'an, Al-'Adala al-Ijtima'iyya fi al-Islam* and *Ma'rakat al-Islam wa al-Ra'simaliyya*. Thus, Sayyid Qutb – the poet, literary critic, the socialist and the philosopher – has been reduced to a personality who excommunicates society and who is the main source for groups calling for excommunication and migration.[12] The challenge still exists today: Who will succeed Sayyid Qutb as an Islamic thinker who wants to unify Muslims, is progressive and socialist, and who would again unite Islam and revolution?

The Contemporary Roots of Political Islam

Within the same period, the Free Officers formed their own secret apparatus in order to seize power and to end the rule of corrupt parties, the Palace's misuse of the national government, the interference of the British in political life and the presence of their forces on the bank of the Suez Canal and at the Tal Kabeer. The objectives of the Free Officers' secret organization also included investigating the malfunctioning weapons and the defeat of the Egyptian army in Palestine, and even the killing of Hasan Al-Banna. All of this was included in the first six principles of the revolution: to eliminate colonialism, monarchy, feudalism and capitalism, to constitute a strong army and to establish a sound democratic life.

[67]

When the revolution broke out in July 1952, half of the Revolutionary Council was from the Muslim Brothers, including 'Abd Al-Mun'im 'Abd Al-Ra'uf and Rashad Mahana. Officer Abu Al-Makarim 'Abd Al-Hay was the link between the Free Officers within the army and the Muslim Brothers. Jamal 'Abd Al-Nasir and Al-Sadat had relations with Hasan Al-Banna and the Muslim Brothers, and they all had the same objective: to change the political regime in Egypt which was controlled by the British, the Palace and feudalism, to a national regime that would liberate Egypt from these forces.

After the dissolution of the Muslim Brotherhood in 1954, some Brothers were jailed, others moved to the Arab states in the Gulf or went underground, and a new phase of underground political Islam started with *Ma'alim fi al-Tariq*. The Muslim Brothers were thinking about their sad experiences and waiting for the moment to take revenge from Nasserism. They considered all its achievements to be losses and its failures to be successes—except the nationalization of the Suez Canal, the stopping of the tripartite aggression against Egypt in 1956, and the release of the Brothers from prison to arm them to participate in the defense of the Suez Canal. After its liberation, the Brothers went back to prison having performed their national duty. However, the unity with Syria, 1958–1961, was made on a national non-Islamic basis, and this was why it was severed in 1961. The July socialist laws (1962-1963) were promulgated in the name of secular socialism or Marxism that was allied with 'Abd Al-Nasir. This is why they were abrogated after the imposition of the law of investment and the open-door economy of 1975. The Yemeni war led to bloodshed between Muslims – Egyptians and Yemenis – and was one of the reasons for the defeat of 1967. The Islamic coalition between Riyadh, Tehran and Karachi in 1965 did not succeed in isolating Nasserite Egypt from the outside world, and the success of the Israeli aggression on Egypt in 1967 put on halt the Nasserite experience that ended with the death of its leader in September 1970 and with it the experience of the first republic.

When the second republic started in 1971, it started to liquidate the Nasserite experience in the coup of May 15, 1971, which was named the rectification revolution. The Muslim Brothers, the enemies of 'Abd Al-Nasir, were freed from prison so that they could be used to dismantle his policies, to constitute one front against the common enemy of atheist socialism and to defend belief and capitalism. The October war of 1973 broke out under the pressures of student demonstrations in 1972, of the war of attrition (1967–1969) and people's expectation of a decisive battle. The Egyptian forces crossed the Suez Canal and the sand barrier to Sinai calling "Allah Akbar."

After its success, the war was construed in religious terms in order to take revenge against 'Abd Al-Nasir, even though he had originally formed the liberation plan 'Badr' and had prepared the army for the war of liberation. The conclusion was drawn that because of atheism during the Nasserite period, defeat had occurred and because of belief in the Sadat period, victory had been achieved. The Virgin appeared in Zaytoun after the defeat to share in the sorrows of the Egyptians, and the believers crossed the Suez Canal in the victory of 1973 while chopping the heads of the Jews, as they had done in the Badr conquest.

The slogan of "knowledge and belief" became the motto of the second republic, for those without belief cannot be trusted. This slogan was used in order to purge the regime of the communist remnants of the Nasserite period. The laws of investment and open-door policy were published in 1975, and the Muslim Brothers started cooperating with the new regime against the old regime. The Nasserites were purged from the universities by the Islamists in 1976–1977 and the Islamic movement was able to impose itself on the campuses and lead the elections of the student union.

Religion was used by the two parties: by the political regime as a tool to add political legitimacy after the coup of May 15, and by the Islamic movement who continued the propaganda and Islamic activities in order to gain popularity that would prepare it for either a democratic victory – because the regime allowed multi-party politics – or a military coup with popular support when time was ripe, that is, when the political regime was weakened and the Islamic movement stronger.

In prisons, discussions between the members of the Islamic movement took place about the course of the Brotherhood and its losses and successes.

A trend that was more radical than the generation of the pioneers was forming, one that wished to avenge what had happened to the movement and wanted to use violence by way of secret armed organizations and assassination—for violence can only be met with violence. The contemporary Islamic groups began to practice this new vision as manifest in the attempt to seize a military technical school in 1974 and then the seizure of the Asyut province a few years later. The death of Sheikh Al-Dhahabi in 1977 also had an impact. The Islamic movement splintered into many small groups, like al-Takfir wa al-Hijra, under the leadership of Shukri Mustapha, which was the name given by the security departments for Jama'at al-Muslimin, and the groups Qif wa Tabayyan, Qutbiyyin and al-Amr bi al-Ma'ruf wa al-Nahy 'An al-Munkar. All are grouped under al-Jama'at al-Islamiyya, if they are united by external or internal reason or al-Jama'a al-Islamiyya, if they act individually according to their peaceful or militant means.

After the popular uprising of January 1977 and the realization on the part of the new regime that Nasserism and the pictures of Jamal 'Abd Al-Nasir were still prominent in the movements of the masses from Alexandria to Aswan, Sadat started to look for new allies outside Egypt—Israel and the United States of America. He visited Jerusalem in November of the same year and concluded the Camp David Accord in 1978 and the Egyptian-Israeli peace agreement in 1979. Furthermore, to increase his control and power, and after the Arab Rejectionist Front cut relations with Egypt, Sadat issued new laws that restricted freedom in addition to the emergency, suspicion and shame laws. He also raised the motto of "Egypt First" and "Knowledge and Belief."

He took on the role of father of the family who defended the values of the village, put on the traditional gown, held a stick and sat on a stool, and was given the title of "The Believing President" and "Khamis al-Khulafa' al-Rashidin." He was referred to as "Muhammad" Anwar Al-Sadat, in imitation of the Prophet, and he started his speeches with the words "In the Name of God," and not as 'Abd Al-Nasir used to do, "O, Citizens, Brothers." He would end his speeches with a Qur'anic verse to give the impression of modesty and humility, so that he could hide his repression and despotism, "Our Lord, Do not punish us if we forget or err; our Lord, do not hold a grudge against us as You held a grudge against those before us; our Lord, do not make us carry more than we can shoulder, forgive us, pardon us, have mercy on us, You are our Lord, make us victorious over those people who do not believe."[13]

The political authority used the weapon of religion to excommunicate its political opponents, like the Nasserites and the communists, and accused them of atheism and materialism, using the slogan "Those who do not have a belief cannot be trusted." Therefore, both the opponents of the political regime and the Islamic movements were both excommunicated through the same logic.[14]

The Islamic movement realized that it could not go along with Al-Sadat after the peace treaty with Israel, his surrendering to the West, especially the United States, the rupture of relations with the Arabs and the promulgation of laws restricting various freedoms. This ended the period of reciprocity between Sadat and the Islamists, during which he used them to liquidate the Nasserites from the universities and public life and to take over the centers of power in the media and society. They then decided to stand against him and ally themselves with the Nasserite, Marxist and liberal opposition. The opposition forces united to formulate alternative policies for rejecting peace with Israel and resisting the United States of America, while calling for Arab unity and rejecting the laws restricting freedoms.

Sadat wanted to get rid of the coalition of the opposition forces in order to prove that his people were behind him after Manhim Begin shed doubt on the support of the Egyptian people for the Egyptian–Israeli peace treaty. Sadat wanted to show that the opposition was a wicked elitist minority that did not represent the majority of people who supported peace, and that he was capable of arresting and jailing them in twenty-four hours. He did that, in fact, and arrested all the representatives of opposition movements, including the Islamists, Nasserists, Marxists and liberals. He also dismissed university professors and journalists from their work and removed Pope Shounuda, the head of the Coptic Church, from his post in what was referred to as the September 1981 massacre. Sadat was assassinated one month later, on October 6, 1981, by army officers and soldiers who belonged to the Jama'at al-Jihad al-Islamiyya.[15]

From 1981 until the beginning of the twenty-first century, the Islamic movements followed the same path, that is, armed conflict against the ruling political regime in Egypt. Sadatism continued without Sadat, and the relations with Israel continued notwithstanding the refusal of Egyptian political forces, unions, syndicates, and civil organizations to normalize relations with Israel. The Luxor massacre of 1999 cancelled the tourist season. Other incidents that contributed to this include incidents against tourists at the pyramids, the throwing of bombs in Liberation Square (*Al Tahrir*) and gunfights between the police and the Islamists in Upper Egypt. This illustrates that the Islamic groups have control over public life and can affect the economy, create political strife and seize the media through the backdoor by being on the front pages of daily newspapers. Tensions between the Islamic groups and the political regime lessened because the groups reconsidered the use of violence and the shedding of innocent blood through the attack on tourists as in the Luxor incident. This was facilitated by the emergence of a new wing that prohibited such actions because the innocent should not be treated as guilty. Nonetheless, tension continues because the Islamic groups are still the main opposition force in the country, and the security departments are watching them closely.

The Slogans of Political Islam

The analysis of the slogans of contemporary Islamic movements as signs of their political ideologies and psychological moods shows that they are more negative than positive. They indicate a great deal of anger and rejection, the desire for an escape to the alternative and a quest for a savior. There are four slogans: the governance of God, Islam is the alternative, Islam is the solution, and the implementation of the *sharia*.

The first slogan, "the governance of God," is the rejection of the governance of humans that persecuted the Islamic movement, whether in the liberal period that witnessed the assassination of Hasan Al-Banna or the nationalist period that witnessed the martyrdom of 'Abd Al-Qadir

'Awda, Sayyid Qutb and others from Jama'at al-Jihad such as 'Abd Al-Salam Faraj and Khalid Muhammad Al-Islambuli. God is the governor who does not do injustice and He knows the interests of His servants. His governance is manifest in applying His will, commands and prohibitions, which are made clear in the *sharia*. This position is clarified by the Qur'anic text in three verses: "And those who do not govern by what God has revealed they are the unbelievers,"[16] in another verse, "they are the unjust," and in a third verse, "they are the heretics." The governance of God is against the governance of human wishes and class interests. The governance of God cannot be wrong but human governance could be wrong or right. Therefore, this slogan connotes the rejection of all human systems of government, liberal, nationalist, socialist, Marxist, democratic, republican, royal, princely, statist, sultanic and popular. The slogan means rejection and negation.

If you ask the Islamic group what the governance of God means in a positive manner, the answer is difficult because God does not rule directly but through the *sharia*. People understand and deduce the *sharia* from its fundamentals and apply it in place and time according to necessity. When greater detail is required, the principle of *shura* is transformed into a system of government, the principle of social justice into a theory of economics and the principle of the right to differ into a theory of political pluralism. When the Islamic movement comes to power, as is the case in Sudan, Afghanistan under the Taliban, and Iran, it is transformed into an authoritarian regime that does not differ from the secular political regimes; authoritarianism is a social structure and a cultural tradition used mostly by both the political regimes and opposition movements, including the Islamic movement.

The second slogan, "Islam is the alternative," also represents a massive rejection of all available alternatives that have been tried in the life of Muslims: liberalism, socialism and then Arab nationalism. Perhaps, liberalism has offered some achievements at the level of freedom of thought, expression, journalism, and party and parliamentary life. In the meantime, the national movement was strengthened and the revolution of 1919 was made in its name. Nonetheless, feudalism, capitalism and orientation to the West dominated. The corrupt parties repressed each other, elections were falsified and parliament could be dissolved whenever the king wished, the constitution was a gift from him, and the British were still in the country. Furthermore, during that period, the treaty of 1936 was signed and the catastrophe of 1948 took place.

Liberalism was then followed by socialism or Arab nationalism, which realized some achievements, such as the nationalization of Suez Canal in 1956 and foreign companies in 1957, the unity with Syria during 1958–1961, the implementation of the July socialist law during 1962–1963, the support of the Yemeni revolution in 1964, the Iraqi revolution in 1958, the Libyan revolution in 1969, the rejection of peace and negotiations with the Zionist entity in 1967, the war of attrition during 1968–1969, adopting free education and the beginning of industrialization. It also included uniting the Arabs and taking liberation movements to their conclusions, building the public sector, the foundation of the non-allied movement under the motto "Neither East nor West" since the Ban Dong conference in 1955 until the Belgrade conference in 1964, and the conferences in Algeria, Cairo and New Delhi. However, it ended in a catastrophic defeat in 1967 following the dominance of the new class that comprised of officers, technocrats, senior state employees and party men, and the spread of massive corruption, repression and looting of the public sector. Sinai, the rest of Palestine and the Golan Heights were occupied and greater Israel was established. Soviet migrations to Israel followed as well as the recognition of Israel and the alliance with the United States of America.

The same continued in the second and third republics—the public sector was privatized, free education was privatized, national planning was transformed to foreign investment and national sovereignty gave way to globalization and market economies. The Islamic movement was incriminated and its leaders were martyred; the Islamists were excluded and imprisoned and then were used against the political opposition, becoming the victims of political games. The legacy of this age is alive; it agitates loathing, incites hatred and is waiting for revenge.

The third slogan, "Islam is the solution," is like the previous slogan. When crises intensified and disasters followed, and when the regimes were incapable of resolving them, the slogan of Islam as the solution surfaced as a search for the unknown and the magic key to open all gates to resolve the inability to find the proper solutions for the crises that mounted day after day. Liberalism did not succeed in liberating Palestine, of which half was lost in the liberal period in 1948 and the other half in the socialist period in 1967. The Islamic movement was persecuted in the liberal period in which Hasan Al-Banna was assassinated. It was also persecuted in the socialist period and 'Abd Al-Qadir 'Awda, Sayyid Qutb and 'Abd Al-Salam Faraj were executed.

The nation was divided during the liberal period after World War I, which saw the defeat of Turkey and its occupation by the Western powers and the division of the treasures of the Sick Man. The nation was fragmented into Arabs, Berbers, Kurds, Sunnites, Shi'ites, Maronites and Copts, and civil wars in Sudan, Lebanon and Algeria took place. The borders between Morocco and Algeria were closed, clashes between Egypt and Sudan occurred, differences between Yemen and the Kingdom of Saudi Arabia and between Qatar and Bahrain happened, as did the Iraqi invasion of the state of Kuwait where a group of Arabs joined the Western coalition and another was opposed to it. Israel transgressed against Lebanon, Tunisia, Iraq, Syria and Egypt, and still wanted to reach Iran and Pakistan.

The ideologies of liberalism and socialist nationalism could not resolve the issues of development, neither through capitalism nor through socialism. They also could not resolve the issue of identity after it had become Western in the liberal period or in the third republic through the impact of the age of globalization and openness. Since experience has shown the failure of secular ideologies to modernize, and because Islam is the only ideology that has not been tried until now, an Islamic rule is under experiment now in Afghanistan and Sudan resulting in great loss of freedom. The Islamic revolutionary experience in Iran is in danger because of the polarization between the reformists and the conservatives and the attempt of each to control the state sectors, such as the army, the

[75]

parliament, the judiciary and information. The 'Islamic' coup in the Sudan ended in conflict between the two leaders, 'Umar Al-Bashir and Hasan Al-Turabi, in addition to the armed conflict that is going on between the North and the South.

The fourth slogan, "the implementation of the *sharia*," represents people's dissatisfaction with the set of civil political, social and economic laws that rule over them. People do not know the reason for their promulgation, for changing them or the interests that they represent. All of these laws are equally bad in terms of injustice and incompatibility with and harm to the interests of the people. People call for the implementation of Islamic *sharia* as an escape from civil laws. If humans are unjust, God is just; and if civil legislations express the will of the rulers and their desires, the divine *sharia* is just and does not commit injustice—it expresses the divine will that cannot be partial.

Political regimes follow the wills and choices of the rulers, whether liberal or socialist, and the ruler himself may change them depending on his mood, development, interests and alliances. The capitalist and socialist economic systems depend on either private or public property and on economic freedom or orientation. All of this is decided by the rulers without due consideration to the interests of the people. The wage policy changes everyday and people do not know its criteria—it leads to poverty and destitution, there is no parity with prices and it is not based on the value of labor alone, but gives the white collar more than it gives the blue collar. The educational systems and their rules change every few years, and they do not change for educational reasons, nor do they lead to research, but to obeying the rulers and the traditions of the elders. The citizen is at the mercy of the governmental institutions, whether to get a building permit, a driving license or an identification card, or his right to a court or to complain to the police department. He longs for a system that does not oppress people and for a just law.

Since Islam is still alive and the *sharia* is accepted as a means of worship, it is right, both existentially and psychologically, that people should raise the slogan of implementing the Islamic *sharia*, although it is only implemented by men who do not understand it and implement it literally, as is the case in many conservative Islamic regimes in Sudan, Iran, Afghanistan, North Nigeria and Chad, where the Islamic majority established itself and sacrificed the unity of the country for the implementation of Islamic *sharia*. This is also the case in some Indonesian regions.[17]

When analyzing the early traditional slogans of the Muslim Brothers – "God is our leader," "the Prophet is our example," "the Qur'an is our constitution," "*jihad* is our way" and "dying for the sake of God is the highest of our hopes," which constituted the collective and principal motto of the Brotherhood – we find that they also express the social, economic and political conditions. "God is our leader" means the dissatisfaction with human leadership, for all humans are domineering, repressive and unjust, and want only to maintain their power, whether a king or an officer, Quraysh or the army, delegated from God or elected by the people. All rule by false delegation and election. The leadership of God therefore is better than human leadership. "The Prophet is our example" means that the human example is rare and that all humans are imperfect and that the rulers are not examples that should be followed. The Prophet is the example, both in his life and behavior, along with his family and companions, and in his words and deeds.

"The Qur'an is our constitution" means the dissatisfaction with human constitutions that express the will of the rulers, for they change and include articles that provide the rulers with absolute powers and restrict the freedom of people. This is why popular uprisings take place in order to abrogate the constitutions or to amend some of their articles. The Qur'an is a constitution because it does not discriminate or favor anyone, and it is a divine constitution that transcends time, place and age. "*Jihad* is our way" means the rejection of subjugation, of yielding to the enemy, of acceptance of humiliation and of having relations that harm the interest of the country. Thus, *jihad* is the best way for attaining our rights. Finally, "martyrdom for the sake of God is the dearest of our wishes" means love of death instead of a shameful life, that the martyrs are alive in the eye of God and that the martyrs of resistance in southern Lebanon and Palestine are capable of holding out before the strongest of armies and the most modern weaponry by using their booby trapped bodies and vehicles against the enemy.

The analysis of the mottos of a political movement leads to the same conclusion, that is, dissatisfaction with reality and the rejection of its imperatives, and the longing for a new reality. For example the slogan "God is Great, and Praise be to God" means that God is greater than any great personality, God is greater than any oppressor and is the eliminator of arrogant powers. This is the slogan of the Islamic revolution in Iran that was directed against the deification of humans, revering the rulers and sanctifying the tyrants. At the same time, it means humility and thanks and praise to God for his support of what is right over what is wrong and justice over injustice.

The motto "Khaybar, Khaybar, O Jews, Muhammad's army will return" is a rejection of the nation's inability to face the Zionist entity and its settlements, expansion, repression of the Aqsa uprising and the killing of the children who are throwing stones. History is a connected series, and as the Prophet was earlier victorious over the Jews in Khaybar, Muslims will be victorious now in Palestine by the same weapon, that is Islam. The motto "By our spirit, by our blood, we sacrifice for Islam" has the same meaning of "By our spirit, by our blood, we sacrifice for Palestine" and the same as the mottos of martyrdom "By our spirit, by our blood, we sacrifice for the martyr" and "There is no god but God, and the martyr is loved by God."

The Dialects of Legitimacy and Illegitimacy

The relation between the Islamic movements and the political regimes is defined by the concepts of legitimacy and illegitimacy and this is a reciprocal perception. When the political regimes are legitimate and genuinely elected by the people, the Islamic movement emerges and takes its share of representation in parliament, in the parliamentary systems. Violent practices then become the exception on both sides because of the new democratic experiences of Islamic movements in Muslim societies. When the political regimes are authoritarian and repressive, and exercise control through security and police departments, this reflects negatively on the Islamic movements, which resort to violence. Public violence is countered by secret violence, and repressive violence by liberation violence. Repressive violence can only be countered by revolutionary violence, as is the case in the relations between the revolutionary organizations and the dictatorial regimes in Latin America.[18] The political regimes started violence, not only against the Islamic movements but also against liberal, national, Islamic opposition movements. Violence as a beginning leads to violence as an end, and violence as an action produces violence as a reaction.

There is visible violence, as practiced by security departments against the Islamic movements, as well as invisible violence, like distorting their image in the media, excluding them from the decision-making center and interfering in the elections of unions, syndicates, non-governmental organizations and political parties in order to defeat the Islamist candidates. It is also manifest in not allowing them to publish their daily newspapers and weekly magazines or engage in their regular activities, putting their members under surveillance and preventing them from traveling and suspecting their leaders and their way of life and practices—the beard, the gown, prayer beads, headscarf, closed groups, and the manner of marriage and kinship. The Islamic movements are also attacked by the governmental preachers of enlightenment and accused of darkness, backwardness, reactionary thought, fundamentalism and formalism. It results in repressed violence that could spontaneously explode when there is a social trigger factor.

There are four types of relations between political regimes and Islamic movements. The first is the parliamentary type that allows the legitimacy of the Islamic movement and regards it as part of the political system and as one of the opposition forces. The democratic political regime produces a democratic Islamic movement that does not practice violence and accepts the results of the elections. Sometimes, the Islamic movement transcends its representative role to perform the national mission of the state in defending the unity of national territories and the independence of the country. The best example of this is the Lebanese experience and the role of Islamic movements in the Lebanese political regime where Hizbullah carried the main burden for the liberation of southern Lebanon from Israeli occupation, with the agreement of the state, within the framework of a constitutional legitimacy and with the appreciation of the state and the people for its role.

The second type is represented by the military and royal regimes that allow the legitimacy of Islamic movements, not out of favoring democracy or believing in the legitimacy of the Islamic movements as well as their organizations, programs, or practices, but out of expediency in order to bring about some stability to the political regime, social life and the security of the state. Examples of this are the Jordanian, Yemeni, Kuwaiti, Moroccan and Bahraini experiences. Jordan started this experience by allowing the Muslim Brothers and other Islamic groups to run for parliamentary elections and to accept the rule of the democratic process—successes and failures, the majority and the minority. If the Islamic movement is successful in achieving some of its professed objectives, its representation in the next round of elections increases, but if it has achieved nothing and people have not felt the practical implementation of its professed objectives, its representation in the next round of elections decreases. The second probability is closer to what the parties in the autocratic, military or royal, regimes would want, but is very difficult to achieve because the main political decisions are monopolized by the political regime.

The Kuwaiti experience is similar to the Jordanian experience due to a long democratic history of the political regime and the strength of opposition on the street, journalism, and the parliament with all its Islamic, liberal and national groupings. Notwithstanding the radicalism of some groups of the Islamic movement like Jama'at al-Islah and the dissatisfaction of the political regime with opposition, democratic practices are still dominant.

Bahrain was aware of the political dynamics and followed the same democratic experience in the form of changing the political regime from a non-constitutional princedom to a constitutional monarchy, just as reformists like Al-Afghani had called for a century and a half before. The opposition outside of Bahrain, whether national, Islamic or liberal, returned to the country, and the university professors who were expelled returned to their jobs.

The royal regime in Morocco was the first to permit political participation, when the king allowed the organization of the Muslim Brothers, which supported the throne, to have a nominal presence without any effective power in political life. The king was the "Prince of the Believers," and Muhammad V and ‘Allal Al-Fasi were national religious personalities. The Hizb al-Istiqlal was composed of the scholars of the Qarawiyyin. Religion existed in the political sphere in the name of the political regime and not because of the pressure of the Muslim Brothers. If an Islamic movement moved out of this type of relationship, its members would be excluded, marginalized, chased out and sentenced to execution, as happened to the Islamic Youth movement. They could also be placed under house arrest, as was the case with ‘Abd Al-Salam Yasin, the leader of Jama‘at al-‘Adl wa al-Ihsan, after he sent a letter of advice to the young King, Muhammad VI, who moved away from the democratic opening at the beginning of his rule and again stifled Jama‘at al-‘Adl wa al-Ihsan. The King had done this because he depended on the socialists in government who had a parliamentary majority, and acted in a style similar to the Middle Eastern rulers who made the different groups of the opposition fight each other in accordance with the perception of their relative threat, the most dangerous being eliminated first.

The political regime in Yemen followed the same democratic approach after it received new legitimacy by maintaining the unity of the South and the North against the danger of secession. Although there were some violent practices by Hizb al-Islah in Yemen, which is connected with the Muslim Brothers, the experience of multi-party politics continues, even though the ruling party has received a majority in parliament. There is also tension between the two groups of national and Islamic opposition, which also indicates that the game of pitting political forces against each other continues, as is the case in Egypt.

There is a third type of relationship between political regimes and Islamic movements found in the experiences of Egypt, Syria, Iraq, and

Libya, which are military regimes. A political regime of this type emerges from a military coup and derives its legitimacy from revolution. The military coup leads to an un-Islamic regime, since it is not based on contract and free choice of the people. Therefore, it lacks legitimacy, which again results in the slogans of Islamic movements, such as "divine governance," representing a threat to it. This third type does not legitimize the Islamic movements because they represent simultaneously a danger and an alternative to it.

There is a repressed conflict between the political regime and Islamic movements that simmers constantly, and surfaces from time to time, as is the case with the expatriate Shi'ite Islamic opposition in Iraq and the Islamic opposition in Libya, which reached the level of armed conflict in the mountains near Benghazi a short while ago. The same happened to the Muslim Brothers in Syria after the massacre of Hamah and their imprisonment, then their release in order to enter into a government coalition. Other examples are the Islamic movements in Egypt, especially Jama'at al-Jihad al-Islamiyya, which still views the political regime as an illegitimate one that should be resisted, even if the innocent die, as happened in cases such as the attack against foreign tourists and symbols of the state.

The third form of political relationship also exists in the royal regimes of the Kingdom of Saudi Arabia, the Sultanate in Oman, the government of the United Arab Emirates, and the princedom of Qatar. The regimes derive their legitimacy in one way or another from Islam. The king of the Kingdom of Saudi Arabia is the Custodian of the Two Holy Shrines, and Islam is the culture, behavior and civilization of the people in the Sultanate of Oman, the Princedom of Qatar and the State of the United Arab Emirates. The distinction is due to the emergence of reformist trends within the traditional Islamic movements, such as the neo-Wahhabism in the Kingdom of Saudi Arabia, which reject some political practices that occur in the kingdom in the name of traditional Wahhabism. Examples of these practices are the increasing dependence on the United States of America after the second Gulf war and the bringing in of foreign troops. In this case, there is no difference between the Islamic forces and other liberal, national, patriotic forces, as well as religious scholars, intellectuals, human rights groups, civil societies and women's movements.

The fourth type represents the most tense relationship between the political regime and the Islamic movement, as exists in Sudan and Algeria. In Sudan, a coup took place that was led by the Islamic movement and the army, that is, the religious authority and the military authority. In its aftermath, many parties went into exile outside Sudan and formed an opposition front, the National Democratic Alliance (NDA), which included members of the Sudanese Peoples Liberation Army (SPLA), with the leader of the Rally, Muhammad 'Uthman al-Mirghani, as the head of the opposition forces. The conflict continues after the arrest of Hasan Al-Turabi because of his agreement with John Garang, the leader of the SPLA. The civil war between the North and the South has been going on for some time, and may be compounded by a situation of North against North. At the same time, Sudan is under foreign sanctions, and the Al-Shifa' factory for medicine was bombed because of the charge that it was producing biological weapons. The people in the South are facing famine because of the war between the government and the opposition, that is, Islam and the rebel groups.

The most dangerous case, however, is Algeria where a civil war is occurring between the antagonistic brothers, the Islamists and the state, after a democratic opening brought about through a popular uprising during the rule of al-Shadhili Bin Jadid. This resulted in the success of the Islamic movement in the elections for legislative councils, which were then cancelled by the military. The movement turned to armed struggle to regain the electoral victory cancelled by the army, bringing about the death of around seventy thousand martyrs, including women, children and old people. The law enacted to promote national harmony has not succeeded in ending the war. Furthermore, the disagreements among the leaders of the Islamic movement about the purpose of the war and its ugliness did not make it less acute. The state incriminates the Islamists because they kill innocent fellow citizens, and the Islamists excommunicate the state because it does not rule by Islamic law and because it follows an authoritarian system. Each party engages in excluding and casting away the other, and there is no light at the end of the tunnel.

The Future of Political Islam

It is clear from the dialectics of legitimacy and illegitimacy that there is more political stability in the democratic political regimes where the Islamic movement becomes a legitimate party. The Islamic political discourse is transformed from its rejectionist slogans to a political discourse that is based on a program that builds and does not destroy and that dialogues and does not exclude others. The political regime also feels that its stability depends on democracy and recognition of the Islamic movement's legitimacy, as is the case with other recognized political parties, whether nationalist, liberal or even Marxist—it is not desirable that a party on the margins should have more popular legitimacy than the others. Party life is energized and the democratic experience strengthened in the regimes that recognize the legitimacy of the Islamic movement, for example, Jordan, Kuwait and Yemen; and perhaps Bahrain and Morocco are following the same course.

Political pluralism is of dual nature: it puts limits on the excesses of the ruling party and its absolute authority, and gives people free democratic choice between alternatives. Therefore, instead of having tensions building between the political regimes of Egypt, Syria, Iraq and Tunisia and the secret Islamic movements that work underground or go into exile, and instead of having the occasional outbreaks of violence, the political regime can stabilize and the Islamic movements can live in a healthy political environment if they are given legitimacy and are turned into political parties with social and economic programs. Islam then becomes a popular culture that also acts as a vehicle for political and social concerns.

The main obstacle is still the lack of legitimacy of both the political regime and the Islamic movement, for each side wants to exclude the other. The political regime wants to eliminate all opposition, but so does the Islamic movement because it regards itself as the strongest among opposition forces that want to overthrow and replace the regime. The latter may not be factual but it lives in the hopes of the people and in the media. The historical weight of the struggle in the past precludes a dialogue in the present and a coalition in the future. The two sides are afraid of each other. Each one waits for the other to make a mistake so that it can overpower the other and get rid of it, and does not know that by doing this it destroys itself and the temple the way Samson did.

The condition that the political regime imposes for the recognition of the legitimacy of the Islamic movement is that it should reject violence and accept the rules of party politics. It should also turn its slogan to a political program, like other parties do, because the constitution prohibits the establishment of parties on religious bases, which would make the state a collection of sectarian parties. Some Islamic movements adhered to this condition. For example, in Egypt some wings in the Islamic movement wanted to establish the Wasat party and lodged a request to set up a party with the 'committee for establishing parties' in the *shura* council. Nonetheless, the political regime refused to grant a license to the party under the pretext that the program did not offer anything different from that of the other parties. The political regime arrested the founding members on the charge of establishing an illegal party for the Brothers that had been dissolved in 1954, although the press reported its activities, meetings, victories and losses in the local and general elections, in which the movement's candidates participated as independents. There has now been another attempt to establish the party of al-Adala and the waiting continues, without any approval or refusal. This is also the Turkish scenario in the formation of Islamic parties, like Refah and Fadila, in a secular state, which officially prohibits religious parties. Secularism seems to be an authoritarian, exclusivist, absolute and unilateral alternative theocracy.

The same happened in Tunisia when the Islamic movement formed the Nahda party under the leadership of Rashid Al-Ghannushi. Its program is not much different from Tunisian secular parties. It accepts the democratic process and it is recognized as part of that process. It also rejects violence and recognizes human rights, including, the rights of women, and the right of all people in a just distribution of wealth, which makes it a national, liberal and progressive party. Nonetheless, the political regime refuses to recognize it and harasses its members. It also wants to arrest its leader who lives abroad in Western capitals with freedom of expression and movement—which form part of good Western political culture. The leader is still waiting to change the political regime through a counter military coup or a massive popular revolution so that liberalism, political pluralism and human rights may return.

The Muslim Brothers were released in Syria under the new regime after the massacre of Hamah and the destruction of the city that followed the uprising of the Muslim Brothers under the old regime. The Muslim Brothers asked the regime to forget the past and to start a new period, in which they would have legality and the right to form a group and practice their activities. Nonetheless, the political regime refused to accept the legitimacy of the group, except as part of a governmental coalition, as individuals but not as a group, and as members but not as an organization. The new regime was still wavering between openness and rejection, between the old practice and the requirements of the new regime, and between sole control of the political system and multi-party politics.

The Islamic movement has been put between a rock and a hard place— if it defends its existence and practices its activities, it is accused of planning a coup against the ruling regime, practicing violence, committing crimes and threatening the domestic security from the inside and national security from the outside. If it gives up violence, accepts the rules of democratic process and wants to be part of the social fabric and the course of history, the political regime refuses out of fear that the movement might get the parliamentary majority. In both cases, the political regime stands to lose, but it would be a short-term loss and a long-term victory for the country.

The political regime is also between the hammer and the anvil. If it accepts the legitimacy of the Islamic movement as a political party, the regime will be the victim because the new party will gain the parliamentary majority and the ruling party will be the big loser in the short term. If the regime refuses to license the Islamic movement as a political party, the regime will be the big loser in the long term, and the movement is left with nothing but violence, resulting in counter violence by the political regime, and the killing of the innocent, as is the case in Algeria.

In fact, there is no alternative to political pluralism as a ruling system and a national coalition front composed of all political forces, including the Islamic movement, whether it is a party or a group, in accordance with the result of the ballot box. It would then be impossible for government parties or opposition parties to have a majority.

There are four political forces that are originally intellectual trends in the Arab world: liberalism, nationalism (Nasserism and Arab socialism), Marxism although its regimes collapsed more than a decade ago, and the Islamic movement. Each of these ideologies ruled alone. Liberal parties ruled in the Arab world from the 1950s, before the Arab revolutions, and some of them still rule in Yemen, Egypt, Jordan, Morocco, Lebanon and Sudan, whether in royal or military regimes. People still yearn for the political freedom of liberalism, not only economic freedom. The national regimes resulting from the Arab revolutions took the form of military government in Egypt, Syria, Iraq, Yemen and Libya, and later the national liberation movement, like Algeria. Most of them turned into a liberal military regime after the June 1967 defeat or into a pure military regime, like Tunisia.

Militarism stayed, but socialism turned into liberalism without its values, and corruption, theft and looting of public money dominated. This happened first in Egypt, then in Syria and then in Yemen. Only Iraq maintained it, although the country was besieged after its invasion of the state of Kuwait, and Libya was besieged because of the charges of Lockerby and support for terrorism. Marxism has only one voice in the coalition front in Syria and Iraq, and only remnants of parties in Lebanon. The Islamic movement is more prominent in Lebanon, Sudan, Kuwait, Yemen, Morocco and Jordan. It also exists through opposition groups outside their countries, such as in the case of Iraq and Tunisia, or inside, as is the case in Egypt and Algeria.

Political pluralism is a fact in modern Arab political thought, and one group cannot exclude the other. Political groups may differ in their representation and practices. They may agree with each other on some common national objectives as well as the means to attain them, but they do not transcend the theoretical framework and motive. The groups

[87]

representing the four intellectual ideologies agree on the liberation of Palestine—in the name of Arab nationalism for the Nasserites and the nationalists, and in the name of a free Palestine for the liberal nationalists, in the name of the peasants and laborers and against settler colonialism, which is the highest stage of capitalism for the Marxist, and in the name of *jihad* to liberate the holy lands and the Al-Aqsa mosque for the Islamists. The political regimes, whether liberal or Islamic, royal or military, statist, sultanic or republican, do not differ on these issues. The objective is one but the theoretical frameworks and the practical means are many.

Moreover, the four groups agree, even if nominally, on the freedom of citizens and their protection against repression and authoritarianism. The slogan of liberalism stresses freedom of expression, movement and party formation, and derives its legitimacy from freedom. Freedom, socialism and unity are the main banners of the national movement, with some focus on the freedom of people rather than the freedom of individuals—for there is no separation between bread and freedom. Marxism is also based on liberating individuals from exploitation and peoples from colonialism. The goal of a command economy – based on planning and state direction as well as public ownership of the means of production – is the liberation of individuals from the control of capital. The Islamic movement embodies in its slogans of freedom and equality the saying of 'Umar Bin Al-Khattab, "When did you enslave people while their mother gave them birth as free people," and the testimony "No god but God," which is a declaration of freedom of the human conscience from all sorts of human repression by negation "No god," then affirmation "but God."[19]

Furthermore, the various orientations agree on achieving the unity of the Islamic nation in the name of Islam and divine unity, which is reflected in the unity of the nation, the unity of the Arab nation that transcends the borders of the national state, and the unity of the working class, that is the laborers and peasants under the banner "Workers of the World, Unite" as in Marxism. They also agree on pursuing the unity of the market and its laws of liberalism, through free imports, exports and multi-national companies. In the age of globalization the smaller entities unite in greater regional associations, for the national state cannot compete except through more comprehensive and wider regional associations.

They also agree on developing human and natural resources, in the name of man, the master of nature, in liberalism, and the dialectics between man and nature in Marxism, planning in Arab nationalism, and divine utilization of the earth for the good of man, who may build and enjoy its fruits, according to the Islamic conception. The literature of different intellectual and political trends emphasizes independent development as a condition for sustainable development, establishing equilibrium in the balance of payments, increasing the rates of development and decreasing the rates of inflation in order to absorb the population increase without lowering the standard of living.

Defending identity against alienation is a principal aspect of the Islamic movement that has reached the level of exclusion, as in, for example, "You have your religion, and I have my religion"[20] and opposition to imitation of the other. It is also the pivot of nationalist thought, which is based on nationalist glory and independence from the two main camps in the age of polarization, a position that was called "positive alignment," "non-alignment" or "The Third World states." Marxism achieves this through the identity of the worker, preventing his alienation through his work and preventing his subordination to the capitalist. Liberalism believes in a common human identity, an identity of civilization and urbanization, that is based on the achievements of the modern age, an identity that is balanced and brings together the old and the new, and the authentic and the contemporary since the dawn of Arab renaissance.

The political forces did not differ on the mobilization of the masses against indifference and apathy. Man, according to the Islamic view, carries the trust that the heavens and earth could not shoulder. Arab nationalism is the message of history that expresses the sentiments and movement of the masses. Marxism moves the masses through social awareness and feeling of injustice. Liberalism, by its very nature, is a free activity that is committed to production and competition, and these move humans and release their energy.

[89]

The Islamic revival that started after the defeat of 1967, the Islamic revolution of Iran, the spread of Islam in both Eastern and Western Europe, in North America and Africa, and the Islamic republics in Central Asia indicates that Islam is coming and that the Islamic world is perhaps on the verge of its third phase, which began in the fifteenth century of Hijra. The first phase was completed in the first seven centuries, ending with Ibn Khaldun, then the second phase that was completed with the dawn of modern Arab renaissance in the seven centuries after Ibn Khaldun. The third phase may witness a golden age for Islamic civilization that is similar to the golden age in the first phase and which reached its zenith in the fourth century of Hijra, the age of Al-Bayruni, Al-Mutanabi, and Ibn Hayan Al-Tawhidi.[21]

The challenge is not in the acceptance or rejection of Islamic revival but is in defining the formulation of the new Islam. Is it the traditional conservative Islam that is inherited from Abi Hamid Al-Ghazali and Ash'arism in creed, Shafi'ism in jurisprudence, illumination in philosophy, and the textual literalism inherited from the old and contemporary Salafism? Or is it the enlightened rational Islam that is inherited from the reform movement of Jamal Al-Din Al-Afghani, Muhammad Abdu, 'Allal Al-Fasi, 'Abd Al-Hamid Bin Badis, Malik Bin Nabiy, Al-Tahir and Al-Fadl 'Ashur, 'Abd Al-Rahman Al-Kawakibi and Muhammad Iqbal? Is it perhaps the pluralist Islam that is based on the legitimacy of difference, the acceptance of dialogue and expression of the interests of the nation? Is it the fundamentalist discourse that is much talked about, or is it the post-fundamentalist discourse that is being formulated?[22]

The Islamic movement is not a cohesive whole but includes many wings and trends, from the right, the center, and left, and from tradition and reason, the text and reality, faith and revolution, and literalism and interpretation. It is a natural pluralism that continues the old pluralism, and it is a dialogue with the self before it takes place with the other.

The analysis of "political Islam between thought and practice" does not depend on literature, studies, researches, letters and articles on the subject, for there are many of them. It can be achieved through analyzing the collective and individual existential experiences in order to realize a new vision apart from what has been achieved through numbers, tables, statistics, dates and names of known individuals. The substance is closer to knowledge than data, and internalization leads to more understanding than statistics. This why the 'phenomenological' method became one of the main methods in philosophy and the social sciences that was able to add something new instead of transmitting information from one reference to another and from one source to another.

Since the subject is related to movements and existing political regimes, and because every scientific analysis of the relations between them may anger this party or that on matters of survival and existence, intellectual freedom and a sound objective public search are two conditions for thinking and deduction. It is true that pure and impartial objectivity does not exist, since every researcher has his personal intellectual and political affiliation. Nonetheless, it is possible to arrive at common conclusions that are generally accepted by researchers through analyzing the common collective experience. The researcher is independent from both the authority and opposition, even if one tends to this side or that. The highest national interest is the common objective of all, and then there is no difference between the researcher and the politician. The best theoretical research is that which is based on practice and the best political practice is that which is based on scientific research.

Extremism and Moderation in Islamic Movements: Causes, Motives and Repercussions

Emad Al-Din Shahin

In the official and Western media, "extremism" has been associated with the Islamic movements that have emerged in the Arab and Islamic worlds during the last three decades. While some analysts saw these movements as the beginning of an Islamic awakening and a revivalist expansion that takes the nation out of its predicament, others have ascribed to them value judgments, such as bigotry, backwardness, stagnation, darkness, terrorism and radicalism, as well as labels that reflect an ideological bias and a presupposed political orientation.

These movements have been portrayed, especially in Western circles, as representing a political and cultural threat that has alternately been called "the Islamic threat," "the green threat" and "the Islamic march." The inanimate world has not been spared such descriptions either; thus, it has become common to find expressions such as "the bloody borders of Islam" – launched by Samuel Huntington in the early nineties – or "the Islamic bomb" alluding to the attempts of some Islamic countries to find a nuclear balance with those that already have such weapons and present an actual threat.[1]

The use of these terms without discernment has led to a broad generalization and an intentional obscurity that militate against the objective treatment of Islamic movements, including the circumstances of their establishment and development. The problem with generalization is that it ignores the fact that, for a long time, Islamic movements have manifested pluralism, not only in the Arab world as a whole, but also within each country. It is possible to speak of the Islamic movements in terms of post-politics or post-fundamentalism.[2]

Moreover, Islamic movements have become an important part of the political and social segments of contemporary Muslim societies, and the role of most of them has expanded to include the cultural, civilizational, social and political spheres. Their goals are multiple and their means diverse. Some of these movements have taken the form of legal political parties and have chosen to participate within the legal frameworks and legitimate institutions of the state. Others have taken the form of social or economic organizations. It has become difficult to classify these movements because of their multiplicity and complexity.[3] This does not negate the existence of radical groups, both in terms of thought and behavior, that adopt violence and armed struggle as a means to achieve their objectives. However, these organizations represent a small segment of the Islamic movements as a whole and are marginal in the general reform trend.

The intentional misrepresentation of Islamic movements takes place through the emphasis and focus on the extremist groups and through portraying them as the model for all Islamic movements and as the future alternative prospect to the regimes of the region. The misrepresentation also occurs through treating the moderate movements as protest opposition political organizations whose objective is to seize power and to destroy both the ruling regimes and the Western interests in the region.

Although the political aspect is of interest to the Islamic movements, they represent at the same time a phenomenon that transcends the political dimension. This phenomenon is connected to the political and intellectual development that the region witnessed during the twentieth century and the conflict between the intellectual and ideological trends, on the one hand, and developmental and political models that some times were

[94]

applied by force, on the other. This, in my opinion, is the essence of the conflict.

The Islamic awakening is not just an ephemeral modern or political phenomenon. Rather, it is an authentic and powerful orientation among the trends that have been competing in the spheres of government, politics and thinking in the Arab world. In its intellectual and organic roots, it belongs to the reform trend that was inaugurated by Jamal Al-Din Al-Afghani and Muhammad Abdu, at the end of the nineteenth century and beginning of the twentieth century, from which many orientations evolved. The reform trend was launched as a reaction to direct contact with the West, and identifying aspects of its material, scientific and military progress, as well as a reaction to the perception of threat against the Caliphate and the unity of its regions, and fear of the loss of its provinces and their subjugation to foreign domination.

Islamic reformism focused on the comprehensiveness of Islam and its validity as a complete life system that contains the components of progress, and its compatibility with reason, science and modernity. It called for a return to the authentic fundamentals of religion – the Qur'an and *Sunna* – to adopting *ijtihad* and rejecting traditionalism. It focused on the active dimension and awareness of Muslim individuals. Islamic reformism called for a limited government and for maintaining the unity of the caliphate state.

This dimension of the intellectual trend and its development for the contemporary Islamic movement is not often talked about and has also not been properly explored. There is a continuous attempt to deal with Islamic revivalism as an unexpected phenomenon and not as an enduring and prominent trend that has both its historical roots and authentic ideological premises, as well as its legitimate demands. From what has been said, it is clear that the terms "extremism" and "moderation" are controversial and need greater investigation, in addition to the establishment of criteria that may be used to determine the level of extremism and moderation of one Islamic group or another.

Methodological Introduction

Linguistically, the word "extremism" means being far away from the middle and at one end of the continuum. It is by definition opposite to moderation. In Islamic *sharia*, extremism has been linked to exaggeration, fanaticism and radicalism, that is, to a position that goes beyond what people can tolerate. All of these aspects are prohibited by the law and warned against in Islam. Islam prohibits extremism in religion and excessive severity with the self and others, "Do not exceed the limits in your religion," (Al-Nisa', 171) and in the Prophetic traditions, "Beware of extremism in religion, for people before your were destroyed by their extremism in religion," "And do not be over-strict with yourself." Radicalism and extremism have been linked to destruction, for destruction is the inevitable result of extremism and undue severity, "The unduly severe have been destroyed."

The "middle way" and "moderation" are characteristics of Islam. Islam is the religion of the middle way that calls for a moderate approach in all matters: in worship that regulates the relationship between the individual and his Lord; in interactions that regulate the relations between people themselves; and in the law that regulates the affairs of society. The middle way distinguishes the nation of Islam from other nations, "And therefore, We created you a moderate nation so that you give testimony over people," (al-Baqara, 143). The middle way and moderation are two conditions that allow the nation to give testimony over other nations.[4]

When we analyze extremism and moderation in the context of Islamic movements, we need to focus on various issues: the relativity of extremism and moderation; extremism does not mean religiosity; extremism is not restricted to the Islamic movement alone; and the need to distinguish between extremism and violence.

The Relativity of Extremism and Moderation

There is no consensus on the "middle way" criterion and people may differ with respect to it. The same applies to the criteria for extremism. The previous criteria are relative in terms of place and time. There are many instances where radicalism and not giving up rights are legitimate. Many revolutions and resistance movements adopted an ideological commitment and armed struggle as a means to achieve their objectives. Furthermore, what is regarded as extremism in one age might be viewed as proper moderation in another and is hence adopted by society as a middle ground position that all agree upon. This is the case of most movements that seek to change their societies. They begin in an extremist position until they are able to occupy a middle ground.

There is no doubt that the Islamic call in its beginning represented to the unbelievers of Quraysh extremism and deviation from what they were used to and had received from their parents and grandparents. Moreover, the degree of religiosity with respect to individuals and society plays a role in judging whether some things are extreme or moderate; what some people view as a middle ground, moderation and a common custom might be, according to other criteria, regarded as extremist and against moderation and justice. There are many examples of this: the world financial system is based on either usury or interest, and many view it as part of the nature of things and a feature that cannot be abolished, while Islamic *sharia* views it as exploitative usury, an enormous injustice and an obvious exploitation of people's needs.

This leads us to another aspect of extremism, which is indifference. Extremism, as said before, has the dimension of being away from the center. This has two aspects: one is radicalism and excess, and the other is indifference and leniency. The latter is not focused upon for obvious reasons—it does not frighten the regimes or stir the sensitivities of society.

Extremism Does not Mean Religiosity

Religiosity, commitment to the teachings of Islam and the care to apply the principles of the *sharia* differ from extremism. When dealing with the Islamic phenomenon, some Western studies, along with some local researchers of the orientalist approach, viewed many phenomena as evidence of the spread of Islamic fundamentalism, including the youth going regularly to mosques, the growing of beards, the wearing of Islamic dress, young and old women wearing the veil, and the emergence of many Islamic groups that demanded the implementation of the *sharia* in society. It should be noted that such phenomena should be natural ones in any Islamic society, but they are being classified under "fundamentalism," a term implying extremism and excess in the implementation of religious rules, and intolerance and stagnation in dealing with all matters.

Extremism is not Restricted to the Islamic Movement

There is non-religious, secular and governmental extremism, examples of which abound in the Arab world. For Arab secularism does not only believe in the separation between religion and the state under the motto "No religion in politics and no politics in religion," but also shows animosity to all phenomena of religiosity in society. It calls on many political regimes to dry up the springs of religiosity and extremism in culture, education and teaching methodologies. This includes the closing of religious schools and institutes, the closing of the channels of legitimate activity for Islamic organizations and Islamic groups and sometimes the promulgation of laws that prohibit the Muslim from practicing his religious right, such as the law prohibiting the veil in official institutions and setting up parties on religious grounds. Such an animosity to religion in society does not even happen in Western societies that officially adopt secularism such as the United States of America or France.

Part of the extremism of the political regimes is the excessive use of unjustified force against their political opponents and religious extremists. The state has laws and regulations that define the means and methods of dealing with "the outlaws." In most cases, these laws provide sufficient means to deal with and repress the opponents. The commitment to the legal framework adds legitimacy to the behavior of the state and distinguishes it from those who challenge the legitimacy of the state. Nevertheless, the state's resort to excessive violence that the law does not allow is another form of unacceptable and unjustified extremism. Furthermore, it encourages "the outlaws" to insist on reacting with equal violence.

The Need to Distinguish between Extremism and Violence

There is a form of intellectual extremism at the moral level, such as when some people view their beliefs as the only right ones and seek to adhere to them. This kind of extremism is not worrying if it stays within a legitimate framework, because such a tendency is considered to be natural to the movements that want to bring about change—they adopt a specific vision for reforming and changing society and believe in the validity and applicability of that vision. All social movements started with the aim to bring about change. The scholars of social movements view this kind of extremism as expected because it expresses an ideological commitment to the movement and a means to increase its efficacy and ability to influence. It is logical that people adopt the opinions that they think are right, and this is why Imam Al-Shafi'i says that, "Our opinion is right but could be wrong, and the opinion of the others is wrong but could be right." This saying shows the difference between cherishing one's opinion and extremism. Extremism is the bigotry of assuming one's opinion to be right and accusing others of being wrong even when they are right. There is still a chance for dealing with this kind of extremism at the level of thought by argumentation and debate.

On the other hand, there is material and practical extremism. This entails resorting to violence and armed conflict in order to impose an idea on others by force. It represents a type of action that cannot be tolerated and must be rejected—even when it is regarded as part of the command to enjoin the good and forbid evil, for the latter has its juristic fundamentals and legal rules that regulate its exercise.

Moreover, one must distinguish between violence as a crisis method that is imposed by certain circumstances and violence as a part of the organized thought and ideology, that is when violence becomes a fixed fundamental in the thought and practice that distinguishes it from other movements. An example of the first is the resort to armed conflict by some Islamic groups in certain circumstances, for instance, to fight foreign occupation, as the Muslim Brothers did in Palestine in the late 1940s, or the current *jihad* groups in Lebanon and Palestine, or as a reaction to the

[99]

violence of the state, as is the case with the Islamic Salvation Front in Algeria after the army halted the electoral process and took power in 1992. In these cases, the use of violence stops with the end of its cause, since there would be no further justification for an armed conflict. Quite different are the jihadist groups that use armed conflict and the quest for changing the status quo by force as a core element of their thought and strategy—these include, the *jihad* groups and similar movements in Egypt, Mustapha Bouya'ali in the 1970s, and the armed Islamic groups in the 1990s in Algeria.

In summary, extremism and moderation are two relative terms that should be defined by specific investigation and fixed criteria. In the Islamic experience, the criterion is the *sharia* and its rules and regulations according to the Qur'an, the *Sunna* and the deductions from the legally acceptable rules of *ijtihad*. As Salah Al-Sawi says, "With reference to religious extremism, it should be noted that the judgment that a certain act is moderate or extremist should be left to experts in the *sharia*. In fact, it is the prerogative of the religious sciences to make the distinction between what is clear and what is ambiguous."[5]

In his research on the *Al-Sahwa al-Islamiyya bayna al-Juhud wa al-Tatarruf,* Yusuf Al-Qaradawi mentions many manifestations of extremism, including bigotry, not recognizing the other opinion, forcing on the public what God has not ordered them to do, like following extra religious works as if they were religious duties, and undue severity, abrasiveness, suspicion, as well as falling into the fault of excommunicating the other.[6]

Al-Sawi also observed some of the practices that constitute parts of the phenomenon of extremism, like overdoing the religious duties, and exaggeration or excess in word and deed. This includes going beyond what is legally called for and committing oneself to what the law does not demand, false piety and the like, and not allowing others to exercise *ijtihad*. That is, the arrogance of one opinion with the concomitant rejection of the existence of others, exceeding the legal limits in denouncing the actions of those who err, where the person does not distinguish between what is a clear injunction and what is not.[7] Al-Sawi mentions the view of Shaykh Al-Azhar Muhammad Sayyid Tantawi on the concept of extremism: "It is exaggeration and addition to what is stated in the Qur'an or the *Sunna* of the Prophet, and it is an exaggeration that all religions reject, which includes extremism in worship where we force ourselves to do what we cannot endure. The Prophet outlawed this kind of extremism in worship."[8]

Causes of Extremism

The Islamic movements can be viewed as social movements that seek to bring about change in society and its institutions. There are many academic studies and social theories on this matter that seek to define the concept and nature of social movements and the causes for their emergence. They also seek to analyze their ideological discourse and the symbols that they use. They explore the internal interactions of these movements, their transformation and their relations with the existing regimes. While one can recognize the specific nature of the Islamic movement, it shares many manifestations with other social movements, and therefore we can benefit from these studies in our analysis of the nature of Islamic movements and the reasons why some adopt moderate methods and others extremism and violence.[9]

The concept of social movements is tied directly to the issue of social change and the belief of some individuals in the possibility of changing society through an organized collective action. Sociologists describe a social movement as a collective action aimed at bringing about change in society in any direction and by any means, including violence, illegitimate ways, revolution and even isolation from society.[10] One of the features of social movements is that they reflect a certain amount of organized effort regardless of its degree or level. It might range from natural and intermittent organized effort – for example, demonstrations, strikes, sit-ins – to tightly structured organizations that are recognized, such as groups, bodies, legitimate legal unions or a political party. The conscious will and individual commitment to the ideas and objectives of the movement and the active participation of its members reflect the extent of commitment of the movement to change. This commitment also provides the principal justifications for the existence of the movement in the arena. For the social movement to become effective and active, it must reflect the culture of the society it belongs to, and this in itself makes it an acceptable and active instrument for change.[11]

It is possible to say that the phenomena of violence, revolution and extremism do not deny the social movements their specific quality and the existence of legitimate demands. Furthermore, it is natural and expected that any social movement, Islamic or otherwise, reflects a conscious commitment at the theoretical and organizational level and at the level of practice. A young movement with such commitment is a small part of a larger society and its members posit a different or distinct interpretation for the conditions and problems of that society. They seek to offer an alternative to solve these problems, which normally leads to great tension and sometimes to a conflict within the society—the latter might hesitate, for many reasons, to accept and adopt the change, while the members of this movement believe that they possess the truth and the means of salvation for this society.

Sociologists have classified social movements into four types. The first consists of isolationist and utopian groups that focus primarily on the individual and his internal transformation and not on the transformation of the institutions and structure of society, because they do not aim at political action to make this transformation or to solve the problems of society. These groups tend to isolation and separation from society to protect their members from falling under the influence of its corrupt values. They believe in the truth and correctness of their positions and the wrongness of the positions of others. From among the Islamic movements, groups with such positions emerged, such as Jama'at al-Takfir wa al-Hijra and others, which perceived themselves as the Society of Muslims or the saved group and were convinced that other groups were wrong. These groups did not hesitate to excommunicate the entire society and to separate their members through actual migration or by creating an existential severance from society.[12]

The second type of social movement is known as the protest movement, whose nature is more spontaneous, discontinuous and intermittent. These movements appear suddenly for a specific cause and to achieve a demand, then disappear with the same speed, immediately after receiving the proper response to their demand or as a result of the success of the regime in their repression and dispersion. Demonstrations, strikes, and sit-ins are examples of this kind of movement. These movements might be successful in bringing about some sort of change but they are distinguished by the absence of an organized and continuous collective action. When considering this kind of movement in isolation from other social movements they normally lack ideological coherence and a clear vision for change.

The third type of social movement is the revolutionary movement that is distinguished by its total rejection of the values and institutions of society and the existing regime, and seeks to bring about the comprehensive change of society in a radical fashion and through the extensive use of violence. This kind appears to include the jihadist Islamic movements, that is, those that adopt *jihad* and violence as the instrument of change. This is partly true in terms of the use of violence, but the specific nature of these groups and their difference from other revolutionary movements must be carefully evaluated. In reality, we find that these groups do not aim to change the values of society in a radical way, for, as Islamic and religious groups, their ideological base is not different from the values of the other members of the Muslim society.

The fourth type of social movement is the reform movement that is distinguished by legitimacy or seeking to acquire it and the readiness to act from within the regime and its existing institutions, through the margin of action allowed to the movements. These movements adopt gradualism and peaceful means to realize their goals. They may go as far as accusing the regime of giving up some basic principles and values of society and even casting doubt on the legitimacy of the existing institutions. Nevertheless, the strategy for change depends on focusing and attracting attention to the existing problems of society and proposing and developing programs that facilitate solving these problems.

Sociologists agree that in order for these movements to maintain their original nature – that is, not resort to violence and extremism or adopt underground action – they must practice their activities in a society that allows a reasonable degree of pluralism and accepts difference and rejection. However, the objectives and demands of the social movements normally represent a challenge to the authority and the stability of the regime, which attempts to contain the rising movement or, if necessary, to repress it. The regime normally resorts to denying and concealing the power of the reform movements and their effectiveness within society by dismissing them as a gang, a bunch of outlaws or secessionists, or by portraying them as extreme movements that want to bring evil into society and then destroy the state. The regime also compares the movements with heretics, sinister forces and terrorists—all of which are also descriptions used by the official media. Furthermore, they portray the conflict between the regime and the movements as a struggle between civilization and the barbarians.

It must be noted that such a classification of social movements is neither inevitable nor fixed—one movement can bring together more than one description of different types of social movements, especially if the movement has many wings, segments or apparatuses. Furthermore, under certain conditions, a revolutionary movement can practice a moderate reform policy, or a reform movement may adopt a violent and extreme method to express its demands.

Extremism has many diverse and interwoven causes, and Yusuf Al-Qaradawi mentions many causes for the extremism of some Islamic movements. Some of these are related to a lack of understanding of true religion, while others are related to the environment that the movements work within. Examples of the former are the weak understanding of true religion, the tendency to understand the texts literally, preoccupation with peripheral instead of central issues, over-emphasis on prohibition, the confusion of concepts (belief and unbelief), pursuing what is ambiguous while not adhering to what is clearly prohibited, as well as a lack of knowledge of history, reality and the rules of the universe (like the concepts of gradual change and predestination). Examples of the causes related to the environments of the specific Islamic movement include the alienation of Islam in the land of Islam, the public attack and secret

[104]

conspiracy against the Islamic nation, prohibiting free call to comprehensive Islam, and resorting to violence and repression to resist the Islamic movements.[13]

Sociologists do not agree on one unified theory that interprets the causes of extremism or moderation of the social movements or on the factors that lead some movements to resort to violence whereas others that go through the same conditions refrain from exercising the same method. There are still more theories that attempt to interpret the phenomenon of the use of violence and extremism, including the psychological theory that focuses on the self and on the individual motives of the person because of his feeling of injustice and the inability to reach an acceptable status in society. This creates a feeling of identity loss, alienation, hopelessness and powerlessness, all of which contribute to the acceptance of extremism and violence as legitimate weapons against society. There is the social theory that refers extremism and the tendency of some individuals to use violence back to the existence of social pressures that might arise from political and economic crises and the feeling by some social segments of rejection and injustice.

In order not to limit the research to theoretical frameworks, in the second part, we will follow the roots of extremism of contemporary Islamic movements at the intellectual and practical levels and the relationship of that with the post-independence state. We will then analyze some prevailing political phenomena that encourage the spirit of extremism and violence.

Roots of Extremism of Contemporary Islamic Movements: Qutbist Thought and the Post-Independence State

Many analysts refer the roots of religious extremism back to Sayyid Qutb and his conclusion that society reneged from Islam and thus has fallen into a state of *jahiliyya* because of its refusal of divine governance and its preference for human governance. Qutb called for the foundation of a unique group of believers that separates itself existentially from the *jahili* society and attempts to change it radically by whatever means it sees fit, including non-peaceful means. Many analysts referred the emergence of this thought back to the conditions that Qutb went through in prison and the torture that he underwent that made him believe that its perpetrators could not be part of the Muslim society. The leaders of the Muslim Brothers refuted directly, and also from prison, this orientation for fear that the group would follow the path of extremism and violence, which would in turn lead to the dispersion of the group and its fragmentation.[14]

However, a segment of the youth and some groups accepted this way of thinking and attempted to find an effective instrument for bringing about change. They started by condemning and rejecting the prevailing reality totally and worked towards changing it by force. Some groups saw the solution as resorting to armed struggle—for example, the group of the Technical Military School in Egypt, the group of Bouya'ali in Algeria and the Islamic Youth in Morocco in the 1970s. There were also those who called for excommunication and migration, and a change of society from the outside. In addition, there were those who launched *jihad* against the existing regimes, a duty they regarded as lost by Muslims and one that they should restore and perform. All of these groups remained on the periphery of the moderate Islamic movements that took the call for reform as their objective.

What concerns us here is the attempt to link the Qutbist thought with the major transformations that were going on in the Arab world, especially after the emergence of the post-independence state and its distinguishing features, without denying the validity of those who considered other factors – individual, social, economic or political – as causes for the extremism of some movements. Nevertheless, we see that these factors may encourage extremism but do not create it.

What is meant by the post-independence state is the Kamelist or Kamel Attaturk's model that many Islamic countries adopted, although it is applied differently from country to country. This model is based on many foundations that contradict what Islam calls for, and differs in many respects from the form of many existing modern Western states. Some of its features are:

- The separation of religion and state, either by declaring that there is no religion in politics and no politics in religion, or by secularizing state institutions and subjecting religion, its scholars and symbols to the authority of these institutions.
- The centrality of the state, its domination over society and its replacement of the nation. It is the leader or organizer of economic development, the sponsor of intellectual and cultural innovation and the controller of social mobilization.
- The domination of one party, the prevention of true pluralism and prohibiting differences even when there is political pluralism.
- The nationalism that is based on race and the bias towards the land, as well as glorifying the pre-Islamic history, as is the case with Pharaohism, Phoenicianism and Ashurism, and reproducing and sometimes inventing that history.
- The demagogic popularity that does not refrain from deification of the individual, which is controlled by the state and driven by the charismatic individual, "the inspired leader," or still the "great Muhjahid" who came at the preordained time to represent the hopes and ambitions of his nation and to move it from backwardness to progress and from subordination to independence.
- It is a state that is independent from its society and linked to the outside. A model of this state is Egypt that stresses its independence from society so that it does not become a hostage to one of its classes—for example, Jamal 'Abd Al-Nasir who wanted to build a socialist state without real socialists and the current model that claims to have made a democratic transformation but without democrats.[15] The state is run by a military, cultural and political minority, separated from the common values of its society and maintaining complete allegiance to the head of the regime. Even the middle class that expanded after independence is still controlled by the state because it lacks material and economic independence. This state is tied to the outside either through following a method of development that integrates it with the world economy and hinders its true independence, or through direct foreign security or economic support to ensure that the regime remains in power.

By exhibiting a tendency towards secularism, domination and dependency, this model contradicts the Islamic system. Moreover, the model cannot maintain this form and receive the support and goodwill of the public. However, in order to perpetuate this model the state resorts to force, violence and economic and intellectual fabrication, that is the falsification of history and cultural and religious awareness through distorting education. It also resorts to changing the values of society and keeps people extensively occupied with earning their livelihood, which prevents them from having the time and resources to enter into politics and to attempt to bring about change.

The post-independence state in Egypt and other Islamic states came close to this model in one way or another. Sayyid Qutb was deeply aware of this and maintained that some states proclaim their secularization and separate themselves completely from religion, while others declare that they "respect religion" but remove religion from their social system, rejecting metaphysics and building their system on secularism because it contradicts metaphysics. Some Islamic states ascribe governance to frameworks other than God and legislate as they wish. The position of Islam on all these *jahili* societies can be summarized in one sentence: Islam refuses to acknowledge the Islamicity and legitimacy of these societies. Therefore, Qutb declared that all existing societies are *jahili* and un-Islamic. He said that Islam does not accept compromise with the *jahiliyya*, nor the ideas or positions arising from such a concept—it is either Islam or *jahiliyya*.[16]

Qutb realized that complacency with and silence about this model would give the state the legitimacy that it needs and stabilize its foundations. This is why he rejected these regimes and their supporters outright. He called for their eradication and the establishment of the Islamic system. Qutb maintained that there must be a source of power to face the *jahili* society, and it is the power of belief and insight, the power of creation and psychological construct, the power of organization and collective mobilization, and other forms of power that are used to confront the *jahili* society and to overcome or at least resist it.[17] The function of Islam is to eradicate *jahiliyya* from the leadership of humankind and to

[108]

ensure that this leadership accords to Islam's particular approach, which has independent principles and authentic characteristics.[18]

The dichotomy will prevail for as long as the state stays separate from the values of its society and while its systems continue to contradict the values and ambitions of that society. The regime should seek to obtain people's approval and acceptance for itself and its institutions, so that the dichotomy disappears and political competition over government, style of rule and programs is not reduced to aspects of the dominant regime itself, but reflect preferred approaches to governance.

In addition to the differences on the nature of the regime as one factor that may lead to extremism, there are political causes related to the political structure and practices within the political entity that might fuel the tendency to extremism or moderation of the opposition organizations:

- The degree of stability and regulation of state institutions, and the administration of these institutions within a rational and constitutional framework, which provides the necessary legitimacy and predictability, and establishes the legal independence between the different political institutions of the state. The state of flux and the inherent instability of these institutions hinder the development of a constitutional opposition, since the latter falls victim to arbitrary, spontaneous and subjective decisions. This results in opposition forces lacking trust in these institutions. Such is the case of most political opposition in the Arab world, whether Islamic or non-Islamic, which exists by decree and fiat that could be withdrawn at any time. Also, most opposition operates within a set of exceptional laws that restrict its activities and limit its ability to become an active opposition.

- The insistence on not integrating the moderate opposition, which enjoys an active existence and popular support, within the legal channels. The decision to not recognize the existence of such parties and to close down the legitimate framework within which they could work, transforms the opposition parties, which would otherwise be moderate and adhere to political procedure, into an extra-governmental opposition that is irresponsible and radical in its positions, since the possibility of participation in the political process and arriving at power through peaceful means is reduced. There is no doubt that recognizing the opposition groups is not a condition that prevents extremism but is a precondition for the emergence of an opposition that is responsible and committed to the rules that have been agreed upon so that violence does not become the only tool available for change.

- The incoherence of state policies vis-à-vis the opposition groups that are allowed to exist and act during any period. The clash between the regime's policies and those of moderate opposition – at times encouraged to exist and perform within the political arena for expediency, and thereafter limited and suppressed – weakens the moderates and strengthens the radical wings within the opposition, which regard resorting to violence as the appropriate means towards resisting state violence and bringing about regime change.

Repercussions

These policies have known and expected repercussions on society and directly influence its stability and development. They are also reflected on the Islamic movements that have tried to express their demands in a legitimate way and to implement their programs to change society through the legal framework. It is possible to reduce the intensity of the existing unjustified polarization between many political regimes and the Islamic movements, if a political settlement is reached that is based on consideration and respect for the main values of society. This settlement is regarded as an essential condition for the stability of any society and to preclude any political group from resorting to violence and extremism as a means of effecting change or retaining power. The policies of exclusion and repression provide sufficient justification for rejecting moderation and result in the creation of irresponsible opposition groups and movements. It is known that whenever the opposition has enjoyed legitimacy and the ability to increase its support base, it moves towards moderation and establishes the foundation of a unifying position for the majority. Legitimacy and recognition produce a responsible opposition while repression and exclusion produce a radical opposition, both in terms of positions and demands.

In the context of the Islamic movements, the administration of social movements and political opposition is not an easy matter, as is known. It requires a high degree of political skill and insight to maintain the cohesion and survival of the groups and to acquire acceptance and popularity in society. As we indicated earlier, the emergence and activity of any social movement produces tension in society. The timing, form and organization of the movement's participation in society are considered to be important matters that the leaders of the movement need to decide upon. To ascribe the terms 'moderation' and 'middle ground' to any movement, the latter must extend its hand to all segments of society, encompassing all its sects, trends and classes. It must not be forgotten that Islam is not only politics. With this understanding, these movements can bring about their own comprehensive, cultural and reformist uniqueness.

4

The Views of Islamic Movements on Democracy and Political Pluralism

Ahmad Moussalli

The focus of this chapter is the role of Islamic discourses in the political stability of the Arab world. Islam's compatibility with pluralism and democracy is of major interest to Western scholars and politicians, as well as to Muslims in general, including the fundamentalists. The possibility of combining modern Islamic thought with democracy and pluralism seems to be a rising and controversial topic, since several Muslim fundamentalist thinkers have been introducing democracy and pluralism into Islamic thought. In the Islamic world, the quest for democracy and pluralism is very apparent: a substantial number of political and intellectual conferences have been held to study the possible ways to democratize and liberalize politics, society and thought. A large number of fundamentalist theoreticians are now engaged in the Islamization of democracy and pluralism. They argue that social and political tyranny and oppression are the main catalysts for the defeat and underdevelopment of the Islamic world and are detrimental to the rise of Islam.

The collapse of the Soviet Union has added to the urgency of implementing democracy, upholding human rights and accepting pluralism. Secular and fundamentalist Islamic thinkers alike attribute the unhealthy and harsh economic, social and political conditions to the absence of democracy and pluralism. A new political process that stresses the importance of political democratization and liberalization is on the rise and is reflected through the media, conferences, universities and other institutions. A few conferences, such as the one held in 1981 in Morocco on "The Democratic Experience in the Arab World," or the one held in Cyprus on "The Crisis of Democracy in the Arab World" and the conference held in Amman in 1989 to discuss the subject of "Political Pluralism and Democracy in the Arab World," clearly show the emerging interest in democracy and pluralism. Other conferences have taken place, and many studies have been conducted on the same issues.[1]

Notwithstanding this interest in pluralism and democracy, the West in general has focused principally on Islamic fundamentalist dangers, without taking into consideration the oppressive nature of most Middle Eastern regimes or considering political discussions over democracy and pluralism. Sensational titles in magazines and newspapers, such as "Will democracy Survive in Egypt?" or "The Arab World Where Troubles for the US Never End" or "The Clash of Civilizations," have increased fear in the West and driven the East and the West further asunder. While quite a few Western academics concerned with the Middle East deal with the real concerns of the people, the West in general prefers to look at these concerns as being trivial insofar as they pertain to a specific people far away.[2]

However, current events in the Muslim world, particularly in Egypt, Algeria, Tunisia and the Sudan, have produced political and academic discussions on the compatibility of Muslim fundamentalist discourses – especially the doctrines of an Islamic state – with democracy, human rights, pluralism and "the emerging world order."

This chapter therefore aims at highlighting some of the important debates that have been going on in modern Islamic fundamentalist discourses about democracy and pluralism. It argues that while a majority of Western media and scholars – along with a majority of their Middle Eastern counterparts – treats fundamentalism as exclusivist by nature and definition, and while a few widely publicized fundamentalist groups are truly exclusivist and adhere to the notion of change through radical programs and uncompromising revolutions, most mainstream and major fundamentalist groups are indeed pluralistic, democratic and inclusivist. The origins of exclusion are neither Islamic metaphysical perceptions of the universe nor abstract extrapolations from some theological doctrines of Islam. Furthermore, exclusion is not limited to Islamic fundamentalist groups and includes the champions of the new and the old world orders. However, it is only with Islamic fundamentalism that the doctrine of exclusion is transformed into a part of a new Islamic theology of metaphysical perceptions and abstract doctrines of belief.

This chapter shows also that Islamic fundamentalism is, in fact, an umbrella term for a wide range of discourses and activism that tend to move from a high level of moderate pluralism, and thus inclusive democracy, to extreme radicalism and intolerant unitarianism, and thus to exclusive majority rule. While some fundamentalist groups are pluralistic in terms of inter-Muslim relations and between Muslims and minorities, others are not. Moreover, while some fundamentalists are politically pluralistic but theologically exclusive, others are accommodating in religion, but direct their exclusivist programs to the outside, to the West or imperialism. Even at the scientific level, some fundamentalists argue that Western science and technology are Islamically sound, while others exclude them because of their assumed un-Islamic nature. More importantly, while the majority of fundamentalists calls for pluralistic democracy and argue for it as an essentially Islamic point of view, the radicals brand it as unbelief.

Why then do the fundamentalists – given their agreement on the usage of the fundamentals of religion, the Qur'an and the *sunna*, as well as a philosophical and political framework – have these basic and substantive divergent views? The answer, to be argued below, is that the inclusive democratic and exclusive authoritarian policies of most Middle Eastern states, along with those of international powers, reinforce and in fact create that dual nature of fundamentalist political thought and behavior. While Arab regimes hold the international order responsible for the harsh situation in which they find themselves, the fundamentalists attribute the economic, social and political failures of the states to the regimes

[115]

themselves. They view the regimes as conductors of multi-layered conflicts between the dominant world powers against the ambitions and hopes of indigenous populations, in this case the Muslims and their most vigorous spokesmen, the fundamentalists.

Fundamentalists in general believe that their governments do not serve the ideological, political or economic interests of their people but those of the dominant world powers. Imperialism, colonialism, exploitation, materialism—all these are charges brought against the West. Liberalization, whether economic, political or cultural, as well as social justice, political freedom and democracy are major demands of both radical and moderate fundamentalist groups. Fundamentalists consider modern national states as the link between what is unacceptable and inhumane in both Western and Eastern civilizations, namely Western materialism and Eastern despotism. An Islamic state, they believe, can withstand and even correct Western materialistic domination and Eastern political authoritarianism. This notwithstanding, the way a fundamentalist theoretician or movement creates its discourse and argues for a particular method of establishing that state, its political system and its basic ideology can provide us with cues to classify one theoretician or movement as an exclusivist, non-liberal and radical antagonist of pluralistic democracy, or as an inclusivist, liberal and moderate protagonist of pluralistic democracy.

This chapter then answers the following basic questions: what are the conditions that make a fundamentalist theoretician and movement develop a discourse on or reject ideological and political doctrines of pluralistic democracy? What is the role of comparable inclusive or exclusive policies of Middle Eastern states as well as the international order in reinforcing one doctrine or another? Part one of this chapter contextualizes at length some general academic and political discussions on inclusion and exclusion, and on pluralism and democracy in the West, particularly in the USA, and in the Arab world, particularly in Egypt. Part two deals with the theoretical foundations and development of inclusion, exclusion, pluralism and democracy, with reference to the more comprehensive political framework that was elaborated in part one. The chapter then explores the inclusivist and pluralist discourse of the most profound fundamentalist movement yet, that of the Muslim Brotherhood in Egypt.

This discourse, however, has become the basis of two contradictory discourses: one that is very radical, anti-liberal, exclusivist and militant, and another that is very moderate, liberal, inclusivist and non-militant. Further, the section on this topic explains why the liberal development of the inclusivist discourse of Hasan Al-Banna and the Muslim Brotherhood was not possible under 'Abd Al-Nasir's regime or the governments of his successors, and why it was logical that it would be transformed into an exclusivist fundamentalist discourse, of which the most exclusive is that of Sayyid Qutb and the theoreticians who followed him and set up armed radical groups.

I argue that the development of the radical discourse was originally a reaction to the political, economic and international conditions of Egypt and the way in which the government handled the basic issues of freedom, social justice and religion. However, the radical discourse nowadays cannot be understood only in terms of its origins but has become a theology of politics that stands on its own. The chapter concludes with a theoretical assessment on the future of the on-going dialectics of pluralism and democracy.

The World, Pluralism and Democracy

Theoreticians and Islamic activists, in addition to Western and Muslim academics and press circles, discuss the issues of inclusion and exclusion within the context of "pluralist democracy." Timothy Sisk outlines the basic interests of the West regarding the rise of fundamentalist Islam. He asks "how, if and when can pluralism and democratic institutions survive compatibly with the rising tide of Islamic fundamentalism?"[3] He places fundamentalism in its global comparative context and views it as a world phenomenon. He also reduces tendencies towards liberalism and democracy to two basic views: a progressive fundamentalist view that accepts liberal democracy; and a non-liberal fundamentalist view that essentially seeks social justice, though not in direct conflict with democracy.

[117]

In *New Perspective Quarterly*, the whole issue of pluralism and tolerance is discussed under sensational titles that make the reader shy away from reading the articles on Islam. For instance, who wants to travel "From Beirut to Sarajevo. . ." to fight "Against Cultural Terrorism" or to witness "Galileo Meets Allah."[4] However, the editor of the journal puts his concern in the following way:

> Islam, alone in a plural world, remains monotheistic in faith as well as, in many places, in practice. In today's globalized cultural space, Islam will inevitably be faced with a host of challenges that will pit "the word" not only against the mere language of Western literature, like Salman Rushdie's novel, but also against non-dogmatic, for example, Hindu beliefs, not to speak of the radically free style tolerance of Europe and America that so riles the mullahs. Faced with these challenges, will Islam turn toward pluralism and the West back to faith?[5]

The answer came from Akbar S. Ahmad. He argues that only one civilization, Islam, will stand firm in its path. The Muslim world provides a global view with a potential alternative role on the world stage. Islam seems to be set on a collision course with the Western world. While the West is based on secular materialism, the scientific reason of modernity, and the absence of moral philosophy, Islam, argues Ahmad, is based on faith, patience and equilibrium. He puts up a picture of non-conciliation between Islam and the West; it is "a straight-out fight between two approaches to the world, two opposed philosophies."[6]

Ahmad's exclusionary views of civilizations are not just Islamic, but have their equivalence among prominent Western intellectuals, such as Samuel Huntington, who argue that the future will witness a clash of civilizations. In his "The Islamic–Confucian Connection," as well as his more celebrated article "The Clash of Civilizations," Huntington considers the conflicts that took place since the Peace of Westphalia in 1648 up to the Cold War as "Western civil wars." Now the "cultural division of Europe among Western Christianity, Orthodox Christianity and Islam has re-emerged."[7]

Disregarding any diversity in the interpretation of Islam as well as its historical schools and different modern tendencies in religion and politics,

[118]

Huntington, who served at the White House under President Carter in the National Security Council and witnessed the collapse of the Iranian regime under the Shah and the establishment of an Islamic state, proclaims that Islam is

> "a militant religion in which there is no distinction between what is religious and what is secular. The idea of "render unto Caesar what is Caesar's, render unto God what is God's" is totally antithetical to Islam. This theocratic proclivity makes it extraordinarily difficult for Islamic societies to accommodate non-Muslims. It makes it very difficult for Muslims to easily fit into societies where the majority is non-Muslim."[8]

In addition to showing very little knowledge of Islamic history and philosophy, he disregards the comparison of Islam with other religions, which, though they look at politics and religion as Islam does, are nonetheless included into the Western culture and not the Eastern. Although Judaism, for instance, is more like Islam, it has been nonetheless included, accepted and incorporated into Western culture. The West until recently excluded and persecuted Jews politically and culturally, with Zionism being a direct consequence of this fact. In fact, exclusion was mutual, with the Jews also not wanting to be assimilated into Western culture. After Hitler, 'anti-Semitism' became an pejorative term in the West and Zionist propaganda gave impetus to this. Again, Protestant America with its emphasis on the Old Testament as an integral and very important part of the Bible, as opposed to the Vatican, was potentially very receptive to Zionist propaganda.

In general, the Islamic world has been included, albeit in a negative way, that is by military force originally employed by the colonial powers and now by dominant world powers that use the threat of economic sanctions and sophisticated weaponry. Why then do these powers not try to include the Islamic world economically, morally and philosophically, especially if one of the features that distinguishes the West is its inclusive pluralism? Or is the non-Islamicity of Muslims the precondition for inclusion?

Judith Miller advocates a non-democratic exclusivist attitude towards the Muslim world since, in her opinion, Islam is incompatible with the values of pluralism, democracy and human rights. This means that Western policy-makers should not support democratic elections since they may result in radical Islamic fundamentalists coming to power. She exhorts the American administration and others to reject any sort of conciliation with, or inclusion of, radical political Islam.

> "Western governments should be concerned about these movements, and, more importantly, should oppose them. For despite their rhetorical commitment to democracy and pluralism, virtually all militant fundamentalists oppose both. They are, and are likely to remain, anti-Western, anti-American and anti-Israeli."[9]

She further rejects any distinction between good and bad fundamentalists. Accepting Martin Kramer's idea of the non-compatibility of militant Islamic groups with democracy insofar as they cannot be by nature "democratic, pluralistic, egalitarian or pro-Western" and Bernard Lewis' argument that liberal democracy and Islam do not keep company. Miller concludes, along with Lewis, that autocracy is the norm and postulates that,

> "Islamic militancy presents the West with a paradox. While liberals speak of the need for diversity with equality, fundamentalists see this as a sign of weakness. Liberalism tends not to teach its proponents to fight effectively. What is needed, rather, is almost a contradiction in terms: a liberal militancy, or a militant liberalism that is unapologetic and unabashed."[10]

Fortunately, not all American thinkers, policy-makers and diplomats think along the same lines. Edward Djerejian, former assistant Secretary of State and US Ambassador to Israel, puts the matter differently. He states that, "the US government, however, does not view Islam as the next "ism" confronting the West or threatening world peace. That is an overly simplistic response to a complex reality."[11] He goes on to say that,

> "The Cold War is not being replaced with a new competition between Islam and the West. It is evident that the Crusades have been over for a long time. Indeed, the ecumenical movement is the

contemporary trend. Americans recognize Islam as one of the world's great faiths. It is practiced on every continent. It counts among its adherents millions of citizens of the US. As Westerners we acknowledge Islam as a historic civilizing force among the many that have influenced and enriched our culture. The legacy of the Muslim culture which reached the Iberian Peninsula in the 8th century, is a rich one in the sciences, arts, and culture and in tolerance of Judaism and Christianity. Islam acknowledges the major figures of Judeo-Christian heritage: Abraham, Moses, and Christ."[12]

The US differs, according to Djerejian, with those groups that reject political pluralism, that would rather adopt religious and political confrontation than engage with the world, that do not accept the peaceful resolution of the Arab-Israeli conflict and that adopt terrorism to achieve their goals.[13]

Some scholars on the Middle East and the Islamic world go beyond this general statement. Augustus R. Norton, in his "Inclusion Can Deflate Islamic Populism," argues that democracy and Islam are not incompatible since it is the demand of the people of the area to be included in the political system. While skeptics deny the usefulness of democracy for the people, based on the fact that existing regimes are inefficient and suffer from a lack of legitimacy and that the fundamentalist political movements are anti-Western, anti-Israeli and anti-democratic, Norton pins down the criticism against the skeptics by saying that "to argue that popular political players are irremediably intransigent and therefore unmoved by tenets in the real world is at best naive and, at worst, racist."[14]

> "So long as the fundamentalist movements are given no voice in politics, there can be no surprise that their rhetoric will be shrill and their stance uncompromising. In contrast, well-designed strategies of political inclusion hold great promise for facilitating essential political change."[15]

Norton concludes his article with a sober reflection:

> "The rulers have no intention of stepping aside, but they must be encouraged to widen the political stage and to open avenues for real participation in politics. For the West, and especially the United States, the issues are complex and vexing, but the basic choice is

simple: construct policies that emphasize and widen the cultural barriers that divide the Middle East from the West, or pursue policies that surmount the barriers.[16]

William Zartman argues that the two currents of political Islam and democracy are not necessarily incompatible. The Qur'an might be interpreted to support different political behaviors. A synthesis might emerge between Islam and democracy where constitutional checks can be employed. He suggests five measures to democratize and make sure that democracy will triumph, including "to practice the forms of democracy whenever scheduled, let the most popular win, and let them learn democracy on the job."[17]Again, in "Democratization and Islam," John Esposito and James Piscatori argue that the process of liberalization and democratization in the Muslim world requires, as happened in the West, a process of reinterpretation of the divine texts. While Islam lends itself to different interpretations, some important fundamentalist thinkers have already started the process of accommodating Islam with democracy and liberalism,[18] which is in itself an inclusive process.

The above discussion indicates the emergence and indeed the existence of a fundamentalist tendency to include some principles of Western civilization, such as liberalism, democratization and a free economic system, which in itself represents features of an inclusive view of political Islam. It also shows that there is a major and influential tendency among Western politicians and scholars alike to reject the Islamization of democracy and liberalism, and to insist on the Westernization of raw materials and markets under the pretext of national security or the clash of civilizations. The same actors that stand opposed to the ascendancy of fundamentalism through democracy, because of its assumed fundamentalist authoritarian nature, support authoritarian regimes for the sake of maintaining a non-existent democracy—an indication of an exclusionary attitude and intolerance directed at Islam under the guise of fundamentalism and a sign of twisted logic.

It seems that most international and regional actors so far have had a vested interest in pushing away fundamentalists from any legitimate role in internal, regional or international affairs. The argument against the fundamentalists outlined above has its counterpart in the Middle East. In "Liberalization and Democracy in the Arab World," Gudrun Kramer shows why Arab regimes are not yet ready for democracy. However, democracy is now one of the common themes among political movements and differs in nature and extent from one movement to another, ranging from the adoption of a liberal pluralistic Western model to "an Islamic model of participation through consultation." However, the two streams "converge on the issues of human rights and political participation."

Although some regimes have adopted certain classic mechanisms to liberalize and democratize, such as the *infitah* (open-door policy) and the multi-party system in Egypt, the limitations are nonetheless classic. Formal constraints also limit the scope of legitimate political expression and action, usually a party law restricting the bases of party formation and a national charter defining the common and inviolable intellectual and political ground. Thus, for instance, the moderate Muslim Brotherhood in Egypt is not legally allowed to form a party, but is nevertheless allowed by the regime to participate informally. Kramer goes on to say that "even an Islamic political order may be able to incorporate Western notions of political participation and human rights." Furthermore, "liberalization," she adds,

> "will inevitably give more room for maneuver to political actors critical of the West and openly hostile towards Israel. While the public demands a greater distance from the West and a tough stand vis-à-vis Israel, the socio-economic crisis intensifies dependence on Western governments and international agencies."[19]

The Arab regimes are no longer capable of relying on repression. Supporting this argument is the fact that the Egyptian government has decided to intellectually counter-attack the current tide of political Islam by having the General Egyptian Authority for Books publish a series of books under the broad title *Confrontation* or al-*Muwajaha*. The series focuses on republishing books of scholars and intellectuals that have in common the goal of refuting the doctrines of radical groups by using the moderate religious and political thought prevalent in Egypt in the late 19th and early 20th centuries, including that of Jamal Al-Din Al-Afghani,

Muhammad Abdu, 'Ali 'Abd Al-Raziq, Taha Hussein, 'Abbas Al-'Aqqad and others. The specific objectives are outlined in the following points:

- to circulate the opinions of the pioneers of "enlightenment" (*al-tanwir*);
- to focus positively on the moderate views of Islam; and
- to refute the radical ideas regarding Islam's view of government and state and the application of the s*haria*.[20]

However, this "intellectual" governmental activity is only a belated supplement to the doctrine of confronting the fundamentalists, that is, the "security confrontation" doctrine that has been officially adopted by the Arab and Foreign Affairs Committee of Parliament, the highest judiciary council in Egypt. The security solution, to be developed through the consolidation of security apparatuses, comes first and foremost, followed by a religious confrontation that should be launched by the religious officialdom and then, most surprisingly, the legislature, which must produce a state-of-the-art law against terrorism. However, no substantial reference is made to address the severe economic conditions of poverty, to limit political manipulation through liberalization and democratization, or to respect human rights. When the report of the Committee suggests paying greater attention to the social development of poor and isolated rural areas with special focus on the youth, the objective is to control the hotbed of fundamentalists. The committee also proposes a further supplement to the law, already passed by the Egyptian Parliament, restricting the number of trade unions and the communication of local parties with foreign parties without official permission.[21]

The "religious confrontation," led by the late Sheikh Al-Azhar, seems to camouflage the measures taken by the government and also seems to provide indirect legitimacy to political Islam, in addition to weakening the modernist and secular tendencies in Egypt. In an interview, Sheikh Jad Al-Haq Ali Jad Al-Haq categorically rejects the separation of the state from Islam. He argues that Islam consists of both *din wa dunya* or, loosely translated, a religion and a way of life — basically identical to the fundamentalist interpretation. The Prophet Muhammad did not differentiate between the political and the religious. Again, the ruler should be appointed by *shura* (consultation) that may be conducted through different methods and approaches. After accepting the ideology of the Muslim Brotherhood as being Islamic, he only objects to the use of violence by some radical groups. However, the Azhar considers the Egyptian government's policies as Islamic and defends its actions against criticisms by radical and moderate fundamentalist groups.

In 1994, Sheikh Jad Al-Haq convened the first general conference for sheikhs in charge of official mosques with the specific objective of counterbalancing the activities of radical groups. The conference was attended by 1500 sheikhs, along with, very interestingly, the Ministers of Foreign Affairs, Interior, Religious Endowments, Information, Housing and Agriculture. The Interior Minister emphasized the organic link between the security confrontation and the religious one through the collaboration between the mosques and the media to curb terrorism. The Information Minister confirmed that the media had plans to uncover terrorism, but according to the "true" explanation of Islam. While refusing to lift media censorship and to license private television stations, he affirmed the role of the Azhar as an "information authority" to confront "foreign fundamentalist" dangers, for an information revolution had been going on with fundamentalists outside Egypt corresponding with those in Egypt by fax.[22]

With the tacit approval of the government, the Azhar plays the role of a modern "Court of Inquisition." Naguib Mahfouz, a Nobel Prize winner, has announced his readiness to rescind his book, *Awlad Haritna* (*The Children of our Neighborhood*) if the Azhar convinces him that it contains any blasphemous remark against Islam. Although Ri'aft Al-Sa'id, a secular leftist intellectual, condemns the fundamentalists for banning the book – in fact it was banned 34 years ago by the Azhar under Nasir's presidency – he calls on the government to face "the terrorists" not only by security measures but also by curbing their media. As one of the "enlightened thinkers" – a term used by Sa'id to describe himself and his intellectual colleagues – he calls for the suppression of whatever media freedom is left to Islamic thinkers because radicalism begins with an idea,[23] forgetting that inclusion, tolerance, pluralism and democracy started as ideas as well.

Furthermore, the case of Nasr Hamid Abu Zayd, an associate professor at Cairo University, who was not promoted to the rank of professor but was brought to a "secular" – and not a fundamentalist – court in Egypt, because of his heterodox views, shows how the government fights not only the intellectual "terrors" of fundamentalism, but also those of modernism. Because he has been convicted of the charge brought against him, he is considered an apostate that should be separated from his wife. The charge focused around his books which showed "animosity to the texts of the Qur'an and the *sunna*, non-belief and recanting Islam."[24]

While the government uses its legal apparatus to exclude major modernist figures and trends, it also uses it to exclude moderate fundamentalism. An Egyptian newspaper, *Al-Sha'b*, published an article on capital punishment stating that the Egyptian government has moved from civil and penal law to emergency laws. This allowed it to employ the "iron fist" policy to contain fundamentalists. During Mubarak's presidency, from 1981 until 1993, the policy resulted in the political execution of 48 individuals, almost double the number (27) of those who were executed for similar political reasons during a whole century in Egypt, extending from 1882 until 1981, including the presidencies of both Nasir and Sadat. In 1995, the number increased to 58.[25]

A member of parliament stated in a parliamentary session that Egypt lives on the margin of democracy, for democracy means the peaceful and voluntary hand-over of power, a feature that does not exist today. The State Minister for Parliamentary Affairs responded by saying that it is unbelievable that the parliamentarians should talk about the succession of power because it is elections and not governmental decrees that bring about political authority. With this remark, the minister insulted the intelligence of the parliamentarians. The party that receives the highest votes becomes the ruling party, he adds. It is well known, however, that the converse is true—the ruling party gets the highest votes. This notwithstanding, both officials forget, for instance, that one of the most popular movements, the Muslim Brotherhood, is excluded from official representation in government, parliament or party systems, though at times tolerated when running under the labels of other parties.[26]

Again, when the Egyptian government wanted to conduct a national dialogue, it launched it essentially with itself. Thus, twenty-six of the forty individuals who were "appointed" by President Mubarak as a preparatory committee to set the agenda for the conference on political dialogue were from the ruling party, Al-Hizb al-Watani. Worse than this, 237 out of the 279 conferees were from the ruling party; major political blocs were excluded. Though one might understand the exclusion of the radical groups that rejected "inclusive" policies, one cannot really understand the government's exclusionary policies towards the Muslim Brotherhood, which has exhibited – intellectually and politically – inclusive tendencies by accepting pluralism and democracy, as well as the legitimacy of the regime. So who is talking with whom?

The Muslim Brotherhood sought to be included in the much publicized national dialogue during 1994. While the government refused the official representation of the Muslim Brotherhood in that dialogue, the Brotherhood nevertheless tried to be included through its unofficial representatives in professional unions such as lawyers, medical doctors and engineers. The Muslim Brotherhood's view on the dialogue can be deduced from what Ahmad Sayf Al-Islam Hasan Al-Banna, the General Secretary of the Lawyers' Union and Hasan Al-Banna's son, said about that the movement's willingness to participate in the political dialogue if the government were to include it. Later on, the government rejected its participation and pressured political parties to disassociate themselves from the Brotherhood. The Brotherhood's view was that, although excluded as a political party, it could still be included as a representative of civil society. Instead, the government resorted to the repression of the Brotherhood through sweeping security measures that resulted in the death of a pro-Ikhwan lawyer while under arrest, an event that produced a strike by the Lawyers' Union and direct confrontation with security forces in 1994.[27]

Ma'mun Al-Hudaybi, the spokesman for the Egyptian Muslim Brotherhood, said in an interview that excluding the Muslim Brotherhood from the dialogue, along with independent fundamentalist thinkers such as Muhammad Al-Ghazali, was an example of exclusion of those who did not adopt or conform to the government's views. While the government does permit some thinkers to attack religion, it does not allow any open criticism to be directed at the slanderers. He characterized the cause for violence in Egypt as being the result of the government's policies of exclusion. Excluded from peaceful participation in political and public affairs, some groups were bound to turn into radicals because of the "closed-door policy." He expressed the Brotherhood's opinion that they were oppressed because of a governmental prohibition on holding public meetings, an act considered by the government as rebellion against the state.[28]

Following the same line of thinking, Muhammad Salim Al-'Awwa, a moderate fundamentalist thinker, lawyer and university professor, formulates the problem of exclusion in the following way: the government imposed new laws, such as the law against terrorism, emergency laws, the law of Shame (al-'ayb), established the Values Court (for the violation of social norms) and others in order to prevent society from moving ahead. There have been two types of political parties in the Arab world: governmental parties that were created by and served the government but did not represent the majority, even when claiming to do so; and other kinds of parties, which may be unlicensed such as Egypt's Muslim Brotherhood, or recognized by the government such as the Muslim Brotherhood in Jordan. These other parties should have been encouraged and managed, but this was not the case.

However, would the establishment of a recognized fundamentalist party in Egypt resolve the problem of radicalism? 'Adil Al-Jawjari argues that the concept of *shura* provides the Islamic movement with the method that allows for peaceful coexistence between the government and an Islamic party. The alternative to radicalism must be a party where fundamentalists can voice their grievances and participate in the political life of Egypt. The containment policy that is being imposed from above by the government has proved its futility, and the only meaningful and peaceful solution is to establish a legal fundamentalist party where the rights of minorities, political pluralism and other essential issues became part of the party's constitution.[29]

The Muslim Brotherhood published a manifesto condemning violence and terrorism, which is in fact its proclaimed public policy. The manifesto was published in Islamabad and not in Cairo because the Brotherhood's name cannot be undersigned publicly in Egypt. Nevertheless, it seems now that neither dialogue nor political life is developing or leading to any real positive change. The Muslim Brotherhood is increasingly being excluded from normal public life, and the possibility of them being included in public political life under the current regime seems limited. It might be appropriate here to cite a few articles of the manifesto:

- The Brotherhood affirms its stand to condemn any sort or source of violence and affirms the need to put an end to it. The Qur'an calls on people to use wisdom in propagating God's path.

- The Brotherhood condemns using revenge and vendetta and calls for implementing the *sharia* that prohibits bloodshed and maintains honor, in addition to the sacred things that people cherish.

- The Brotherhood adds its voice to all those who want to see a real end to violence. The Brotherhood declares that any solution that does not include real popular participation is defective.

- Restrictions on popular participation in politics should be lifted, and freedom to form parties and expression of all political forces should be permitted in order to achieve comprehensive social, economic and political reforms.

- All popular and political forces are required to stand united in order to extricate themselves from the vicious circle of violence and seek real reforms that fulfill people's hopes.[30]

Fundamentalist Discourses on Pluralism and Democracy

Inclusive Discourses

The ideological and political discourse of the Muslim Brotherhood's founder and first supreme guide in Egypt, Hasan Al-Banna, lays down the bases of inclusive views of the theological and political doctrine of God's governance or *hakimiyya*. While it has been used at times, both historically and presently, to exclude whatever is considered un-Islamic and, for some, even non-Islamic, Al-Banna transforms it into a source of both legitimacy and compromise. This feature has been more or less followed and developed by the majority of moderate fundamentalist political movements. Taking into account the circumstances of Egyptian society during the first half of this century, and given the relative freedom that the Egyptians had therein, the question of a forceful seizure of power was not on the agenda of the Brotherhood. Though interested in the Islamization of government, state and society, Al-Banna aimed essentially at being included in the existing political order and also competed with other political parties.

His call for inclusion was not a fabricated slogan but was applied in practice. Al-Banna himself stood twice for elections along with his party, the Brotherhood. Some of the Brotherhood's founding members were simultaneously members of other political parties; and the same applies to members of the contemporary Brotherhood. The peaceful involvement of the Muslim Brotherhood in Egypt's political life is well documented. It was involved in the struggle of the Azhar during the twenties and thirties and also sided with the king against the government. During that period, Al-Banna cooperated at times with Isma'il Sidqi, the on-and-off prime minister, and was engaged in teaching and lecturing.

The Brotherhood built its headquarters from voluntary donations, after which it built a mosque and schools for boys and girls. In 1946, the government provided financial aid, free books and stationery to the Brotherhood schools, with the Ministry of Education paying for all their educational and administrative expenses. In addition, Al-Banna established holding companies for schools, which became a success since most of the Brotherhood's membership was composed of middle class professionals and businessmen. Only a year after the establishment of the Brotherhood in Cairo, it had 50 branches throughout Egypt. Worried about the spread of Christian missionary schools in Egypt, the Brotherhood called on King Faruq to subject this activity to state supervision. However, after a meeting with a priest in one of the churches, Al-Banna wrote on the necessity that men of religion should unite against atheism. During the same year, the Brotherhood decided to set up a press and publish a weekly, *Al-Ikhwan al-Muslimun*.[31]

Al-Banna also included Boy Scouts in his organization. The Scouts' pledge was essentially of a moral nature, and not political or revolutionary. It centered on faith, virtue, work and the family. Al-Banna never denied that the Brotherhood was a movement that sought the revival of religion and had its own political, educational and economic aspirations. This did not mean, however, that the Brotherhood would isolate itself from society. In 1936, for instance, the Brotherhood participated in the coronation of King Faruq. During 1948, the membership of its Scouts exceeded 40,000 and had spread all over Egypt, working to eliminate illiteracy and to eradicate cholera and malaria epidemics. By 1948, the Brotherhood had established 500 branches for social services as well as medical clinics and hospitals and had treated about 51,000 patients.

Al-Banna also formed a women's organization in the forties whose membership in 1948 reached 5,000—a high number according to the standards of the time. It played a central role during what is referred to as *al-mihna al-ula* (first ordeal) in 1948–1950, when it looked after the families of the thousands of members of the Brotherhood in jail. The active membership of the Brotherhood was around half a million, with supporters counting for a similar number, and by the time of its dissolution, it had 1,000 branches in Egypt.[32]

In politics, the Brotherhood did not originally resort to violence, but followed the rules for as long as it was allowed to do so. It only became involved in violence when violence became prevalent in political life. It was not only the Brotherhood that established secret apparatuses. Such structures were a common feature of other parties as well as the state, which used political assassination to resolve many problems. This violence manifested itself against the Brotherhood through the assassination of Al-Banna, the jailing of thousands of its members, the dissolution of the organization and liquidation of its assets.

Before then, the Brotherhood had played by the rules. More importantly, the Brotherhood has always accepted the legitimacy of the existing regime and Al-Banna described King Faruq as the legitimate ruler. Al-Banna developed his organization into a political party with a specific political agenda in order to compete with other parties that were, in his opinion, corrupt. In 1942, Al-Banna along with other members of the Brotherhood stood for election, but the then Prime Minister persuaded him to withdraw. In exchange, he was supposed to receive more freedom for his organization and a promise from the government to shut down liquor stores and prohibit prostitution. However, later that year, Premier Al-Nahhas closed down all of the Brotherhood branches, except its headquarters. Again, in 1945, Al-Banna and five other members of his organization stood for election, but lost. The Brotherhood competed with the Wafd, the communists and others.

Al-Banna became a powerful player—for instance, he was called to the Palace in 1946 for consultation regarding the appointment of a new prime minister. At the time, the Brotherhood was especially encouraged in order to stand against the communists and the Wafd.[33] Again, Al-Banna's condemnation of Egyptian parties was based not on their neglect of religion but on their widespread corruption and collaboration with the British. His denunciation of Egyptian pre-Nasir parliamentary experience was therefore a rejection of Egyptian party life and not of the principle of constitutional life or multi-party politics. He expressed his belief that Egypt's constitutional life had failed and was in need of reorientation.[34]

During the seventies, the Muslim Brotherhood was used by Sadat to boost the legitimacy of his government, though they were still not allowed to form their own political party. However, Sadat's trip to Jerusalem in 1977 and the Camp David agreement and its aftermath resulted in a definitive rift between the Muslim Brotherhood and Sadat's government.[35] Their protest led to the imprisonment of hundreds of the organization's members in addition to members of other radical groups (discussed below). Nevertheless, the Muslim Brotherhood has not officially sanctioned or used violence to achieve any political or religious objective. Since 1984, the Brotherhood in Egypt and elsewhere, and similar movements like Al-Nahda in Tunisia and the Islamic Salvation Front in Algeria, have sought their inclusion in the political process and have been involved in establishing civil institutions. In Jordan, however, as the Brotherhood has functioned as a political party since the 1950s, some of its members have become well placed in government and parliament.

Inclusion and recognition in the state's hierarchy, as well as the Brotherhood's attempts to become part of the state administration, made *hakimiyya* basically a doctrinal organizing principle of government and a symbol of political Islam, all the while allowing inclusive and pluralist policies. Al-Banna's emphasis on the proper grounding of political ideology does not exclude individual and collective, social and political reformulations of Islamic political doctrines in accordance with modern society's needs, aspirations and beliefs.[36]

According to Al-Banna, while Islam contains basic legal material, its denotations and connotations cannot be restricted to or derived only from historical paradigms. More importantly, he attempts to show that Islamic thought must account for and deal with modernity as a worldview, not only as a law. Both the law and the worldview must deal with the real world, not in abstract terms, but in practical terms. They must therefore take into account and include other interpretations, political ideologies and philosophies. Because Islam is a religion, society and state, it must deal effectively with religion and the world. This means the inclusion of diverse substantive and methodological pluralistic interpretations, while maintaining the basic doctrines of religion.[37]

Since the *sharia* is viewed as a social norm, Al-Banna frees its application from specific past methods and links its good practice to maintaining freedom and popular authority over the government and separating the executive, legislative and judiciary authorities. Western constitutional forms of government do not contradict Islam if grounded in the fundamentals of the *sharia*. Constitutional rule is transformed by Al-Banna into *shura* by a subtle reinterpretation in the light of modernity and in a spirit not contradictory to the Qur'an. *Shura*, as the basic principle of government and the exercise of power by society, becomes inclusive by definition and is employed to empower the people to set the course of political action and ideology. For Al-Banna, because the ultimate source of the legitimacy of *shura* is the people, its representation cannot be restricted to one party, which usually represents only a fraction of people.

A continuous ratification by the community is required because governance is a contract between the ruled and the ruler.[38]

Al-Banna's theoretical acceptance of political pluralistic, democratic and inclusive interpretations sowed the seeds for future acceptance by the Muslim Brotherhood of political pluralism and democracy, notwithstanding its link to *tawhid* and its political connotation of unity. For Al-Banna, party politics and political systems do not preclude the acceptance of substantial differences in ideology, policies or programs. An Islamic state, however, does exclude parties that contradict the oneness of God.[39] The illegitimacy of atheistic parties does not represent, in Al-Banna's view, an infringement on freedom of expression and association, because these parties stand in opposition to the majority, or even minority, that believes in God. Atheistic parties would be outside the consensus of society and therefore threaten its unity. If Islam is chosen as the basis of government and society, then opposition to it becomes a matter of opposition to society, not a practice of freedom. Nevertheless, this is not a negation of pluralism in Islam, since foreign ideas and systems of thought can be incorporated.[40] The state must reflect social agreement and provide a framework for resolving conflicts peacefully.[41]

Furthermore, Al-Banna's system includes different social and religious groups, such as Christians and Jews, who, along with Muslims, are united by interest, human good, and the belief in God and the holy books. Where religion is acknowledged as an essential component of the state, political conflicts ought not to be turned into religious wars and must be resolved by dialogue. In Al-Banna's view, individuals enjoy equal religious, civil, political, social and economic rights and duties. The principle of individual involvement, to enjoin good and forbid evil, is the origin of pluralism, leading to the formation of political parties and social organizations or, simply, to the democratizing of social and political processes.[42]

Another important thinker, Taqiy Al-Din Al-Nabahani, the founder of Hizb Al-Tahrir in Jordan and Palestine, follows in Al-Banna's footsteps. While accepting in his *Al-Takatul Al-Hizbi* multi-party politics as a contemporary synonym of the duty to "enjoin good and forbid evil," he laments the many opportunities that political movements have lost. This is due to the lack of proper awareness of the role of parties in communal renaissance. According to Al-Nabahani, for the functioning of a party to be optimally effective, the party must be based on a set of principles that commits the community to act. Only in this manner can a real party rise, represent the people and push for major positive developments. Without popular support, civil actors cannot work properly.[43]

Al-Nabahani imagines a gradual process of development that centers on a three-fold program: first, propagating the party's platform to acquaint people with its principles; second, social interactions to sharpen the awareness of the people concerning essential issues; third, the quest for power in order to rule in the peoples' name. The party must always play the role of a watchdog and must not dissolve itself into state apparatuses. Its independence from the government is essential for its credibility. While the government's role is executive and must represent the people, the party's role is ideological. In this sense, the party must always watch the government. The government should not isolate itself from society, but must be responsive. Even when represented in government, the party must remain as a social force that supervises state actions. Put differently, to Al-Nabahani, civil institutions are social constructs and the government must yield to public demands and interests. Nonetheless, this situation must not be in contradiction to any Islamic principle.[44]

Al-Nabahani views the institutions of the community at large as the legal source of authority. Therefore, the government must respect the wishes of the community and enact its will. People are free to give or to withdraw authority, especially since a consultative council (*majlis al-shura*) must be the outcome of elections and not appointment. Al-Nabahani downplays the importance of the executive power and highlights the pivotal functions of elected bodies. They simply represent the people and protect their inalienable rights, including the right to form parties.[45]

However, since the 1950s, Hizb Al-Tahrir has not been able either in the East or West Bank, to carry out its program and fulfill its desired role. In 1976, the Jordanian government banned the party because its actions were perceived as threatening the stability of the monarchy, due particularly to its emphasis on the need for elections as an instrument to legitimize government. As a result of persecution, Al-Nabahani went to Damascus and then to Beirut. His party did not get a license, because the Jordanian government considered it to be against the monarchy.[46]

Another fundamentalist thinker, Munir Shafiq, argues that the relationship between governments and their societies is encumbered by major obstacles, like the lack of social justice, human dignity and *shura*. These issues transcend the Western ideas of human rights, the rule of law and democracy, and form the base for a proper relationship between the ruler and the ruled. He does not accept any justification for the conditions that beset the Muslim life, such as the absence of political freedom and the existence of widespread economic injustice. Thus, any modern resurgence must address these issues by spreading social justice, respecting human dignity and the law, and extending the meaning of *shura* and popular political participation by developing representative institutions.[47]

Similarly, Sa'id Hawwa, the Syrian Muslim Brotherhood's leader and thinker, argues that in an Islamic state all citizens are equal and protected from despotism and arbitrariness. The distinction between one individual and another should not center around race or belief. As for the exercise of power, it should be based on *shura* and freedom of association, specifically political parties, unions, minority associations and civil institutions. The one-party system is unworkable in an Islamic state. Furthermore, he adds that the rule of law must reign supreme, and people should be able to have access to courts to redress their grievances. More importantly, the state must guarantee freedom of expression, whether on the personal or the public level.[48]

In particular, Hawwa shows sensitivity to the importance of arguing for equal rights for Syrian minorities. While ultimate authority should be within the confines of Islamic teachings, and while individuals from minorities can be members of cabinets or parliaments, political representation must be proportionate. However, the administration of the minorities' internal affairs, such as building educational institutions and having religious courts, are the domain of the minorities themselves and must not be subject to others.[49]

Other thinkers, like Muhammad S. Al-'Awwa, a distinguished Egyptian member of the Brotherhood, go beyond these general statements and directly address the standing issues of democracy and rights. Starting from Al-Banna's discourse, Al-'Awwa elaborates further on the absolute necessity of both pluralism and democracy. According to Al-'Awwa, Islam is falsely accused of being opposed to pluralistic societies.[50]

Al-'Awwa accepts, broadly, that despotism was the general practice of the historical Arab-Islamic state, but this does not mean that Islam is by nature opposed to pluralism and democracy. He uses historical examples, like the first state in Islam founded by the Prophet, to show that despotism as a political concept, although tolerated by the general populace, has not enjoyed any legitimacy. He emphasizes that the historical state is not the sole representative of legitimacy and its model must not be imposed on the people. For Al-'Awwa, the first step to major changes is the reorganization of the society in a way that allows civil institutions to develop freely without any state control, since the current conditions hinder the development of pluralistic societies where real civil institutions serve the interests of groups. Islamic states have now created their institutions in order to preclude the real representative institutions and consequently force them to go underground. Thus, Al-'Awwa calls for revitalizing civil society as a means of freeing society from the grip of the state and its unrepresentative institutions.[51]

Pluralism, to Al-'Awwa, is the tolerance of diversity—political, economic, religious, linguistic and otherwise. This diversity is a natural human tendency and an inalienable right, especially when considering that even the Qur'an allows differences in identity and association.[52] Al-'Awwa identifies six doctrines that make Islam tolerant and pluralistic: it does not specify a particular social and political system but provides general principles; a ruler must be elected by the people through *shura*; if Islam permits religious freedom then all other kinds of freedom are legitimate; all people are equal in terms of both rights and duties; God's command to enjoin good and to forbid evil is a communal religious duty;

and, rulers are accountable to their communities.[53] However, to Al-'Awwa the legitimacy of pluralism hinges on two conditions: first, it should not contradict the basics of Islam and, second, it should be in people's interest. In all other respects, individuals and groups may associate with each other in any manner deemed necessary, especially as political parties which act as a safety valve against limiting freedom and a means for limiting despotism.[54]

Hasan Al-Turabi, the leading and powerful fundamentalist thinker of contemporary Islamic movements, breaks many taboos about the state in his theory. He drops many conditions about the nature of institutions that may be allowed by an Islamic constitution and in an Islamic state. More than Al-Banna, he imposes "Islamic" limitations on the power of the state and equates them with those of liberalism and Marxism. The state must not go beyond formulating general rules enabling society to organize its affairs. Accepting the idea that the *sharia* limits the powers of the state and frees society, he grounds it in the religious command "to enjoin good and to forbid evil."[55]

To Al-Turabi, this command becomes parallel to pluralism, because its performance is obviously of communal nature. Since the powers to exercise *shura* and *ijma'* are people's prerogatives, this primarily requires the existence of many opinions (*ijtihadat*) so that a community can choose from among them. This task is more urgent today, as Muslims are beset by dire conditions and unprecedented challenges. The current situation demands a new understanding of religion that transcends mere addition and subtraction of particulars and that accords to the need to provide new organizing principles appropriate for modernity.[56]

Al-Turabi theoretically justifies such a need by arguing that both the specific prescriptions and the organizing principles of religion are historically developed and are consequently subject to change according to the community's needs. The historical nature of these principles means that no normative standing is attributed to them and that their replacement with new prescriptions and principles is not in violation of religion. While this replacement does involve the Qur'an and the *Sunna*, the new *usul* (organizing principles) must be the outcome of a new *ijma'*, itself the consequence of a popular choice in the form of contemporary *shura*.[57]

For Al-Turabi, if *shura* and democracy are viewed outside their historical conditions, then they might be used synonymously to indicate the same idea. While it is true that ultimate sovereignty in Islam belongs to God, practical and political sovereignty centers on the people. For Al-Turabi therefore, s*hura* does not take away communal freedom to select an appropriate course of action, a set of rules or even representative bodies. However, Al-Turabi cautions against breaking any fundamental Qur'anic principle.[58]

Thus, Al-Turabi reserves ultimate political authority to the community, which in turn concludes a contract with an individual to lead the community and organize its affairs. This is done only through delegating power for the well being of the community. Al-Turabi accepts any state order that is bound by and is based on contractual mutuality, where the ruler never transgresses against the individual or communal freedom provided for by the Qur'an. The main Qur'anic discourse is not primarily directed to the state but to people, and more specifically to the individual. A proper Islamic constitution must guarantee individual and communal freedom. Proper representative bodies must then be set up to counter the possibility of despotic rule.[59]

Al-Turabi looks at the freedom to organize political institutions as an absolute necessity for an Islamic revival. A reformation that lacks a true philosophic and political reformulation of Islam will not give impetus to the sought-after cultural revolution. Mere religiosity along traditional lines would not be conducive to revolution. Nevertheless, a revolution must be based on religion, transcend temporary interests and be underpinned by social consensus. Consensus must be the source of communal interests and the social setting is the environment that enables the individual to enjoy freedom.[60]

While the *sharia* is pivotal to Al-Turabi, it does not exclude non-Islamic doctrines and institutions, especially if an Islamic society needs them. Al-Turabi exhorts Muslims to keep in mind the objectives of religion. Justice, for instance, does not mean one thing throughout history and, therefore, its individual interpretations must change from one time to another. However, there must be no opposition to a Qur'anic text.[61] As an example, Al-Turabi explains the "true" Islamic position on woman by arguing that Islam has provided her with complete independence. The Qur'anic discourse speaks to her without a male mediator; her faith, like that of the male, could not be meaningful without her sincere conviction. If the Qur'an postulates her complete religious freedom, it stands to reason that she is also free in other spheres of life, in society and state, as well as in economics and politics. She has equal rights in public life. While Al-Turabi acknowledges the historical lower status and mishandling of women, he attributes all of this to the misinterpretation of Qur'anic verses on women, in addition to negative social environments. However, these two aspects must be rectified, both theoretically by a re-reading of the text and practically by giving women their proper place in society.[62]

This kind of change cannot take place through minor adjustments, but requires, according to Al-Turabi, comprehensive mental adjustments and social restructuring of the community's experiences within a modern program. This program does not only lead to redressing the peculiar grievances of women, but also all other contemporary problems. The starting point, however, relates to freeing individuals and groups to pursue what they consider as new means toward development, since the historical experience of the Muslims is now defunct and cannot be of major utility. Muslims are experiencing what is not developed by them; simply put, it is a new world that requires new thinking.[63]

This call even leads Al-Turabi to aim at creating a modern jurisprudence that is not based on past history but rather on modern experience. A modern Islamic jurisprudence that is based on freedom of research without past restrictions imposed by jurists and state seems, to Al-Turabi, capable of providing Muslims with the necessary instruments to initiate revival. In this process, the state's role should be formal, that is to conduct *shura* and therefore to codify communal opinions. It must refrain from forcing its views on the public and must allow a new breed of '*ulama*' to develop and restructure Islamic thinking. Official institutions have no right to seize the communal rights of legislating and thinking.[64]

Al-Turabi further postulates comprehensive freedom as a fundamental right and formative principle in the life of people. More specifically, he denies the government any right to impose recognized legal views on the community. Such an action constitutes an uncalled-for interference by the state in the community's life and a breach of *shura*. Again, enjoining good and forbidding evil is the source of people's legitimate authority over the state.[65]

For Al-Turabi, this does not mean that the views of the community should be one and the same. On the contrary, he believes that the existence of only one public opinion may constitute an obstacle to progress and flexible change. While public opinion expressed in the media or by other means does not constitute an alternative to *shura*, policy-makers should take that into consideration. Furthermore, while jurists' *ijma'* on a specific issue is not binding on the community, the state should not dismiss it altogether. However, the community should neither be subject to jurists nor to outspoken public opinions. A democratic interpretation of Islam requires, in Al-Turabi's view, the existence of proper and free relationships between the state, individuals and community.[66]

According to Al-Turabi, without freedom human beings lose their true essence and become indistinguishable from animals. The original freedom includes freedom of expression and belief, for God convinces and does not force man to believe. Moreover, if this is the case with religion, so should it be with political matters. Tyranny from an Islamic point of view cannot be justified, and the *sharia* calls on people to voice their views. Today's powerful rulers, however, force people to follow certain ideologies and political programs. This contributes to the marginalization of people and their aspirations. In theory then, Al-Turabi stands against identifying the individual with the state. For the individual's inherent freedom cannot be given to institutions and to society, and any institutionalization of freedom means its destruction. For Al-Turabi, the only normative individual commitment is to Islam, which frees the individual from having to yield to imposed principles and ideologies.[67]

Al-Turabi cites a few examples of the powers that Islam has given to both the individual and society. For instance, Muslim society has the power to legislate and impose taxation. While the West, according to Al-Turabi, has surrendered such powers to the state, Muslim societies have reserved them for themselves, and there is no delegation as such. Strictly speaking, these are social and not political powers. Their surrender to the state negates the possibility of independent social development and subjects society to the state. As an example of a modern manifestation of the social power to legislate, Al-Turabi mentions political parties and legal schools. A political party expresses the individuals' desire for cooperation and unity, while multi-party politics may be the expression of *shura* in a complex system.[68]

Such freedom must not in any way lead to the division of Muslim society into warring ideological groups as happened in the history of Islam, which resulted in the community being split essentially into Shi'ism and Sunnism. While pluralism is recommended by Al-Turabi, its good practice revolves around its consensual context, based on a set of principles that is agreed upon. This context will also guarantee the indivisibility of society and provide a balance between freedom and unity.[69] Al-Turabi cites the mosque as a typical place where the true spirit of Islamic democracy is exemplified. It is a place formed by ideological bonds and unified by social and political orientations. More importantly, it is a prototype for communal unity, solidarity, unified organization, communication and leadership. The democratic aspect of religion is so obvious that even prayer leadership is subject to the selection of people and cannot be legitimately forced on the community. In addition, in spite of color, origin, wealth and languages, equality permeates all aspects of religious life. This is to Al-Turabi a good example that ought to be copied into politics.[70]

The leader of Al-Nahda in Tunisia, Rashid Al-Ghannushi, holds similar views to Al-Turabi. Al-Ghannushi argues for the need to maintain public and private freedom as well as human rights. Both freedom and rights are called for by Qur'anic teachings and ratified by international covenants. They are not contradictory to Islam and involve primarily freedom of expression and association as well as political participation, independence and condemnation of violence and of suppression of free opinion. Such principles, to Al-Ghannushi, should become the center of peaceful co-existence and dialogue between society and the state.[71]

However, Al-Ghannushi ties the political legitimacy of any political system to its provision of freedom for political parties and different elements of society. They should be allowed to peacefully compete over social, political and ideological agendas. The political system must permit free elections to representative councils and institutions so that they may contribute to state administration. If this takes place, the Islamic movement lends its popular support to and provides legitimacy for this system. Popular authority, grounded in God's governance, is the highest authority in society. Accepting freedom of association leads Al-Ghannushi to accept parties even like the communists who do not believe in God.[72] His rationale is that some groups may find it in their best interest to form parties and other institutions that might be irreligious. This does not constitute a breach of religion since pluralism, and more specifically freedom of belief, is sanctioned by religion. To Al-Ghannushi, the sacred text represents a source of reference for truth and its embodiment, while its human interpretations are grounded in diverse discourses representing different understandings under changing social, economic, political and intellectual complexities. Unfettered possibilities of systematic development should be encouraged.[73]

Openness and dialogue become a must for Al-Ghannushi, not only within the Muslim world but also within the world and with the West in particular. He argues that the world is transformed by scientific advancements into a small village that cannot tolerate war any longer. This matter poses the necessity of serious rethinking about the future of this village since it has a common fate. This is true if the inhabitants of this village are committed enough to a common fate and presupposes, among other things, putting an end to the abstract geographic and cultural division of the world into East and West and to the idea that while one of them is rational and democratic, the other is perverse and despotic. Such a division is nothing but a recipe for war. Any objective analysis testifies that negative and positive values and forces exist everywhere. The forces of good are invited to dialogue and to search for avenues for intercourse.[74]

The views of the fundamentalist trend that legitimizes pluralistic civil society and democracy can be aptly derived from the circulated text of a charter (*mithaq*) that was published and distributed by Muhammad Al-Hashim Al-Hamidi to other fundamentalists. He states that the success of the Islamic movement after it comes to power hinges on its establishment of a just and democratic system in the Arab world. Liberating the community from the tyranny that it has been subjected to necessitates that the Islamic movement puts down limits and a program for justice, *shura* and human rights. The program must include the rights of life, equality, justice, women, minorities and the right to political participation, to a fair trial, as well as freedom of thought, belief, expression and religion. His suggestions about the basic principles governing the formation of parties and associations include the freedom to form parties and political associations for all citizens without exception. Moreover, parties do not need to be licensed by government. Internal party life must also be governed by democracy. The call for dictatorship and totalitarian rule is prohibited under any circumstance, or in any slogan or political propaganda. Furthermore, all citizens, including communists, have the right to form parties, to promote their ideology and to compete for power. Finally, racial, tribal, sectarian or foreign affiliations cannot be the base of any legitimate political propaganda.[75]

The political program of Jabhat Al-Inqadh in Algeria also calls for adherence to *shura* to avoid tyranny and eradicate all forms of monopoly — political, social or economic. Political pluralism, elections and other democratic means of political and social life are called for as the means for liberating the community.[76]

Exclusivist Discourses

More than anything else, the discourse of Sayyid Qutb, the founder of radicalism in the Arab world, develops the underpinnings of radical

Islamic fundamentalism in the Arab world—the second major trend. The study of Qutb's thought shows us why many Islamic groups moved to religious radicalism. Qutb himself was both its foremost theoretician and victim; he was transformed under 'Abd Al-Nasir's regime from a very liberal writer in Egypt to the most radical fundamentalist thinker in the Arab world. His imprisonment and ferocious torture were transformed into a radical political jurisprudence of violence and isolation. It may be that this was his psychological compensation for the violence and repression inflicted by the regime.

Sayyid Qutb, born to a middle class family, received his Bachelor of Arts degree from Dar Al-'Ulum, like Al-Banna. Thereafter, he worked as a teacher and columnist and was associated with Taha Hussein, 'Abbas Mahmud Al-'Aqqad and other liberal thinkers. From the time he started writing in journals and magazines, he showed a general tendency to be in opposition to the government and critical of Egypt's state of affairs. He was very daring in his opposition to the government and in his 'radical liberalism,' manifested in writing free love stories and in his call for nudity. His first writings revealed existential, skeptic and liberal orientations. Because of his opposition to the government, he was first sent away to the countryside, and the two journals of which he was editor-in-chief, *Al-'Alam al-'Arabi* and *Al-Fikr al-Jadid*, were closed down. In 1948, he was sent by the Ministry of Education to the United States of America to continue his studies in education.[77]

His first book that adopted fundamentalism as a way of life, along with a political agenda, *Al-'Adala al-Ijtima'yya fi al-Islam* (Social Justice in Islam), which appeared during his stay in the United States, was far removed from radicalism and closer to Al-Banna's discourse. His stay in the United States, 1948–1951, made him review his previous attitude to and adoption of Western thought. His dislike of materialism, racism and the pro-Zionist feelings of the West, which he personally experienced in the United States, seemed to provide the impetus for his alienation from Western culture and his return to the roots of the culture in which he was raised. Upon his return to Egypt, that is, after the death of Hasan Al-Banna and the first ordeal of the Brotherhood mentioned above, he joined

[145]

the Brotherhood, became very active in its intellectual and publishing activities and wrote numerous books on "Islam as the solution." However, until that point, no radicalism or violence was involved. His priority was to write a modern understanding of Islam and the solutions it provided to the basic political, economic, social and individual problems of Egypt and the Arab and Islamic worlds.[78]

In 1953, Qutb was appointed editor-in-chief of the weekly *Al-Ikhwan al-Muslimun*, which was banned in the following year upon the dissolution of the Brotherhood. This followed the rupture between the Muslim Brotherhood and the Free Officers. He was arrested in 1954 and then released, and arrested again after the Manshiyya incident where an attempt was made on 'Abd Al-Nasir's life. Qutb and others were accused of being affiliated with the movement's secret military section. In 1955, Qutb was sentenced to 15 years in prison. He, along with thousands of the Brotherhood and their supporters were subjected to terrible torture that has left scars up to this very day. During this time, he shifted to radical fundamentalism and exclusiveness. Again, isolated from the outside world, under daily provocative pressures such as witnessing the slaughtering of tens of the Brotherhood in a jail hospital, Qutb could not but blame those who were free outside the jail but would not defend the unjustly imprisoned and viciously tortured. For Qutb, these people became accomplices in the crimes of the regime and therefore, like the regime, infidels. His most important books or the gospels of radicalism, *Fi Zilal Al-Qur'an, Ma'alim fi Al-Tariq, Hadha Al-Din, Al-Mustaqbal li Hadha Al-Din,* and others, were written because of and despite the torture that he and others endured year after year. Qutb was released in 1964, but was arrested soon after on charges to overthrow the government and was executed in 1966.[79]

In order to be able to endure his suffering and poor prison conditions, Qutb transformed his discourse into an exclusivist discourse so that it was not the state and society that were excluding him, but rather he, as the leader of the believing vanguard, who was excluding individuals, societies and states from the true salvation. The whole world became a target of his condemnation and isolation. The state's vengeful exclusion and repressive intolerance to any sort of popular opposition was counterbalanced by his desperate spiritual, moral, social, and political exclusion and intolerance. This is a clear contextual and historical example of how the parameters of radical fundamentalism developed. From there on and from his cell, he started developing his theoretical exclusivism.

Qutb argues that divine governance, the essential political component of *tawhid*, must be upheld at all times, when forming a virtuous and just society or providing personal or social freedom and must prevail under all conditions—in prison or outside of it. Freedom is perceived in a prescribed way—people are free insofar as their choice of social and political systems does not violate divine governance and does not hinder religious life. He perceives the state as the agent for creating and maintaining morality, both individually and collectively. Because of the sanctity of legislation, individuals, societies and states cannot legitimately develop normative rights and duties, whether related to political freedom, pluralism, political parties or even personal and social freedom. Qutb views universal divine laws as outlined in the Qur'an as the bases for all forms of freedom and relationships. In other words, all people, Muslims and non-Muslims alike, must link their views of life with the Islamic worldview, and Muslim and non-Muslim countries must finally submit to the divine laws without exception. The state and civil institutions as well as individuals may only codify legal articles if the need arises.[80]

Though this perspective postulates communal precedence over state control, the legitimacy of both is linked to the application of divine prescriptions. Qutb argues that because obedience to the government is not absolute, people should revolt when any government violates Qur'anic prescriptions, since it then loses its legitimacy. Thus, for Qutb, while ultimate sovereignty is reserved for God, its human application is a popular right and duty. This leads Qutb to argue that state authority is not based on any divine text, but must be popularly endorsed. Only free popular consent makes social, political and intellectual institutions legitimate. Adherence to Islamic law must be from a popular and not an official perspective. For it is the people who represent the divine will.[81]

Qutb's view of jurisprudence as a practical discipline severs it from its past theoretical golden pedestal and links it to contemporary needs. People are then freed to reconstitute modern Islamic political theories and institutions. His rejection of the historical normative compendium of Islamic disciplines leads him to uphold people's freedom to re-order their systems and lives.[82]

Consequently, Qutb rejects the unique legitimacy claims of any specific system or form of government; for instance, he would legitimize any form, republican or otherwise, insofar as its base is consensual agreement.[83] However, theocracy cannot be a sound Islamic system because no elite may claim divine representation. To Qutb, a proper Islamic state is both communal and constitutional; the judiciary, the legislature and the executive rule only through delegated powers by means of *shura*—the central political, theoretical and practical doctrine of government and politics. Any social agreement that does not contradict *sharia* is Islamically sound and can be included; however, elitism is excluded and rejected in principle.[84]

Qutb's discourse, thus far, gives the impression that even radical fundamentalism respects and honors communal choices. While this may be partially true, it still excludes pluralism, free civil society and multi-party systems in particular or liberal democratic tendencies in general. According to Qutb, the basis of freedom, the command to enjoin good and forbid evil, must be subjected to general communal interests like unity. In turn, these interests must override particular political, social or personal interests, like political elitism and economic monopoly. Personal freedom linked to communal interests and united in broad unitary ideological orientations is the source of social peace. To Qutb, a good religious society cannot rise on the basis of ideological and religious conflict, but requires goodwill, solidarity, security, peace and equality.[85]

As an example Qutb cites self-interest. Self-interest weakens communal solidarity, while mutual responsibility (*takaful*) strengthens that solidarity and is in itself a religious duty for society. Although Qutb argues that this responsibility is social in nature, it may turn into a political responsibility carried out by the state. This responsibility includes education, health and proper jobs. While, in Qutb's view, the state's interference must theoretically be limited, any failure of society to take care of its own affairs leads in practice to the state's moral responsibility to control society. Furthermore, while state institutions are of supplementary nature to Qutb, they ultimately replace as well as exclude the institutions of civil society. Interest groups are allowed only if their objectives are broad, such as caring for the poor or the sick. Others, like women liberation movements developed along Western models, are not welcomed or included. He argues that women's freedom to pursue their personal interests without regard to family weakens society. Moreover, Qutb argues that Western political systems are false in practice and in theory, and he thus excludes them, prohibiting group formation along Western models. A good society to Qutb is composed of religious groups sharing similar interests and perceptions of life as well as unified political orientations.[86]

Qutb excludes not only the legitimacy of multi-party systems, but also of one-party systems, and replaces the two with a religious 'vanguard' whose job is primarily salvation. Thus, any ideological group or system that is not based on Islam is not allowed to operate. Religious minorities are included insofar as they can keep their faith, but are excluded politically since they are not given any right to form political parties or even a 'vanguard.' Qutb also links any valid free expression to the parameters of Islamic ideological understanding. All those societies and parties that do not conform to such an understanding are described as *jahili*.[87] Thus, only an Islamic ideology may be represented in a political party (the vanguard or *tali'ah*). His book, *Ma'alim fi al-Tariq* (Signposts on the Road) is specific about the mission that this vanguard should carry out with an exclusive and uncompromising attitude regarding all other ideologies, societies and ways of life. However, establishing an Islamic system permits the involvement of different institutions in political processes so that the public will is known in the context of an Islamic ideology.[88]

The particular issue that Qutb uses to exclude Western models of unions and federations is their self-centered and materialist nature.

Conversely, he argues that *al-naqabat* or unions in Islam, which were originally the models for their Western counterparts, are based on brotherhood and solidarity. Thus, Qutb, like Miller and Huntington, sees only a mutual exclusivity between Western philosophies, ideologies and institutions on the one hand, and those of Islam on the other. The former are *jahili* and, as such, belong to *hizb al-shaytan* (the party of Satan); the others are Islamic and, as such, belong to *hizb Allah* (the party of God).[89]

Once out of jail in 1964, he started forming a "party" that adhered to the above-mentioned rationalizations and included the following principles: human societies do not follow Islamic ethics, system and *sharia* and are in need of an essential Islamic education; those individuals who respond positively to this education should undertake a study course on Islamic movements in history in order to set a program of action to fight Zionism and colonialism; in addition, no organization should be established until a highly ideological form of training has been undertaken.[90] Qutb's implementation of this vanguard program ended with his execution by hanging in 1966.

Most of the radical fundamentalist groups in the Arab world, and specifically in Egypt, have been influenced both directly and indirectly by the radical exclusivist discourse of Qutb and by his notions of paganism of the "other." A few examples may suffice here.

In Egypt, the Liman Tarah prison played an important role in Qutb's radical education of himself and others. Mustafa Shukri, a fellow-inmate of Sayyid Qutb, accepted the latter's views and established the exclusivist Jama'at al-Muslimin (the Community of the Muslims), notoriously known as Al-Takfir wa Al-Hijra, as a fulfillment of Qutb's vanguard. Shukri denies the legitimacy of pluralism and calls on people to adhere to the Qur'an and the *sunna* only. In his trial before a martial court in Egypt, he explained the exclusivity of his group in its rejection of theories and philosophies that are not textually derived; the Qur'an and the *sunna* are the only criteria of legitimacy and truth and, therefore, the government is in violation of divine governance. Furthermore, Shukri branded as unbelievers all other Muslims who did not view Islam in his way and turned migration (*hijra*) from Egyptian society into a religious duty.

Hence, he claimed that his isolated group is the only true Muslim community.[91]

Salih Sirriyya, the leader of Tanzim Al-Fanniyya Al-'Askariyya, was also a follower of Qutb. His exclusionary stance can be seen in his categorization of mankind into three groups only: Muslims, infidels and hypocrites. Any dereliction of an Islamic duty makes the individual an apostate and subjects him to death. Multi-party systems and diverse legal schools negate unity and lead to basic conflicts.[92] While Shukri turned his back on the *jahili* society, Sirriyya allows the temporary use of democracy in order to establish an Islamic state. If the activists are persecuted, then it is possible for such activists to secretly infiltrate the political system and even become cabinet ministers. This is legitimate since the struggle to topple un-Islamic governments and any irreligious organization is a religious duty that ends only on the Day of Judgment. Sirriyya maintains that the defense of un-Islamic governments, participation in un-Islamic ideological parties, and adhering to foreign philosophies and ways of life are as obvious instances of unbelief that incur death. He uses the sovereignty of God to divide mankind into the inclusive *hizb al-shaytan*, consisting of all individuals and institutions that do not believe in or practice Islam, and the exclusive *hizb Allah*, consisting of those who struggle to establish the Islamic state. Based on this logic, Sirriyya attempted a coup d'état against Anwar Al-Sadat that resulted in his execution in 1974.[93]

A further example of Qutb's influence is the case of 'Abud Al-Zumar, a former army intelligence officer, the military leader of Tanzim Al-Jihad, as well as the leader and one of the founders of Jama'at Al-Jihad Al-Islami. He follows Sayyid Qutb's reasoning about the importance of active opposition to the state. His program of action focuses on the implementation of an Islamic vision that consists in uniting Islamic movements within one framework, foregoing individual and public differences. Employing Qutb's key political term, *ma'alim al-tariq* (signpost of the road), he urges the Islamic movement to concentrate on its basic objective, the Islamic state. This requires an uncompromising and exclusive attitude towards all aspects of *jahili* systems and societies. The alternative for him is to employ a radical transformation and a total Islamization of all facets of life and the unequivocal rejection of secularism, nationalism and parliamentary life. However, this change has to begin with the ousting of current rulers who do not adhere to the *sharia*. In line with his exclusionary radical ideology, Al-Zumar tried but failed to kill President Sadat.[94]

Not less exclusionary is Al-Jama'a al-Islamiyya al-Jihadiyya, a branch of Tanzim al-Jihad in Upper Egypt, headed by 'Umar Abd Al-Rahman, now jailed in the United States. 'Abd Al-Rahman divides the Islamic movements themselves into two trends. The first trend, headed by the Muslim Brotherhood, accepts the existing Egyptian regime as legitimate and therefore adopts pluralism and democracy as legitimate tools of political action to establish an Islamic state. The other trend, headed by Al-Jama'a al-Islamiyya, denies legitimacy to the regime and publicly follows a course of total confrontation. 'Abd Al-Rahman accuses the Brotherhood of complicity with the government, since it worked with Sadat and Mubarak, condemned Sadat's death as well as acts of violence, and paid visits to the Coptic Pope. He further rejects the Brotherhood's inclusive and compromising attitude in allying itself with the Wafd party, as well as the Al-'Amal and Al-Ahrar. Instead, he calls for replacing the inclusiveness of the Brotherhood with the exclusionary policy of the Jama'at by rejecting integration in democratic institutions and by adopting a course of forceful resolution regarding basic issues of identity, ethics and values.[95] Also in line with Qutb's argument, he describes any system that adopts foreign principles as belonging to *kufr* and *jahiliyya* and legitimizes its overthrow.

This view leads al-Jihad to declare war against the Egyptian parliament, since, through Article 86 of the Constitution, it accorded itself the right to legislate and permitted democracy, a concept that treated the believer and non-believer equally as citizens.[96] 'Abd Al-Rahman explains, "The 'assumed democratic system' in Egypt wants us to enter into party politics in order to equate Islam with other ideologies." However, the Islamic movement believes in its distinctive superiority and rejects the *jahili* positive law. He further rejects any role for representative bodies as avenues for Qur'anic interpretation and adjudication. Qur'anic legitimacy stands on its own. Thus, any violation of Qur'anic texts leads a ruler to *kufr* punishable by death. 'Abd Al-Rahman himself was viewed as the instigator of Sadat's assassination.[97]

Conclusion

It is clear throughout this chapter that fundamentalism, though perceived as being one exclusive phenomenon in both theory and practice, is in fact diverse. Fundamentalism, whether Jewish, Christian, Islamic or even Hindu has become a world phenomenon. However, it is essentially only Islam that is identified with fundamentalism. Agreements on the framework of Islam – which are dealt with in the chapter on epistemology and political philosophy – might even lead not only to confusion of radical fundamentalism with moderate fundamentalism, but involve Islam as well. If an ordinary practicing or non-practicing Muslim is asked whether the Qur'an postulates God's governance in all aspects of life, the answer is "yes, of course." However, this belief does not necessarily make a Muslim a fundamentalist, or, conversely, depending on interpretation, it may render all Muslims fundamentalists by definition.

What must distinguish a radical view from a moderate one is the method used to transform a political agenda into a way of life. As we have seen, even fundamentalism employs diverse methodological and practical processes to create intellectual and political formulas. One formula is conceptually based on theoretical and practical exclusiveness that permits the use of violence against the other. Because radical fundamentalism lives in isolation from society under conditions of social disunity, corruption, exploitation, political violence and undemocratic regimes, it has transformed its political discourse into an isolationist theology of politics. From this point of view, Islam demands a political contextualization.

Shura becomes to the radicals not merely a religious doctrine or a mechanism for elections—it reflects the public will, a far superior doctrine to individual freedom or social agreement. More importantly, it represents the divine will and, as such, any deviation from the divine is a religious violation. The individual cannot but submit to this will; in fact, he is only an appendage to it, with his freedom depending on it. While this will may opt for a political contract with a ruler, it cannot, because of what it represents, allow pluralism and basic differences leading to disunity. For radicalism, the establishment of an Islamic state becomes the fulfillment of this divine will, and individuals and groups are therefore subordinated to the state.

Processed through the lenses of the *sharia*, the institutionalization of *shura* and *ijma'* provides the state, which expresses the general will, with a normative role in making basic choices in people's life. The formal legitimacy that the state acquires makes it, in fact, unaccountable to anyone but God or compliance with *sharia*, which is in itself institutionalized in the state. Henceforth, legitimacy becomes an affair internal to the state, and not a social and public issue, even though originally it was so. In addition, insofar as the state is not going against the *sharia*, no one can legitimately overthrow it. Because the state supervises public morality and the application of *sharia* in this context, individual religiosity is subject to the communal public will, itself transformed into state control, both moral and political. Parties, associations and other civil institutions have no intrinsic validity in this hierarchy but operate only in a supplementary manner. In the final instance, such an elaboration seems to demand an exclusionary approach. Indeed, there is no possibility of a pluralistic understanding of religion, since politicizing Islam, according to the proper Islamic interpretation, cannot be represented except by the state. The establishment of inclusive pluralistic civil democracies and ways of life then seems unworkable.

The descriptions that Miller, Lewis, Huntington and others attribute to fundamentalism and to all other Islamic movements might be more appropriately restricted to Islamic radicalism. However, to use the radical groups as representatives of Islamic and Arab culture is both factually erroneous and culturally biased. Other non-Islamic religious interpretations suffer from very similar phenomena, but are never treated in the same manner. The use of violence by radical groups is not theoretical in origin, but the theory thereof is a product of history. Put differently, Islamic radicals have been committing violent acts not because of their theories, but rather their theories justifying violence have been derived from the real and imagined violence that they have been subjected to. Thus, practice has been transformed into theory, which has now a life of its own. Both radical groups and most regimes are committed to recycling intellectual and physical violence and exclusiveness. Violence, both secular and religious, has been exercised most of the time in reaction to the tyrannies of political regimes.[98]

On the other hand, those belonging to the moderate sector cite the absence of a pluralistic society and democratic institutions as the real cause of violence. While this group has for long been excluded from political participation, it still calls for its inclusion into politics and formal institutions. Its involvement in civil society and its call for pluralism are still seen as the road to the salvation of the community and individuals. Its inclusive views do not postulate an eternal or divine enmity between Islam's institutions and systems and those of the West. Properly grounded, what is Western becomes indeed Islamic. The moderate fundamentalists are able to blend the culture of the East with that of the West. They provide Islamic arguments for inclusion, not mutual exclusion as some secular and religious radicals do in the East and the West. The conflict between the East and West is viewed as being primarily political or economic, but not religious or cultural. The two sides have common monotheistic grounds upon which multi-cultural and religious cooperation and co-existence might be built.

For the moderates, a popular liberal democracy, grounded in Islamic law, is a political bridge between the East and the West. Authoritarianism and despotism are not specifically cultural or Islamic – they have existed in both the West and the East – but are more prominent now in the Arab world. The moderate sector has started to adopt an Islamic interpretation of liberal democracy, as opposed to popular democracy, or the authoritarian nationalism of the Arab world, or, indeed, the radical fundamentalism tyranny of the majority.

If the weakness of fundamentalism, both in its minor radical and, especially, major moderate trends might lead to free, liberal, pluralistic and democratic societies and inclusive regimes in the Middle East, why did this not happen when Islamic movements were at their lowest ebb and their members jailed? We should bear in mind that the liberal West, along with some Arab political regimes, encouraged the emergence of Islamic movements in the 1970s, at least in Egypt during Sadat's presidency and in Afghanistan to fight the Communist regime. After the fall of the Soviet Union and the Communist regime in Afghanistan, the Arab Mujahidin, known today as the Arab Afghans, returned to Egypt, Algeria, Saudi Arabia and other Arab countries only to stage a new religious war in the Arab world, resorting to violence, both physical and religious, against their new opponents. Therefore, who is responsible for political instability in the Arab World?

5

Islamic Movements and their Role in the Political Stability of the Arab World

Fawaz Gerges

To start with, emphasis needs to be placed on an important theoretical point relating to the tight or causal relationship between the nature of an existing regime and its structure on the one hand, and the role of political opposition forces and their behavior, on the other. The study and understanding of political opposition cannot be properly pursued without analyzing and investigating the material and sociological structures of elites and ruling regimes and how they deal with civil societies. Opposition is no more than a natural expansion of culture and political behavior that is dominant in a specific country. It is the clearest expression of the nature of the relationship between state and society and of the strength of political life in any country.

While liberal governments produce sound democratic opposition based on a peaceful transfer of power and are responsible for implementing the programs and projects of development, authoritarian and tyrannical regimes block the avenues for and control the means of political expression. This compels the opposition either to accept the status quo and become integrated in the existing political regime, or to operate underground and to seize power through undemocratic means—considering that it was undemocratic processes which in the first place led to its oppression and removal from the political scene. Therefore, the opposition is the other face of the existing political regime, in the context of which it develops its style and creates it framework, mechanisms and general behavior.

The importance of this simple and important point is that it centers the research on basic and practical material factors in order to understand the rules of the political game, including the mechanisms and strategies that the opposition adopts to change these rules or co-exist with, refine or improve them. In addition, the emphasis on the close relationship between the structure of the regime and the role of opposition leads to caution about oversimplified reductionist views that try to explain the status of political instability in the Arab world by returning to cultural and civilizational factors rooted in man's intellectual structure and Arab societies. Such an emphasis gives the cultural and civilizational factors a scholarly aura and exonerates its advocates from investigating the main causes for the opposition's resort to violence to seize power, which should take into consideration politics, the economy and political tyranny.

What is at stake here is whether the existing Arab regimes will disengage from confrontation with the movements of political Islam and instead use them in the process of national renaissance. Are the Arab governments going to maintain the status quo in terms of preventing freedom of expression and of opinion and the active political participation of different social groups, including the movements of political Islam? From this point of departure, it is not possible to study and understand the role of the movements of political Islam in the Arab world except through the public behavior of the existing elites and political regimes, reflecting the way they deal with both Islamic and secular opposition.

In this context, the topic will be explored below by analyzing seven principal questions.

The Universal Phenomenon of Religiosity

There is no doubt that movements of political Islam have played an organic role in shaping the political scene in the Arab region since the

1970s to the present. This does not mean that these movements did not exist on the political and social map before the 1970s, but their ability to mobilize the population did not become clear until the 1960s, especially after the June 1967 defeat by Israeli forces in six days, which shook the Arab consciousness and the social and political structures. Without going into detail about the causes that contributed to the rise of the movements of political Islam since the early 1970s – since most of them are well known and documented – I will focus on the phenomenon of religiosity, which is now universal and international, transcending the borders of the Arab and Islamic region. The main question in this context is how to interpret the phenomenon about the spread of religiosity among human societies in the last three decades of the twentieth century.

It must be noted that the most important and influential fundamentalist movements are in the United States of America and India, in particular, as well as in other countries, and are not restricted to the Arab region, as some researchers claim. The role of Christian, Jewish and Hindu fundamentalism in their societies is more widespread, influential, and important than Islamic fundamentalism. These fundamentalist trends are distinguished by their ambitious political, philosophical and intellectual agendas and visions, which transcend spiritual and religious matters and try to introduce dramatic and radical changes in the structure of their societies and regimes, and not only to increase the love of religion among the populace. Religion and politics are two sides of the same coin. Some fundamentalists have had tremendous victories in India and the United States regarding their ability to influence national decision-making and other vital issues.

There is no distinctive characteristic that sets the Arab region apart in terms of the gradual ascendancy of the movement of political Islam in the last three decades. For the Arab world, like the West and the East, has witnessed a massive growth and a qualitative leap of the religious trend and active organizational mobilization, which have shown the real weight of different social and political forces in the balance of power. The Arabs and Muslims are not alone in trying to politicize religion and to use it as an active strategy or mechanism to confront exiting regimes and to change the status quo and the prevailing political discourse using old as well as new theories of sociology, whose legitimacy is derived from the local cultural heritage. In this case, the Arabs are not different from their counterparts whether in relation to religiosity or the politicizing of religion. The Arabs are part of the cultural universe and the trends that influence the universe leave their imprints on their thinking and behavior. Therefore, Islamic fundamentalism is not different in substance and logic from other fundamentalisms in the United States, India or Israel.

Some may ask about the proper method of interpreting the behavior of Islamic fundamentalist movements in Egypt, Algeria or other Arab countries. Have these movements not resorted to violence to seize power? Did some movements not present a threat to political and economic stability in the Arab region during the 1980s and 1990s? There is no doubt that Islamic movements constituted the principal challenge to governing elites and regimes from the late 1970s to the late 1990s; this is especially so since these elites were not prepared to accept any active political participation in the running of state affairs or the peaceful transfer of power to other social forces.

The way the existing ruling regimes dealt with the rise of Islamic fundamentalist movements has increased tension and the dominance of the logic of exclusion and isolation, instead of dialogue, cooperation and constructive participation. The causes for the armed conflict and confrontation between some regimes and Islamic movements cannot be understood outside the context of the state of terror that engulfed the governing elites since the rise of popular fundamentalist trends, which created insecurity around their positions, cadres and achievements. It must be noted that the reactions of political authorities in the Arab region against the Islamic phenomenon are characterized by high tension and violence with the aim to curtail, reduce and paralyze it. Political authorities started the explosive confrontation that is still continues. Nevertheless, this does not mean that the leaderships of the various Islamic movements are exonerated or are only victims of a conspiracy executed by the existing regimes with support from influential Western powers.

[160]

Arrogance and Desire for Power in Islamic Leaderships

Also of note are the arrogance and feeling of power of some among the Islamic leadership in the 1980s and early 1990s, as well as their discourses and provocative actions. This increased the fear of the governing elites and led to their conviction that the stability of their political regimes and their political future depended on their ability to confront the growing Islamic phenomenon. The regimes' awareness of the new threat coincided with the beginning of the collapse of the socialist camp and the failure of development programs in most of the third world countries, including the Arab states. Such a failure showed the fragility of the Arab nation-state regime and its weakness and inability to launch wars, protect the homeland and provide for the basic needs of its citizens. Moreover, regional and international developments removed from the Arab regime its Arab ideological legitimacy and cover, and exposed it to merciless, powerful winds.

Moreover, the ruling regimes and elites were not accustomed to confronting an active internal opposition that had the ability to mobilize the population, to take the initiative and to compete with the authorities over livelihood issues that were of concern to the citizens. Instead of entering into dialogue with the elites to reduce their fears, the leaderships of the Islamic movements increased the intensity of the conflict and threatened them with dire consequences should they seize power. Therefore, the desire for power and dominance replaced the logic of political co-existence in the way the Islamic movements dealt with the existing regimes. This attitude comprises one of the most fatal errors committed by third world opposition, where the logic of exclusion superseded the logic of co-existence. It is improbable that any peaceful transformation can take place within the power centers of the regimes unless the opposition behaves in an intelligent manner and builds some political coalition with the governing elites in order to reduce their fears and secure their future political existence. The governing elites will not voluntarily give up power without such a political coalition since such an act would lead to their exclusion and even annihilation.

One of the important theoretical achievements of the process of peaceful democratic transformation in Latin America in the 1980s and 1990s was the creation of mechanisms for power transfer and for cooperation between the authoritarian military regimes and the opposition on the basis of a gradual transfer of power without punishing or excluding the influential governing elites. This succeeded in many countries of Latin America where a gradual democratic development took place during the 1980s and the 1990s. Nevertheless, it is wrong to compare the Islamic and Arab region with that of Latin America, since the historical experiences and sociological and economic factors differ greatly. However, what is important in this context is that opposition in the countries of Latin America benefited from a long history of struggle against the military regimes and arrived at the conclusion that the best and most successful method for transfer of power depends on guaranteeing the security and life of the influential leaderships, and not to scare, threaten or corner them so that nothing is left but confrontation.

In the Arab case, some Islamic movements have behaved unwisely and generally increased the burden of the influential elites and governing leaderships. They have fallen prey to their own illusions and incorrect analyses and have provided the perfect excuse for the exclusivist members of the elites to consider the Islamic phenomenon a danger that cannot be ignored and an evil that must be eradicated. Thus, some Islamic movements have given the exclusivists and radicals within the power structure an excuse to attack them in an attempt to bring about their destruction.

Islamic Movements and the West

The Islamic movements have not only opposed and threatened the current political regimes but have also launched a fierce campaign against what they have described as their tyrannical masters, that is the Western powers, especially the United States. Thus, some of these movements have entered into a costly confrontation not only with the local governing elites but also with the West, without due attention to the consequences of such a confrontation. Indeed, the radical trend in the West employed the collapse of the Soviet Union in late 1980s and early 1990s to redraw its military and security strategy to locate new enemies that can pose new dangers to vital Western interests.

Therefore, some radicals in the United States and other Western states found their enemy in the Islamic phenomenon, or what is referred to as Islamic fundamentalism. It has been considered to be one of the main dangers that face the West after the collapse of the Soviet Union. Some have even gone beyond this and considered the conflict between the West and Islam to be a cultural conflict that transcends ideology, history and security. Thus, the Cold War is now regarded by some as no more than a marginal civil war within the same European family. However, the conflict with Islam, according to radical propagandists, is natural, civilizational and permanent.

After a short period of indecision and doubt, Western powers, especially the United States and France, have entered the conflict on the side of their allies in the Middle East in an attempt to strike at the Islamic fundamentalist movements in order to bring about their demise or to weaken them. It would be a mistake to belittle or underestimate the importance of moral, political and military Western support to their allies in Egypt, Algeria, Jordan and Palestine in confronting the expansion of the Islamic movements and preventing them from attaining a qualitative penetration that could leave strong imprints and result in negative consequences for the political and economic stability of the region. Regardless of the Western agenda for the region, which is considered by some to be an agenda that clashes with the religious, national and patriotic ambitions, some of the Islamic movements committed some fatal mistakes by providing powers in the West that are antagonistic to the Islamic phenomenon with the excuse that compelled their governments to enter into confrontation along with the current regimes. The logical conclusion for antagonizing Western powers is tipping the balance in favor of the allies of the West in the Arab region, who have been successful in striking hard against the Islamic phenomenon.

[163]

Failure to Renounce Violence

The main Islamic fundamentalist movements in Arab countries have failed to renounce the violence and other mechanisms that the jihadist movements used to confront security authorities. Some Islamic movements issued statements and declarations from time to time criticizing terrorist operations of jihadist movements and especially those that led to civilian casualties. But these statements were not sufficient to convince the regimes and elites in the region and the West that the Islamic phenomenon is a civil social movement that refuses to employ violent means to seize power.

The occasionally ambiguous and non-transparent discourse of the Islamic leaderships led to the impression that the latter tried to achieve public benefit from the outcome of the confrontation between political systems and jihadist organizations, and to make use of this confrontation and lie in wait for the appropriate chance to set on the regime and topple it. It would be a mistake to underrate the importance and effect of the bloody confrontation between jihadist organizations, on the one hand, and the authorities in politics and security, on the other, on public conscience in the Arab states and the international public opinion. In the final analysis, the assassinations and bombings carried out by the jihadist organizations in the 1980s and the 1990s had a negative impact on societies. They led to a feeling of repulsion on the part of the various social layers in the Arab states with respect to these terrorist acts, which convulsed social security, and their attendant losses in the human and economic fields, especially the tourism sector.

The previous terrorist acts also led to confusion about the Islamic phenomenon among Western public opinion and an inability to distinguish the jihadist movements from the mainstream Islamic movements. Violence has been considered the common denominator between the two streams that aim to seize power and establish a theocratic religious state. The media of the Arab regimes have succeeded in misrepresenting the two movements in the eyes of Western and Arab public opinion and they have portrayed the jihadist movements and mainstream Islamic movements as two sides of the same coin, but that have played different roles and missions in order to achieve their strategic goal, which is to seize power and turn things upside down, including changing the relationships with Western powers and intensifying the conflict with Israel. In this context, I met tens of American officials in the departments concerned with the Middle East during the 1990s when the Council on Foreign Relations in New York charged me to prepare a study on US foreign policy towards the movements of political Islam. There was almost a consensus among the US foreign policy elite that the Islamic movements should be distinguished from each other, with respect to their use of violence, their relations with the West and their treatment of their own societies and regimes. There was also a consensus that there was no field coordination between the jihadist organizations and movements of political Islam. Instead, there is a state of enmity and hatred on both sides. Nonetheless, the Clinton Administration was forced then by pressure exerted by Arab countries to cancel its unannounced meetings with some leaderships of the Islamic movements in Egypt, Algeria and other countries, that had been initiated in the 1990s in order to build bridges with the movements and to avoid their going underground in a manner similar to what happened in the 1970s in Iran. Instead, the American Administration started in the 1990s to provide unlimited support to its allies to confront the Islamic movements and indirectly accepted the regimes' views of these movements as threatening international and regional stability. All of the Islamic movements have been grouped together, and the United States has put all of its weight behind its allies in their war against the movements of political Islam.

General Obsession with Power

There is an obsession with power not only among the Islamic movements but also across most political trends in the Arab region. The objective of seizing power blinded many Muslim leaderships from investing their vast intellectual and human abilities and resources in building a solid popular base focused on socio-economic issues that are of a general interest to citizens. Most field studies in this context point to the existence of a causal relationship between the steady but fast development of Islamic movements in Arab neighborhoods and countries, on the one hand, and their ability to provide social and daily services to destitute segments and classes of society, on the other.

The critical question is then, why did the Muslim leaderships not focus on investing all of their capabilities on developing and educating the huge popular bases instead of entering into a useless confrontation with political authorities? The more important philosophical question relates to the political nature of the movements at the expense of the cultural, social and economic needs of societies. How do we explain our excessive interest in what is political while we direly need to emphasize the other bases required to build civil societies that are more solid, educated and able to confront political tyranny? What is important is that by giving priority to what is political has brought the Islamic movements into an inevitable confrontation with the authoritarian regimes that are not used to the voicing of opinion by others but rather are accustomed to monopolizing all the legitimate means related to political participation.

The emphasis of some Islamic movements on the political factor and their competition with the governing elites, in addition to increasing the confrontation and demonstrating belligerence in their political discourses and literature, led to the sowing of the seeds of political instability in the region, at specific times in the 1980s and the 1990s. There is no doubt that these movements should shoulder a great share of the responsibility for the tense environment that they have brought upon their peoples and societies—a tunnel with no end in sight.

There are also a lot of examples of rational Islamic movements that preferred to work gradually, cooperate and participate indirectly in the running of state affairs, instead of threatening the security and safety of existing regimes. For example, the Islamic movements in Yemen, Jordan, Lebanon, Kuwait and other places chose peaceful and positive strategies that rejected costly confrontations with the regimes and governments, even though they have fundamental disagreements with the elites over their agenda and political and ideological principles. It seems that the leaderships of these movements have accepted the rules of the game without the danger of risking the stability of the country and the people. They preferred to wait patiently and to participate indirectly in order to bring about changes in the structures of authority, state and society in the long term.

It should be noted that among the Islamic movements there are pluralistic and qualitative differences in programs and treatments of societies and regimes. While the Islamic movements in Egypt and Algeria have chosen ambitious offensive strategies and mechanisms to seize power, others have preferred cooperation and gradual change, as is the case of Lebanon, Jordan, Yemen and Kuwait. The behavior of the first group of movements has led to a state of chaos, confrontation and political instability, while the second group has developed further. The importance of the latter approach is that it has protected society from dangerous internal trauma that could have arrested the development of the movements and annulled their gains over the last few decades. Also, the general importance of establishing and building upon peaceful rules for political behavior is that it may in the future lead to a peaceful transfer of power to social forces that are more democratic and representative of public opinion than what exists at present.

Losses of the Jihadist Movements in the Field

The jihadist movements have incurred great losses in the field in Egypt and Algeria, brought about by the existing authorities, even though the latter have not been able to disengage the conflict from civil society or succeed in isolating the Islamic movements from the public sphere. The parliamentary and union elections have proved the popular support that the main Islamic movements enjoy and the failure of the regimes of Egypt and Algeria to eliminate these dynamic and vigorous Islamic movements, even though thousands of their members have been jailed and many strikes have been directed at their cadres and leadership. The observers of the Algerian field believe that the Islamic movements will achieve important gains and results if there are free elections. It appears that other regimes in Jordan and Yemen, under local, regional and international pressure, have moved to curtail the Islamic movements even though the latter have not tried to threaten or endanger political stability. With such an attitude followed by Arab regimes, the observer might question the role of Islamic movements in political stability. This question leads to the following point.

Impact of Confrontation on Maturity of Islamic Movements

The experience of confrontation between the Islamic movements and the regimes during the 1980s and 1990s contributed somewhat to the political maturity of Islamic movements. Of note is that the experience of violent confrontation had a positive effect on the political discourse of the Islamic movements and on their agendas. Although there were attempts to exclude the Islamic movements, their young and experienced leaderships have now moved to organize themselves in political parties, shun underground actions and publicly adopt peaceful political activity. More importantly, these leaderships have started revising their old tactics and strategies, recognizing the movements' mistakes committed from their inception to the present.

Some call this method revisionism and others consider it to be a tactical withdrawal because of the defeat that the jihadist movements have suffered and the downsizing of the mainstream Islamic movements. It seems that the Islamic leaderships are seriously trying to reformulate the Islamic project on new bases that depend on peaceful integration and participation in the political sphere, where violence is rejected as a means of arriving at power. The important issue is that these leaderships are seriously trying to construct a theoretical and juristic framework that allows the formation of political parties with rights and duties similar to other parties. What is noticeable in this context is that the young leaderships of former jihadist movements are playing a pivotal role in the process of reformulating a project for political Islam on new bases and foundations.

Conclusion

Thus far, it does not seem that the ruling regimes have a long-term strategic vision that allows them to take the new developments into consideration and try to disengage and absorb the Islamic movements instead of excluding and curtailing them. The regimes are still persecuting the Islamists, arresting their leaders and cadres and refusing to allow them to form political parties to peacefully participate in the political sphere. Thus, some questions become important: How can political stability be ensured and supported when the political authorities close up all the avenues for the constructive participation of the most important social forces in the process of political transformation? Will the shortsightedness of the Arab governments lead to a repeat of the security upheavals in Arab societies? How can a real political change take place under conditions of tension and exclusion between the authorities and the opposition? Do the governments believe that they can eliminate a social phenomenon that is deeply rooted in the cultural and civilizational structure of Arab societies?

These legitimate questions do not mean that the Islamic movements are undergoing some qualitative leap in their relations with states and societies, or that there is some radical transformation of their political discourse. Their discourse is still defensive and characterized alternately by demagogy and formal exaggeration at the expense of content, as well as by the inability to construct critical mechanisms to deal with the process of development, governance and complicated social issues. The fear is that the Islamic movements may move toward a cultural confrontation with their societies after a bitter failed offensive against the existing regimes. Cultural wars are more dangerous, ferocious and destructive of social structures than military clashes with authorities. Can our societies that are oppressed, and politically and economically exhausted tolerate cultural wars that are characterized by exclusion and excommunication? Would the Islamic movements yet again miscalculate and waste their abilities and achievements in marginal conflicts, that only increase cultural polarization and reduce the space for intellectual and personal freedoms, thus benefiting only the authoritarian regimes? Would the behavior of these movements indirectly serve the agenda of the governing elites?

The question over the role of Islamic movements in the political stability of the Arab world is a legitimate question under the prevailing international, regional and local conditions but it does not deal with the larger dimensions of the Islamic phenomenon. There are other questions that are more important than the question of political stability, which should be tabled for discussion. Such questions include: Do the Islamic movements have a project for renaissance that incorporates real change? Do the agendas of the Islamic movements differ radically and organically from other social and political movements in the Arab world? Is the issue of modernity still the difficult dialectic from the perspective of these movements? Is it easy to be integrated with the world and the others when the movements isolate themselves in the name of identity and particularity? Do the Islamic movements have a specific and comprehensive plan to solve the problem of development in Arab countries? Does the discourse on identity and 'the other' as well as culture represent an escape from the vital issues that will define the Arab future in the third millennium?

6

The Future of Islamic Movements in the Context of Changing Regional and International Conditions

Radwan Al-Sayyid

During the last decade, a number academic researchers and strategic analysts have predicated the near end of the Islamic movements, or what they prefer to call "the movements of political Islam." They have started from different assumptions depending on their interests or fields of specialization.

Political and strategic researchers have been following the events of the last two decades and noticed that the movements of political Islam have not achieved any major victory since the Iranian revolution of 1978–1979. On the contrary, what appears very noticeable is the Islamists' repeated failure to seize power, for example, in Afghanistan and Algeria, as well as in Sudan. In Afghanistan, different factions vied for power after the Soviets withdrew. The Taliban, who were not originally part of the *mujahidin*, were able to seize power not because of their own strength but because of Pakistan's support. Later on, the United States launched the war against the Taliban regime on the October 7, 2001, in order to arrest Osama Bin Laden, the leader of the Al-Qaeda, who the United States charged with the responsibility for the explosions at the World Trade Center and the Pentagon. The Taliban regime collapsed and a new government was formed.

In Algeria, the early successes of the Islamic movements were due to the failure of the Algerian authority and the heightened tensions between its different factions. The revolutionary movements that rose after the losses of the Islamic Salvation Front do not have an alternative program or vision, but depend instead on terror and terrorism as a method of struggle. In Sudan, Hasan Al-Turabi, whose party has been a minority party since the 1970s, collaborated with the military as an indirect means to seize power. As is common practice, his colleagues and disciples jailed him.

In all, the ascendancy of political Islam itself was, in essence, the result of the lack of alternatives in the political arena. This in turn was the result of the blows dealt by the ruling regimes to the national and leftist political movements, and the way the social and economic crises exacerbated to the point of hopelessness. Finally, the success of the Islamic revolution in Iran is not due to what is referred to as the Islamic movements but rather to the traditional religious establishment that championed the masses that had been marginalized and negatively affected by both modernization and the corruption of the ruling regime.[1]

The academics from the new and old Orientalist School attribute the failure of the movements of political Islam to one of two causes. Some say that Islamic religion, which produces troubled revolutionary movements in times of crisis, is now producing a movement of protest against the values and practices of modernization and westernization and in strong defense of its medieval identity. However, the Orientalists maintain that such protest movements cannot be a sustainable alternative for Muslims and that they will in fact delay the process of adjustment and development. The Turkish alternative along Ataturk's model and strict containment of traditionalism is the final and real solution. The Arab regimes have problems with the Islamists because of the regimes' middle-of-the-road solutions and weak approach in confronting the Islamists.

Other Orientalists think that to discuss the backward or progressive characteristics of Islam is immaterial and argue that the power of the Islamic movements is derived by default from the weakness of the regimes in promoting and practicing the values of freedom, democracy and human rights. The movements' limited successes are also due to the fact that they are the main party that opposes the authoritarian regimes whose legitimacy is weak. However, the principal reason for their overall failure is the fact that their priority is not to regain democracy but instead to apply Islamic *sharia*. Such a protest slogan cannot be the basis of a program that leads to the forming of government and therefore one cannot speak of a political future for the Islamic movements.[2]

In fact, acquiring or sharing authority might be a sign of success for the future of ordinary political movements. However, the Islamic movements are not just political movements but are revivalist movements of religious nature. Their political orientation came a few decades after their establishment, and this is why the criterion of political success is insufficient for judging their future prospects.

Nevertheless, talking about political failure and success requires precision. The governments of Pakistan, Malaysia, Indonesia and Turkey have for a long time been overshadowed by the ideas and practices of different manifestations of the Islamic phenomenon and its realities, whether at the level of Islamist successes in elections, the ability to form governments or of introducing the minimum of Islamic ideology into internal and external state policies. During the 1980s, a mainstream group appeared that has been very active, although it has been repressed repeatedly and has operated mostly underground. This movement has achieved many gains every time it has been allowed to participate in free elections, while liberal, leftist and nationalist parties have failed. This is why the discussion over the belief or otherwise in democracy as a political criterion is only a discussion of unverifiable intentions on the part of those involved in politics. In this case, this criterion is not useful in understanding the continuation of Islamic movements and the justification for their popular power. The movements participate in elections, whether directly or indirectly, in all countries where such participation is allowed.[3]

For these reasons, it is useful to study the intellectual and cultural fundamentals of the Islamic movements and to search for the emergence of their political views and their development in the 1980s and 1990s. There is no attempt here to discuss the causes for the appearance of the Islamic movements[4] but the focus – after discussion of the ideas, views and circumstances within which revivalist Islamic thought emerged – is instead on the current capabilities of the Islamic movements and their future prospects.

Intellectual and Cultural Fundamentals

Initial signs of contemporary Islamic thought appeared in the 1920s and 1930s. This emergence and subsequent development took place within the cultural and political contexts of a period between the two world wars. It was a period that was characterized by radical changes, both in perplexed Europe and in the Islamic world, which was in a transitional phase. Turkey was cut off from Ottoman Islam, which was in crisis, notwithstanding its attempts to reorganize the state along the lines of a secular nationalist state, following the French model. Indian Islamists allied with Gandhi's Conference for India attempted to revive the caliphate of which they had never been part and then to create a peculiar Islamic entity that later developed into the state of Pakistan.

New regimes were formed in the east and west of the Arab world under different mandates, resulting in a quest for independence and freedom through revolt and revolution. At the time when a new world order was emerging as a consequence of compromise between the victorious European states in World War I, as represented by the League of Nations, the capitalist order was undergoing recession and crisis, as was the case of the stocks of New York, London and Frankfurt, which increased the competition for raw materials. All of this was followed by shockwaves in the spheres of culture and technology leading to developments in physics, economics and psychology, as well as new ideas and forms of expressing social and cultural mobilization.[5]

This universal upheaval was echoed in the Arab and Islamic worlds in the emergence of new realities and orientations. Such realities and orientations did not initially manifest themselves in new issues and prospects, but in the change of the environment and methods of thinking. The desire for independence increased with keen interest in ending European domination in the political and strategic sphere through

[174]

revolution, although the alternative was not clear. In addition to the quest for freedom, there was interest in cultural and political particularism, separation from the perplexed West and the quest for salvation in returning to the fundamental sources of Arabism, Islam and local ideologies. These were seen as solid forces for stability and identity, especially since they were elements which cultural and political colonialism wanted to eliminate or change for its own interest.

While the people working in the national and political domain focused on extracting independence from the colonialists, Muslim elites suffered from what might be called a crisis of conscience that pitted the views of the modernists, which depended on the idea of progress, against the Islamists who focused on puritanism and particular identity. Within this crisis, the Islamists focused on the revival of the caliphate that Mustafa Ataturk had abrogated. They also reconsidered the issue of the liberation of women and feared transcending religious limits, whereas before the Islamists' concern had been about how to establish a constitutional and representative authority to defend the legal rights of Muslim women.

In addition, the position on Orientalism was critical but was open for communication and cooperation, whether in terms of ideas or individuals. While their view of missionary activities was negative, the Manar School developed literature on dialoguing with Western Christianity. During the period between the two world wars, especially after the appearance of the theses of 'Ali 'Abd al-Raziq and Taha Hussein, which were regarded as derivatives of Orientalists' theses, Orientalism was connected to missionary activities. Both were considered to be cultural and religious weapons of the West in confronting Islam, whose followers were fighting to break free from religious and cultural subordination. Here also, they struggled to free themselves from the colonialist domination.[6]

Within this new environment, along with attempts to achieve independence and separation, as well as argumentation with the West and those who promoted the latter's views, associations and parties with cultural and educational dimensions became primarily concerned with the issue of authentic identity and the necessity to protect and defend it. These were the Association of the Muslim Youth, the Muslim Brotherhood, the

[175]

Al-Shar'iyya Association, the Supporters of the Sunna, the Union of Muslim Youth, Muslim Scouts, Young Egypt and Muhammad's Youth. They started establishing schools, economic enterprises and scout camps, which aimed at building an independent Islamic character that competed with the Western institutions, missionary schools and Masonic associations, and all manifestations of westernization and subordination.

At the same time, theses on Arabic and Eastern and Islamic literature upheld the cultural and civilizational heritage and aimed at building another model for the individual and collective character of the people and the nation. The term "awakening" or "Islamic awakening," which was used first in the 1930s, transcended the old and new Islamists to include the general atmosphere. The westernized Taha Hussein was moved to write his two books, *Al-Wa'd al-Haqq* and *'Ala Hamish al-Sira*; 'Abbas Mahmud al-'Aqqad his *'Abqariyyat,* and Ahmad Amin the cultural history of Islam and "Tawfiq al-Hakim" a play on Muhammad. Muhammad Hussein Haykal wrote his books on the biography of the Prophet, Abu Bakr and Omar and Ma'ruf al-Arna'ut on inspiration of the Qur'an and of the Islamic past in the writing of stories. The objective of all these writers was not to explain Islamic history but to build an independent and authentic identity.[7]

The start of World War II led to further belief in the failure of Western civilization and its near collapse among those of Islamic culture. This belief prevailed among the Muslim people before it reached the political circles. Some intellectuals published an exposition of Spengler's book on the collapse of Western civilization and they learned from Indian Muslims about Alexis Carrel's book, *Man the Unknown*, and similar books on the death of Western civilization and its materialism and the way it stirs bestial instincts in the human psyche. The works of Abu Al-A'la Al-Mawdudi and Abu Al-Hasan Al-Nadwi, which spoke of the suicide of Western civilization and the need to reconsider Islam as the alternative, were translated into Arabic. It is known that during the 1940s, and especially in Egypt, there was an increase in the popularity of all radical movements and parties, including the Muslim Brotherhood, which then expanded into Syria, Palestine and Yemen.[8]

[176]

If the 1930s had witnessed a campaign against the West and the westernizers on issues of culture and dress, individual character, enslavement to technology and conflicting struggles, the 1940s saw the comprehensive expositions of both Islamic and Western civilizations, which condemned the latter and adopted the former. Abd Al-Qadir 'Awda, a civil judge and member of the Muslim Brotherhood's Bureau of Guidance, wrote a volume on comparative law, showing the differences and similarities between Islamic criminal legislation and positive law. Not only did he side with Islamic jurisprudence, but he also argued that Islamic legislation was divine, while Western or French law, which constituted the basis of Egyptian civil law, was man-made and was designed for the Western man who was corrupted by whims and material progress at the expense of moral and spiritual development.

The difference between 'Awda's work and that of Al-Sanhuri, Muharram and Hishmat in the field of constitutional and civil law is that the latter wanted to enrich the adopted modern civil law with some articles from the journal *Al-Ahkam al-'Adliyya al-Uthmaniyya* and books of jurisprudence that they discovered from the renaissance thinkers. However, 'Awda was arguing for the adoption of a complete Islamic divine method of legislation or its opposite, and that one should choose between the divine method or the human, much as Sayyid Qutb would later say. It was not sufficient for 'Awda to uphold the divine method in legislation, but he also wrote on the legal economic positions and championed an Islamic approach to resolve social problems. He also wrote on political issues and upheld an Islamic system of government, considering Islam as a comprehensive system that should govern Muslims and human life in the world. This is the idea that dominated the writings of the Islamists in the 1950s.[9]

Thus, under the general conditions between the two world wars, a revival or return to Islam emerged as the basis for preserving identity, as a religion valid for all times and places and as an ideology for Muslims that confronts all other ideologies. During the 1950s, along with Al-Mawdudi, Nadwi and Sayyid Qutb, it was possible to say that Islamic movements emphasized an Islamic approach based on a reconstructed cultural and civilizational model and characterized by the following features:[10]

- A new worldview, where Islam, at a minimum, serves as an independent, separate and sufficient framework, but serves ideally as the opposing and competing alternative for expansion.
- A revivalist Islam, which depends on building its model on revivalist thinking about an integrated and complete civilizational experience that derives its justification and authority from divine sources – the Qur'an and the *Sunna* – and the period of the rightly guided caliphate. To reach this objective it has to employ an authentic method of negation and affirmation as its instrument.
- A comprehensive system with religious foundations whose main problematic centers round a puritan and distinct identity, separate from all other experiences that are plagued with human weaknesses, including the periods of modern westernization and deterioration.

Islamist Political Vision in the Context of the Cold War

Perhaps 'Abd Al-Qadir 'Awda in his short book, *Al-Islam wa Awda'ana al-Siyasiyya*, is the first thinker who spoke of a Qur'anic vice-regency in the political context or as the base for a complete political vision. However, this idea was brought to maturity by Abu Al-A'la Al-Mawdudi and Sayyid Qutb. It is true that Imam Hasan Al-Banna mentioned that Islam is a religion and a state that expands through conviction or conquest. However, he did not explain how Islam takes care of political concerns. Should there be one religious and political institution or two separate institutions, as was the case with medieval Islam?

'Abd Al-Qadir 'Awda maintained that man is God's vice-regent on earth, whose function is to build it according to the divine law. The divine law that the last Prophet brought is the dominant force in Islam. This is why the Muslims called their political authority a caliph or vice-regent in the sense that God empowered him to administer the public domain according to the method defined by God. Al-Mawdudi says that the

Islamic system is based on four pillars: God, the Lord, religion, and worship.[11]

Initially, it does not seem that such a theological understanding has a role in the administration of the public domain, but Al-Mawdudi goes on to explain the matter in the following way: Divinity means the supreme authority in the world of generation and degeneration; and lordship carries the idea of divine providence for the created world through religion that has been revealed. This religion is the task for which God made man his vice-regent and on the condition that he upholds it. Upholding religion includes administering the public domain, which is part of worship, while other parts relate to ritualistic relations between God and man. These ritualistic relations are concerned with divinity, while that of vice-regency and administration are concerned with lordship. Therefore, there is divine governance, on the one hand, and the duty to execute that governance, on the other.

Sayyid Qutb has summarized all of this in three interconnected links: governance, vice-regency and duty. Because of His governance, God Almighty mandated human vice-regency and empowered humankind to build the world; and because Islam is the right religion, Muslims, out of all humans, are those who accepted to put that duty into practice.[12]

Sayyid Qutb explained this idea that he derived from Al-Mawdudi in his lengthy exegesis of the Qur'an, *Fi Zilal al-Qu'ran* and summarized it in his *Khasa'is al-Tasawwur al-Islami wa Muqawimatih*. He then changed it into a political and ideological method in *Ma'alim fi al-Tariq*. Thus, the concern with identity remained of educational and ideological nature with Al-Banna and 'Awda but took on a revolutionary and political nature with Al-Mawdudi, Al-Nadwi and Sayyid Qutb. However, Qutb added an important dimension that became the basis for firmly establishing Islamic partisanship. This version is meant to contrast with the *jahili* (paganist) tyrannical method. It is true that Al-Mawdudi spoke of *jahiliyya*, but for him it is the Western civilization and has nothing to do with Muslims who are in a state of unawareness and subordination. However, the West can be saved by self-awareness, education, the propagation of Islam and *tawhid*, not by revolution.

For Qutb, the Islamic conception of governance is categorical in its clarity and separation from all of *jahiliyya*. This is why disobeying the method of governance reduces Muslims' belief. This is also why the Western *jahiliyya* in the twentieth century, according to Muhammad Qutb, brother of Sayyid Qutb, is universal and includes Muslims and non-Muslims, except the few that are aware of and have persevered in the true method and are therefore responsible for and obligated to fulfill the duty of governance. They are those who believe in their God and who should unite to confront the *jahiliyya* by force, based on the divine promise to empower them over the earth if they are sincere about divine *hakimiyya*.

Consequently, in Qutb's thinking, three transformations took place: first, transforming revivalist Islam to revolutionary Islam; second, transforming revolutionary Islam into an Islamic party; and, third, transforming the charisma of the traditional Sunni community into the charisma of the *sharia*, which became the instrument to put into practice the divine duty or divine governance. Thus, the Islamic state is not the state that is made up of a majority of Muslims and ruled by a Muslim, but is that state – or the system that is worthy of Islamic description – which implements the *sharia*. The Qutbist view of governance dominated the period where the Islamic movements moved from being revivalist movements into a period of party politics and revolution during the 1960s and the 1970s. It has also dominated the views of the analysts of the Islamic awakening until now, regardless of the numerous changes that have accumulated since the 1980s.[13]

The well-known American researcher and Orientalist, Malcom Kerr, called the period of 1958–1968 "the Arab Cold War."[14] By this he meant the positions taken during that period by the Arab progressive states led by Nasserite Egypt, on the one hand, and other Arab regimes led by the Kingdom of Saudi Arabia, on the other. Nevertheless, in confronting the states with a socialist orientation allied to the Soviet Union, the Islamic coalition included many Arab and Islamic states allied to the United States of America, in the context of the Cold War between the two superpowers. Kerr mentions many phenomena of this division, ranging from the Pact of Baghdad or Cento and the Syrian-Egyptian unification, to the collapse of the royal regime in Iraq in 1958, then the separation of Syria from Egypt in 1961, the eruption of the war in Yemen in 1962, then stretching to the war of 1967 between Egypt, Syria and Jordan, on the one side, and Israel, on the other. Of note is that the progressive regimes were not on good terms with each other. Nevertheless, what is important for us here is Islamic party thinking in the international and regional contexts of the Cold War.

Since the late 1940s, in its attempts to acquire independence, Islamic revivalist thinking has fought international capitalism as the greatest danger to the individual and collective identity of Muslims. This is very clear in three of Sayyid Qutb' books: *Al-Islam wa al-Salam al-'Alami*, *Ma'rakat al-Islam wa al-Ra'simaliyya*, and *Al-'Adala al-Ijtima'iyya fi al-Islam*. This line of thinking reaches it apex in Mustapha Al-Siba'i's book, *Ishtirakiyyat al-Islam*.[15] It is not a secret that Islamist authors distinguished between communist socialism and Islamic socialism. However, they focused at the same time on the fact that the main threat is the massive capitalism that Sayyid Qutb tied with *jahiliyya*. The internal and external choices of the revolutionary Arab regimes crystallized internally toward socialism and allied with the socialist camp in international politics, although they upheld the idea of non-alignment.

Thus, while revivalist Islam was turning into militancy because of the struggle with the ruling regimes in Syria, Egypt and Iraq, the conflict with communism marginalized the civilizational and cultural contradiction with the capitalist West. This is very clear in Al-Ghazali's book *Al-Islam fi Wajh al-Zahf al-Ahmar*, Muhammad Al-Bahi's book *Al-Fikr al-Islami wa Silatuhu bi al-Isti'mar al-Gharbi*, Muhammad Al-Hamid's book *Radan 'ala Ishtirakiyyat al-Islam li al-Siba'i*, and finally Muhammad Baqr Al-Sadr' books, *Falsafatuna*, *Iqtisaduna* and *Al-Bank al-la Ribawi fi al-Islam*.[16]

If the international and regional contexts affected the transformations of Islamic thought during the 1960s, the conditions of such contexts and their regional and local dimensions left deep imprints on Islamic ideas concerning the political system and its objectives, and on party organization and goals. The idea of a comprehensive or totalitarian

Islamic system, which Muhammad Al-Mubarak developed as a system of creed, worship and economics during the 1960s, can be understood as a confrontation with Arab totalitarian systems and their practices. The same applies to the concept of divine governance, which aimed at confronting the absolute power of the head of state and the exclusive existence of a one party system in progressive regimes. Moreover, the inevitability of the Islamic solution, developed by Yusuf Al-Qaradawi,[17] confronted the inevitability of the socialist solution that dominated the progressive parties and regimes during the 1960s and the 1970s. However, the exercise of violence in the name of *jihad*, which was mainly directed internally, during the 1970s and 1980s, was more likely affected by revolutionary violence and the tradition of prolonged struggle.[18]

While the killing of Anwar Al-Sadat by *jihadist* men is difficult to understand within the context of the Cold War, the war in Afghanistan, where many Arab and Pakistani Islamists fought, can be understood as a struggle against the communist Soviet Union and in favor of and under the leadership of the United States of America. The impact of this war has affected the Islamists up to the present. The same applies to the Islamist rebellion in Syria until the early 1980s.[19]

The 1980s and 1990s: Contexts and Changes

The publication of Hasan Al-Hudaybi's book, *Du'at la Qudat*, in 1977, heralded the changes that intensified in the 1980s. What is indicative is that this book was not authored by Hasan Al-Hudaybi alone, but also by the elders of the Muslim Brotherhood to face the ideas of Sayyid Qutb and Shukri Mustapha (the leader of the organization of Jama'at al-Muslimin or al-Takfir wa al-Hijra). Equally important is that the book was originally published in prison in the late 1960s, and thus its new public appearance meant reevaluating the previous period and seeking a new horizon. The writers tried to take Islam back to its revivalist non-revolutionary origins, on the one hand, and to correct the relations between the Islamists and the public, on the other. The idea is put across that the error committed by a Muslim and his neglect of some duties does not make him an unbeliever.

[182]

Also, the mission of the Islamists is not to impose their views on people or
the political system but to call with compassion to true Islam. Thus, the
public stays Muslim even when many of its members commit some errors,
and the country stays a Muslim land. Violence is prohibited in the Islamic
homeland regardless of justification, and no Muslim has the right to
exercise violence regardless of his strong ideological convictions.

There is no doubt that the periods of the 1970s and 1980s had a deep
impact on the consciousness of partisan Islamists and others. In Egypt,
thousands of the Islamists were released from prison in 1971 and were
able, with the approval or tacit consent of the authorities, to control many
of the student and civil associations and unions, which were earlier under
the control of the Nasserites and leftists. The radicals among them in
Egypt and Syria entered into violent confrontation with the authorities,
which left deep wounds in the movements' consciousness and cadres. The
Islamists, among whom a mainstream group was formed in Egypt, Jordan
and Tunisia, started to participate in parliamentary elections and were
deeply involved in public and semi-public meetings, in the publication of
newspapers, journals and pamphlets and in creating alliances with the
nationalists and liberals in opposition to the leftists. Although they did not
initially publish writings on transformation and the adoption of
democracy, some issued important treatises on self-criticism and others
spoke of redirecting the Islamic awakening. Other non-partisan Islamists
adopted theories about political pluralism and partisanship under the
banner of Islam, while still others returned to studying the relationship
between *shura* and democracy.[20]

The tendency towards a puritan identity remained strong, as may be
gleaned from the thesis on 'The Islamization of Knowledge' set up by the
International Institute of Islamic Thought, in Virginia in the United States
of America. However, some moderate Islamists from within the
mainstream, both in Muslim countries and in the Muslim community in
the diaspora, started speaking of the national community and rights of
citizenship as well as issuing Islamic declarations on human rights
according to the objectives of the *sharia*.[21] All these individuals and
groups tended to work from within the existing institutions. While the

[183]

system of Islamic *shura* does not correspond completely to democracy, which upholds the sovereignty of the people and not God, they share many points such as the equality of citizens in rights and duties, the possibility of exercising the responsibility of citizenship through the ballot box, and elections that guarantee freedom, transparency, and multiparty and political pluralism.[22]

There is no doubt that the tolerance exhibited by this mainstream group and its practices is the result of many factors, including: first, and foremost, the decrease in the international and regional polarization that characterized the mid-1980s and ended with the collapse of the Soviet Union. Second was the stability apparent at the level of the Arab regimes and their ability to continue, notwithstanding international circumstances and conditions. The Islamic parties are the main opposition forces in the Islamic and Arab domains. These opposition forces struggled for a long period with the regimes and did not have the ability to change or weaken them, notwithstanding the talk about the regimes' reduced legitimacy and popularity. This is why mainstream Islamists have had to adjust their approach and steer a middle course — they realized that violence does not bring about political change and does not command the approval of the majority, notwithstanding the existing tyranny. Third, is the rise of the Islamists' self-confidence after they were able to enter into the institutions and the leadership mechanisms of civil society, and were able to enter political life through participation in elections in some countries and improve their relations with the public and some of the regimes.[23]

Nonetheless, the processes of adjustment and openness did not have the desired results — the international changes that the Islamists responded to positively, because of their enmity to communist forces, culminated in the victory of the United States and of international capitalism and globalization. The Islamist dislike of these changes and the new world order was similar to how the leftists and the nationalists felt.[24] It was unfortunate for them and for the Arab and Islamic public that the features of the new world order started to emerge during the second Gulf war which was considered by most Islamists – and not only the radicals – to be a war against the Arabs and Muslims and a victory for Israeli superiority and American domination. They also understood the ideas of 'the end of history' and 'the clash of civilizations' within the same context.

While it is true that in their response they did not return to the categorical basics of revivalist Islam of the 1940s,[25] many of them incorporated in their criticisms of globalization and its phenomena, and Israel and its enmity, the idea of a Western conspiracy against Islam and Muslims, as seen in Palestine, Bosnia, Kosovo, East Timor, Kashmir, the issue of Salman Rushdie and others. This might be the reason why many radical phenomena, like Osama Bin Laden, the Afghan Arabs and the splinter groups in the internal Algerian conflict, have not disappeared but remain on the periphery. Furthermore, because of the currently charged atmosphere due to anger and resentment, many other groups joined the Islamists in criticizing the double standards and condemning the unjust and aggressive forces that violate legitimate international resolutions and do not abide by human rights and the right to self-determination. No doubt, the phenomena of bias and lack of response to the demands and ambitions that transcend the Islamists to include those of the Arabs and the Muslims generally do not encourage adherence to the international order. In fact they increase the daring of the radical Islamists in their revolt and their resort to violence in self-defense and in attempting to achieve their goals.

Hamas and Islamic Jihad in Palestine represent a special case, for they follow the method of armed struggle in confronting Israeli occupation and settlement, and in upholding the slogan of the liberation of Palestine. The Arab and Muslim observers do not view the struggle of the two movements and Hizbullah in Lebanon from the perspective of ideology and Islamic goals, but from the perspective of their right to fight the Israeli occupation of their land and to prevent the Israelis from establishing an independent state with Jerusalem as its capital. This is the national objective of all of the Palestinians and Arabs. However, Western analysts classify that struggle as terrorism.[26]

The Algerian example brings to mind the return of the Islamic and Arab regimes to narrow-mindedness and disinterest in democratic openness, while they accuse the Islamists of insincerity towards democracy. Islamic parties are still outlawed in many Arab and Islamic countries. In countries where participation in elections is allowed, there is no guarantee for the freedom and transparency of elections. This situation is exacerbated by the fact that not only are the Islamists excluded, but also all other forces that call for democracy. Some analysts assign a degree of the responsibility to all partisan groups and forces of civil society that do not believe in and strongly adhere to democracy and good relations among each other, which could have really exerted some pressure on the regimes to make changes.[27]

Islamic Movements and the Future

In the first Islamic nationalist meeting that was held in Cairo in 1988, I proposed to some Islamists that they should postpone the advocacy of the slogan to implement the *sharia* in their programs. Some people were extremely amused by this, for that slogan is what gives the hoped-for Islamic state its meaning. If what was meant is to create an alliance between the two large groups, then each cannot, according to its viewpoint, ask the other to give up its identity and objective. Such an act would cause the group to lose its public base and supporters.

However, what I meant by postponement was not a call for giving up the identity or objective, but to reconsider the slogan of the implementation of *sharia* itself. For the slogan was put up during a time of crisis in the 1960s that was based on the separation between the *sharia* and the community, because the community was not seen to adhere to the *sharia*. Imposing the *sharia* became a duty that the community must perform in order to regain its Islamic identity according to the partisan Islamists who came to power.[28] Partly, this means that the community is not entrusted with religion and that the *sharia* has been made a law instead of being a system for life. It also means that the main problem is represented not by others' administering the affairs of people but by their giving up their religion and law because of their negligence, at one time, and the control of tyrannical regimes, at another. Thus, the basis of legitimacy in an Islamic system rests on the *sharia* for the partisan Islamists, who moved away from revivalism.

Regardless of the contexts that have led to the separation of the community from the *sharia*, this separation itself becomes the basis of the misunderstanding between the Islamists and the public, and the Islamists and democracy. It is right to say that, since the 1980s, the mainstream groups have again said that the system of *shura* coincides with democracy on many points. Nevertheless, the issue of the origin of legitimacy and the issue of the sovereignty derived from it has remained an obstacle to arriving at a sound and fruitful discussion of this extremely sensitive issue. What is promising in this context is the emergence of a difference between the non-partisan Islamists on this issue. It was brought into public discussion by Muhammad Mahdi Shams Al-Din's thesis of the community's sovereignty over its affairs.[29] This thesis showed various opinions on this issue. Some considered it as a rehabilitation of the community as the legitimate power. Consequently, there is theoretically no justification to have any reservation against the sovereignty of the community and the nation and their freedom to take decisions regarding the administration of public affairs.[30] If the general and formative meaning of Islam is realized in the Muslim community, then the Islamic state or its slogan does not have an ideological and religious significance, a view that has been dominant among the partisan Islamists.

On the other hand, there appears to be another avenue that can arrive at a very similar conclusion. Many Islamists, and some are partisans, argue for the principle of citizenship and its prerequisites. Citizenship does not only include equality in rights and duties but also the diffusion of authority among the citizens and their equality in developing it constitutionally through elections. The Islamists have participated in elections and in executive and representative councils. Thus, there is only one step left to recognize the national community, or the community of citizens as put by Tariq Al-Bishri, as having authority and sovereignty. This seems the necessary step to end the separation between the *sharia* and the community — taking into account the free will and decisions of the community reveals the orientations of the majority, on the one hand, and the general objective of the *sharia*, on the other.

It is known that the reformers of the renaissance used *maqasid* (objectives) *al-sharia* that earlier jurists discussed in order to arrive at the same view. They said that God Almighty sent messengers and revealed the laws in order to realize the necessary interests of the people: the right of life or self, the right of reason, the right of religion, the right of procreation and the right of possession.[31] For a long time, the revivalist Islamists ignored this method or understanding and opted instead for authentication,[32] but they have again been using the mechanism of the *maqasid* since the 1980s to show that, in Islam, human rights consist of entitlements and obligations.

It seems that the current international and regional contexts, which address these rights or necessities, present an opportunity and a possible future for the Islamic movements and Islamic thought in general. They can communicate their message and rehabilitate themselves in order to face current problems and challenges.

As the view of *hakimiyya* led to the separation between the community and the *sharia*, it led also to the integration of the state and the political order. Differences with the head of the system led to suspicion around the concept of the state itself. It is fair to say that the same also happened with the nationalists, where their inability to establish the pan-nationalist state led to questioning of the legitimacy of the nationalist patriotic state, as the Ba'athists would describe it. Such ambiguity is still present even among the non-partisan Islamists. This matter was clear for the medieval Islamic jurists, for the caliphate was the project for the entire nation or the acceptable means toward realizing the nation itself. However, one caliph or another and one sultan or another and one administration or another can be objected to because of injustice or differences with respect to defining necessities and interests. This was the difference, for instance, between Al-Mawardi (450 AH) in his *Al-Ahkam al-Sultaniyya* and Al-Imam Al-Juwayni (478 AH) in his *Ghiyath al-Umam*. Al-Juwayni considered that the irregularity of the functions of the caliph and his inability to perform them for long periods necessitated a change in the concept of the state or the abrogation of the caliphate in favor of the sultanate. However, Al-Mawardi believed that the caliphate or the state was the project of the nation, but the sultanate or emirate – that is the regime or the government – is the institution that should be adjusted or reformed.[33]

The state is the field of organization of the nation and the community and their legitimacy — this is why historical legitimacy is related to the state. The mainstream body of the Islamic movement wants to be included into the known frameworks, without abandoning the idea or concept of governance that merges the state into religion or makes the state an executive instrument for it. No doubt that this has some relation to the origin of legitimacy discussed before. There must be some discussion in order to explain the domain that allows the authority of the nation and the state to manifest in political life, especially in the current contexts where there is much discussion about the dislocation of what is known in modern political history as the national state. I believe that the increasing participation of the Islamists in political life is a supporting factor in achieving some clarity on such issues.

The last few years have witnessed the increasing return on part of the Islamists to constitutional and administrative bodies of the state to realize one demand or another. Although these demands are mostly unsuitable to the general environment, it does, however, mean the Islamists' acceptance of citizenship and that their demands and ambitions can be achieved through existing institutions. More importantly, it also indicates the acceptance of the distinction between the state and the administration or the government and the regime. In fact, a development took place in the ideas and practices of the Islamists in the 1990s, moving from the position that legitimacy rests with the head of the state or the organization, to saying that legitimacy rests to a degree on the *sharia*. In other words, there has been a discrete transition from governance to the state of law.

If the decision over the issue of authority and source of authorities and the decision to distinguish between the state and the regime are helpful in establishing a cultural and political life where the Islamists play a prominent role, then accepting political pluralism and multi-party politics play a decisive role in developing the open environment that our states, regimes and civil societies lack. The partisan Islamists exercise that factually through participating in elections and setting up alliances as a party among many others that are different and diverse. Some non-partisan Islamists published studies on pluralism but the partisans still consider the people to be a silent entity that they alone represent because they apply the *sharia* — this is clear from the labels used in describing their groups and parties.

In fact, the nation that has the same religion includes many groups with different views and interests. These groups resort to building their own organizations based on their different understanding and on the administration of their interests. It is incorrect for this Islamic party or that to consider itself to be the sole representative of all groups of society and that the obstacle for that representation is the regime or the government. Perhaps the best example for this consideration is the conflicts among the Islamists themselves when a group of them sets up a new party or organization. It is true that such a phenomenon is common among the non-Islamist parties, but it acquires greater danger among Islamists since they perceive it as the battle between good and evil, as expressed by Hasan Al-Turabi, when he fought Omar Al-Bashir and ended in prison. The same happened with the Algerian Islamists in the early 1990s, as well as the Egyptians, when some young Muslim Brothers tried to set up the al-Wasat party. I see the ideology of having one group or one party only as a legacy from the Cold War even if it is given Islamic labels, and that getting out of such an ideology opens the possibility for future changes that the Islamists urgently need today.

If we consider the international contexts and future prospects, what comes to mind is the saying of the well known researcher 'Ali Al-Mazru'i in a lecture presented at the faculty of Economic and Political Science at Cairo University a few years ago. He said that we should not hesitate to embrace the great universal values that do not contradict the great values in our civilization, even though we are not responsible for their acceptance at the international level. This saying should be obvious, but it has not been so for the Islamists for decades. Ibn Qayyim Al-Jawziyya (751 AH) said that wherever there is interest there is God's law. In a response to a question in the Al-Manar in 1907 as to why Rashid Rida does not call constitutional rule a *shura* rule if the two correspond, he argues that Muslims should not say that the rule that is restricted by *shura* is one of the fundamentals of religion or that Muslims have acquired it from the Holy Qur'an or the biography of the rightly-guided caliphs. In fact, we have learned this from the Europeans and from studying their conditions. If it were not for them, we would not have thought of *shura* as a true expression of Islam.[34]

Since the 1940s, the culture of identity and particularism that depended on the method of authentication spread through the analysis of what is permissible or prohibited. Furthermore, although the Islamists upheld *ijtihad*, the realities witnessed to the fact that there was nothing that can be renewed or deeply investigated, unless there was an authority for it in the Qur'an or the S*unna*. As a result of the circumstances of fighting colonialism and the attempt by the colonialists to detach Muslims from their culture, from the very beginning, Islamists viewed universal values and international institutions with suspicion and antagonism. At times, it was said that such values were especially Western; at others, it was said that the West had double standards.

In the conflicts of the Cold War and the rise of the culture of particularism and separatism, it was said the values mentioned in the Charter of the United Nations and the International Declaration on Human Rights were based on natural rights, while they were constant values for us because they were only derived dutifully from the religious texts. It is true that our states have entered into the international order and signed its pacts, but the culture that the Islamists propagated denied their validity or tried to issue declarations and constitutions that consider them Islamic because of the spread of Islamization. This would not have been seen to represent an issue or a problem except for the Islamists' belief in the contradiction between the divine method and the human approach.

When the Cold War, which constituted a source for conflict and rejection ended, the theories of conspiracy took over and the campaign against these values became part of the campaign against American domination and the phenomenon of globalization. In fact, the problem in

[191]

all of this is not the validity or invalidity of these values and issues, but our inability to exert the necessary efforts to enter and participate in the new emerging world. For participation, even if it takes the form of protest because of misapplication or takes the form of suggesting amendments and corrections, gives things new meaning and puts them in new contexts. It is true that participation includes the necessity of arriving at a compromise that may not lead to achieving all objectives. Nevertheless, shunning discussion, enrichment and corrections also fails to do so. Constantine Zurayq spoke much about the need to do what is right.

The Islamists have no problem with the issues of knowledge and struggle, but with methodology and fear of being subject to compromise. They have a great fear of democracy, the rigging of elections and failure to get public support. They have experienced all this but have not realized all their objectives. Yet, they have not regretted the experience of participating. What is required is a change in their vision, something that happens slowly and hesitantly every day, but is not sufficient. What is meant by "change in their vision" can be reflected in something like the Islamic declaration of human rights. In principle, this can be done, for it can constitute an Islamic vision of the contemporary world.[35] It is clear that what is meant by the Islamicity of human rights, including that of women and children, is not the support of such values and guarantees, but rather a reflection of particularism and separatism from the world, out of fear of dissolution or repulsive westernization.

In the real world we change, and we accompany such changes with studies that do not alter our consciousness much, but rather produce justifications. Accepting pluralism in the last two decades is an example of that. Since the 1950s, we have insisted that cultural and political pluralism was a conspiracy against the unity of culture and the unity of nation. Then we opened up massively to pluralism and supported it with Qur'anic verses, as we did when we rejected it. For five decades, we insisted that the conflict between the West and us was a deep and everlasting clash of civilizations, but when Huntington surprised us with his "clash of civilizations" we moved quickly to uphold the concept of dialogue among civilizations. So we first rejected an idea, then we adjusted along the same line: alienation and separation from the world. I guess that the Islamists, the nationalists and some leftists started to combat globalization from the same orientation. The stormy changes that are occurring in the world today do not demand absolute acceptance or rejection but active critical participation. The American military and economic domination is not our problem alone but that of the world, and we might have allies from the West and outside of it in our attempts to define and adjust the methods of handling that domination.

The revivalist Islamic generations have bequeathed to us a tendency that is ideological, separatist and uncompromising. For the sake of living in the real world, we resort to partial and technical solutions, without attempting to reconsider the puritan and religious nature of our dominant thought. No doubt, contemporary Islamic thought, which is dominated by the revivalists, is full of attempts and solutions of a technical nature. This is manifest in the revivalists' abandonment of the method of authentication and justification through *maqasid al-sharia*, which had been adopted by the reformers of the twentieth century. There is no doubt that the method of *maqasid* opens a broader horizon when coupled with a change in the worldview of Islamists.

I guess that international contexts today require such a radical change that the Islamists hesitate to bring it about, notwithstanding the infinite possibilities that it can lead to. There are general whole-continent conceptions that constitute a culture. There are also arrangements that take place in the real world, which constitute the medium through which consciousness moves.[36] Lately, we have been overcome by the consciousness of incoherence because of our dissatisfaction with the new arrangements in the real world that our direct consciousness, which must decide how to confront it, rejects. What is required is that this consciousness, which is dominated by ambivalence over the present and the future, should not dominate our conception of issues, such as the reconsideration and acceptance of positive participation in changing not only consciousness but reality as well.

Still, there are many Islamists and some nationalists who write about cultural invasion, self-renewal and about the Arab or Islamic civilizational project. Renewal cannot be achieved by individual states; rather, it is achieved through participation in the worlds of culture, politics and the broader environment. The Arab or Islamic civilizational project warrants this name by virtue of participating in changing and developing the world. In the light of such a vision, there is no room for talking about cultural invasion, since this can only occur when there is an isolated identity.

The last decade witnessed the openness of the Islamic revivalist thought of Islamic movements to many conflicting changes. The movements are undertaking a great deal of work to be an active part of the Islamic and Arab scenes. The changing contexts in the world today pressure these movements, as well as other political and cultural segments. However, the Islamic movements have become so deeply entrenched that it is highly improbable that they will disappear or reduce their influence in the near future. Revivalist thought by its very nature is an ideology of identity and not belonging, and its scope of influence, success and adjustment depends on the ability of that ideology to move from the religious identity that falls easily into crisis and alienation to an ideology of belonging that can maintain its project through participation in the world.

There are two Islamic texts from Syria that I want to use to demonstrate the ability of the Islamic movements and Islamist intellectuals to benefit from the new international and regional contexts and environments. The first text is from the well-known jurist Wahbah al-Zuhayli, entitled *Haq al-Hurriyya fi al-'Alam* ("The Right of Freedom in the World"). The other text is from a group of the Syrian Muslim Brotherhood, and it is a declaration published in May 2001. Jurist al-Zuhayli bases his reservations about democracy on Muhammad Diya' Al-Rayyis' book *Al-Nazarriyat al-Siyasiyya al-Islamiyya*, which was published in 1967.[37] The reservations are that democracy is associated with nationalism, that it is mainly of this world, and that the sovereignty of the nation is absolute.

The Syrian Muslim Brothers say in their declaration that they are one political team from among many groups and parties in Syria and that no body, person or party has the right to claim to represent the homeland or the nation.[38] This is why the group calls for a national dialogue and multipartism based on the constitution, law and free and democratic political action, and believes that Islam in Syria is based on an individual belonging and a civilizational identity. In any case, there will not be discrimination or conflict. An Arab individual may belong to Islam and still belong to Syria, with no contradiction in identity. The Brothers want to work with all other groups to set up a modern state in Syria, which has a contractual and democratic nature where authorities are separated and power is peacefully transferred through elections and party and political pluralism. It is the state of all people that confronts the Zionist project and works for the realization of Arab solidarity and finally Arab unity. Moreover, where there is a clear distinction between the state and regime, the regime does not overcome the state. It is a state where citizens cooperate to realize and preserve freedoms, maintain the civil nature of the regime and its institutions and achieve free development without subordination, which would benefit from the progress of the world and the era. It is a state where violence should not be used in political and state actions, that is not ruled by emergency law with security solutions to political problems and where the citizens cooperate to protect the constitution, the institutions and human rights. The Muslim Brothers announce at the end of the document that, because of their national feeling, they will work with all of the parties in the political scene to realize these objectives gradually because of their perception of reality and its conditions.

The note with which I want to end this exposition of the two texts is that Al-Zuhayli's text was published in Damascus, but the Muslim Brothers' text was published in London, like the texts of Rashid Al-Ghannushi, the leader of the Tunisian renaissance movement. My interest in mentioning the places of publication of the texts is not only to show the local and regional contexts and their impact but also directing attention to the influence of the new international context.

They are two texts: one that imposes obstacles on the nation and the world while the other reaches out and removes barriers. Our future as a nation, and not only the future of the Islamic movements, lies between two extremes: negating nationhood, religion, homeland and democracy and affirming them.

ABDULWAHHAB EL-AFFENDI is the coordinator of the program of Democracy in the Arab World at the Center for Democracy, University of Westminster, where he also lectures. He graduated with a Bachelor of Arts degree from the University of Khartoum in 1980 and received his Ph.D. in political science from the University of Reading in Britain.

Dr. El-Affendi worked as a teaching assistant in the Department of Philosophy, University of Khartoum, then joined the diplomatic service at the Sudanese Foreign Ministry. He was an Adjunct Expert at St. Anthony's College, University of Oxford and a Visiting Fellow at the Institute of Michelsin for Development Studies and Human Rights in Norway.

Dr. El-Affendi has published many books and studies in Arabic, which include *Islam wa al-Dawla al-Haditha* and *Al-Thawra wa al-Islah al-Siyasi fi al-Sudan*. He also published many books and studies in English, which include *Islam and Modernity: A New Vision*; *Islamic Base*; *The Crisis of Modern Islamic Thought*; *The Question of the Muslim Brothers in Sudan*; *Who Needs an Islamic State?*; *Rationalism, Democracy, and Modern Islamic Experience*; *The Concept of Power in Islamic Political Thought*; and *Rationalization and Civil and Democratic Society*.

HASAN HANAFI received a State Doctorate from the University of the Sorbonne in Paris, in 1966. Earlier, he received his Bachelor of Arts in Philosophy from the Faculty of Letters, Cairo University in 1956, where he was Professor of Philosophy and Chairperson of the Department of Philosophy. He was Visiting Professor at the University of Philadelphia in the United States of America from 1971 to 1975 and the University of Fas in Morocco from 1982 to 1984. He also served as academic advisor for the United Nations University in Tokyo, Japan, from 1985 to 1987.

Dr. Hanafi is a member of many associations, including the Deputy Chair of the Arab Philosophical Association, the General Secretary of the Egyptian Philosophical Association, a member of the Afro-Asian

Solidarity Committee, and a member of the African and Asian Writers Union.

Dr. Hanafi published numerous books and studies in Arabic, French and English, including *Al-Din wa al-Thaqafa wa al-Siyasa fi al-'Alam al-'Arabi*; *Al-Qarar al-Dini wa al-Thawra*; *Al-Islam fi al-Asr al-Hadith*; *Al-Din wa al-Thawra fi Misr*; *Humum al-Fikr wa al-Watan*; *Dirasat Islamiyya*; *Risalat fi al-Lahut wa al-Siyasa li Spinoza*; *Dirasat Falsafiyya*; *Al-Turath wa al-Tajdid*; and *Min al-'Aqida ila al-Thawra*,

EMAD AL-DIN SHAHIN is Associate Professor at the Department of Political Science at the American University in Cairo. He received his Bachelor of Arts and Master's degree from the American University in Cairo and also received a Master's in International Economy and a Ph.D. in International Relations from the University of Johns Hopkins in the United States. His Ph.D. thesis was on the Islamic movements in Morocco.

Dr. Shahin taught courses in Cultural and International Affairs, Islamic Societies and the West, and Islamic Civilization at the George Washington University in the United States and the University of al-Akhwayn in Morocco. He worked as a consultant to the Smithsonian Institute in Washington, and headed the research and development department at the Embassy of the Kingdom of Saudi Arabia in Washington.

Dr. Shahin published the book *Political Ascent: Contemporary Islamic Movements in North Africa*, and another book entitled *Bi 'Uyun Islamiyya: Muhammad Rashid Rida wa al-Gharb*. He also published many chapters, studies and articles in books, encyclopedias and specialized academic journals, such as the *Oxford Encyclopedia of Islam* and the *Oxford Encyclopedia on Contemporary Islamic World*. They include "Islamic Movements and Violence," "Islamic Movements in the Middle East: Transformation and Continuity," "Islamic Renaissance Movement: the Emergence and Curb of Islamic Movement," "Algeria: Limits of Democracy," "In the Shade of the Imam: Islamic Movements in Morocco," "Egypt: The Need for a New Social Contract" and "Self Understanding of Contemporary Islamic Movements."

AHMAD MOUSSALLI is Professor of Political Science and Islamic Studies at the American University of Beirut. He received his Ph.D. in Government and Politics from the University of Maryland and a Master's Summa cum laude in Liberal Arts and Philosophy and Islamic Studies from Saint John's College, Santa Fé, New Mexico, USA. His Bachelor of Arts was also received Summa cum laude in Islamic Studies, English Literature and Simultaneous Translation from Al-Azhar University, Cairo, Egypt.

Dr. Moussalli was Senior Fellow at the United States Institute of Peace, Visiting Professor at the Center for Christian-Muslim Understanding, Georgetown University, Washington, DC and Visiting Professor at Carsten Niebuhr Institute for Near Eastern Studies, University of Copenhagen, Denmark. Dr. Moussalli is the recipient of many academic honors and prizes, including in 2001 the selection of his *Historical Dictionary of Islamic Fundamentalist Movements in the Arab World, Iran, and Turkey* as Choice Outstanding Academic Book for 2000; in 1999, the Abd al-Hadi al-Dibs Prize in the field of Islamic Sciences; the 1999–2000 Senior Fellowship from United States Institute of Peace; and in 1998–1999 the Research Grant from the Earhart Foundation.

Dr. Moussalli is the author of numerous books and articles, including the following books *The Islamic Quest for Democracy, Pluralism, and Human Rights*; *Understanding Islam: Basic Principles*; *Moderate and Radical Islamic Fundamentalism: the Quest for Modernity, Legitimacy, and the Islamic State*; *Myths and Realities of Islamic Fundamentalism*; *Islamic Fundamentalism and World Order*; *Qira'a Nazariyya Ta'sisiyya fi al-Khitab al-Islami al-Usuli*; *Al-Khitab al-Idiology wa al-Siyasi 'inda Sayyid Qutb*; and *Radical Islamic Fundamentalism: The Ideological and Political Discourse of Sayyid Qutb*. In addition, he published over 43 articles in international and Arab journals.

FAWAZ GERGES is Professor and Christian Johnson Chair in International Affairs and Middle Eastern Studies at Sara Lawrence University in New York. He received his Ph.D. in International Relations and Middle Eastern Studies from Oxford University. He also taught at Oxford and Harvard.

He worked as a Research Professor at Princeton University in the United States of America and as Visiting Professor at the American University of Beirut.

Dr. Gerges has published many books and studies, including *America and Political Islam: Clash of Civilizations or Clash of Interests?* which was translated into Arabic; and *Arab Regional System and Great Powers: A Study in Arab-Arab Relations and Arab-International Relations*, which was published in English by Oxford University Press and in Arabic by the Center of Arab Unity Studies. He also published *American Policy towards the Arabs: How is it made and who makes it?*; *The Movements of Political Islam and Clinton Administration*; and *The New Danger in the East? American Foreign Policy Towards Political Islam*. In addition, he has published numerous articles and researches in well-known international journals and newspapers.

RADWAN AL-SAYYID is Professor of Islamic Studies at the Lebanese University, Director of the Higher Institute of Islamic Studies and the co-editor of *Al-Ijtihad* in Beirut. He received his Bachelor of Arts from the Faculty of Usul al-Din, Al-Azhar University, Cairo, in 1970, and his Ph.D. in Philosophy from Tubengen, in Germany, in 1977. He has taught at many universities, including Harvard and Chicago in the United States. In 1985, he received the 'Abd al-Hamid Shuman Prize for Young Arab Scholars in Islamic Studies.

Dr. Al-Sayyid has published numerous books and studies, including *Al-Umma wa al-Jama'a wa al-Sulta* (1984); *Mafahim al-Umma wa al-Jama'a fi al-Islam* (1985); *'Al-Islam al-Mu'asir* (1987); *Al-Jama' wa al-Mujtama' wa al-Dawla* (1997); and *Siyasat al-Islam al-Mu'asir* (1998). He has also edited many books and published a few translations, including *The Concept of Freedom*, by Frank Rothensal and *The Images of Islam in Europe in the Middle Ages*, by Richard Southern. He has participated in numerous conferences and workshops and presented many articles on political Islam, Islamic political thought, and Islamic movements and their future.

NOTES

Chapter 1

1. Hugue Didier, "Al-Islam wa al-Muqaddas," *Mawaqif* no. 65 (Beirut: Fall 1991), 101.
2. Ibid., 105.
3. Ibid., 111.
4. Haydar Ibrahim 'Ali, "Al-Usus al-Ijtima'iyya li al-Zahira al-Diniyya: Mulahazat fi 'Ilm al-Ijtima'," in 'Abd al-Baqi Al-Hirmasi et al, *Al-Din fi al-Mujtama' al-'Arabi* (Beirut: Center for the Studies of Arab Unity, 1990), 23–62.
5. 'Ali Al-Kinz, "Al-Islam wa al-Hawiyya: Mulahazat li al-Bahth," in Al-Hirmasi et al, op. cit, 102.
6. See for instance, Karel Dobbelaere, "Secularization: A Multi-Dimensional Concept, *Current Sociology* vol. 29, no. 2 (Summer 1981): 1–21; Peter L. Berger, *The Sacred Canopy: Elements of a Sociological Theory of Religion* (Garden City, NY: Doubleday and Company, 1967); Steve Bruce, *Religion in the Modern World: From Cathedrals to Cults* (Oxford: Oxford University Press, 1996); Bryan Wilson, "Aspects of Secularization in the West," *Japanese Journal of Religious Studies* vol. 3, no. 3/4 (1976): 259–276.
7. See Richard K. Fenn, "The Process of Secularization: A Post-Parsonian View," *Journal for the Scientific Study of Religion* vol. 9, no. 2 (Summer 1970): 117–136; Dobbelaere, op. cit.
8. See Abdulwahhab El-Affendi (ed.) *Rethinking Islam and Modernity: Essays in Honor of Fathi Osman* (Leicester: Islamic Foundation, 2001).
9. See Earnest Gellner, *Conditions of Liberty: Civil Society and its Rivals* (London: Penguin Books, 1994). See also Earnest Gellner, "Fundamentalism as a Comprehensive System: Soviet Marxism and Islamic Fundamentalism," in Martin Marty and Scott Appleby (eds)

Fundamentalisms Observed (Chicago: Chicago University Press, 1995).

10. See Gellner, op. cit.

11. See Zia Sardar, *Orientalism* (Buckingham: Open University, 1999); Edward Said, *Orientalism* (London: Routledge and Kegan Paul, 1978); and Bryan Turner, *Orientalism, Postmodernism and Globalization* (London: Routledge, 1994).

12. See Abdulwahhab El-Affendi, "Studying my Movement: Social Science without Cynicism," *International Journal of Middle Eastern Studies* vol. 23 (1991): 83–94.

13. See Abdulwahhab El-Affendi, "The Long March from Lahore to Khartoum: Beyond the Muslim Reformation," *BRISMES Bulletin* vol. 17, no. 2 (1990): 137–151.

14. Aziz Al-'Azmeh, *Al-'Ilmaniyya min Manzur Mukhtalif* (Beirut: Center for the Studies of Arab Unity, 1992). See also Ira M. Lapidus, "The Separation of State and Religion in the Development of Early Islamic Society," *International Journal of Middle Eastern Studies* vol. 6, no. 4 (1975): 363–385. Sadiq Jalal Al-Azm, "Is Islam Secularizable?" in Elizabeth Ozdalga and Sune Persson, *Civil Society, Democracy and the Muslim World* (Istanbul: Swedish Research Institute in Istanbul, 1997).

15. Shakib Arsalan, *Limadha Ta'akhara al-Muslimun wa Taqaddama Ghayruhum*? Edited by Sheikh Hasan Tamim (Beirut: Dar al-Maktabat al-Hayat, 1975).

16. See Martin Kramer, "Fundamentalism at Large: The Drive for Power," *Middle East Quarterly* vol. 3, no. 2 (June 1996).

17. See Nikki Keddie, *An Islamic Response to Imperialism: Political and Religious Writings of Sayyid Jamal Al-Din Al-Afghani* (Berkeley: University of California Press, 1968).

18. See Muhammad 'Amara, *Al-A'mal Al-Kamila li Jamal Al-Din Al-Afghani* (Cairo: Dar al-Kitab al-'Arabi, 1968).

19. Al-Imam Al-Shahid Hasan Al-Banna, *Mudhakarrat al-Da'wa wa al-Da'iyya* (Cairo: al-Maktab al-Islami, 1983), 353–354.

20. Ibid, 72–76.

21. See Charles J. Adams, "Maududi and the Islamic State," in John Esposito (ed.) *Voices of Resurgent Islam* (Oxford: Oxford University Press, 1983), 100–104.

22. Abu Al-A'la Al-Mawdudi, *Minhaj al-Inqilab al-Islami* (Beirut: Mu'assasat al-Risala, 1979).

23. Ibid. See also Al-Mawdudi, *Al-Islam and al-Madina al-Haditha* (Cairo: Dar al-Ansar, 1978).

24. Al-Mawdudi, *Minhaj al-Inqilab*, op. cit.

25. See Abu Al-A'la Al-Mawdudi, *Islamic Law and Constitution* (Lahore: Islamic Publications, 1969).

26. See William Roff (ed.) *Islam and the Political Economy of Meaning* (London: Croom Helm, 1987). Perhaps the irony is that Kepel says the same thing about the Islamic groups that appeared in the seventies; See Gilles Kepel, *The Prophet and the Pharaoh: Muslim Extremism in Egypt* (London: Alsaqi Books, 1985), 129.

27. Adams, op. cit., 99.

28. See, for instance, Daniel Pipes, *In the Path of God: Islam and Political Power* (New York, NY: Basic Books, 1983). Detleve Khalid, "The Phenomenon of Re-Islamization," *Aussenpolitik* no. 29 (1978): 433–533.

29. Esposito (ed.), op. cit., 11–14.

30. Haydar Ibrahim 'Ali, op. cit., 33–36. See also Mark Tessler, "The Origins of Popular Support for Islamist Movements," in John P. Entelis (ed.) *Islam, Democracy, and the State in North Africa* (Bloomington, IN: Indiana University Press, 1997), 92–126.

31. Salah Al-Din Jourshi, "Al-Haraka al-Islamiyya Mustaqbaluha Rahin al-Taghiyrat al-Jazriyya," in 'Abd Allah Al-Nafisi (ed.) *Al-Harakat al-Islamiyya: Ru'uah Mustaqbaliyya, Awraq fi al-Naqd al-Dhati* (Cairo: Maktabat Madbuli, 1989), 117–147.

32. Gellner, op. cit.

33. Al-'Azmeh, op. cit., 221–248.

34. See Leonard Binder, *Islamic Liberalism: A Critique of Development Ideologies* (Chicago, IL: University of Chicago Press, 1972). Dale Eickelman and James Piscatori, *Muslim Politics* (Princeton, NJ: Princeton University Press, 1996).

35. See John Voll, "Wahhabism and Mahdism: Alternative Styles of Islamic Renewal," *Arab Studies Quarterly* vol. 4 (1982): 110–126; Voll, "Renewal and Reform in Islam History: Islah and Tajdid," in Esposito (ed.), op. cit., 32–47.
36. See Abdulwahhab El-Affendi, *Turabi's Revolution: Islam and Power in Sudan* (London: Grey Seal Books, 1991), 1–22.
37. Eickelman and Piscatori, op. cit., 28–36. See also Al-'Azmeh, op. cit., 312.
38. Jourshi, op. cit.
39. See Olivier Roy, *The Failure of Political Islam* (Cambridge, MA: Harvard University Press, 1994); Tessler, op. cit.; Kramer, op. cit.
40. Malcolm Kerr, *Islamic Reform: the Political and Legal Theories of Muhammad Abduh and Rashid Rida* (Berkeley, CA: University of California Press, 1966); Compare with H.A.R. Gibb, *Modern Trends in Islam* (New York, NY: Octagon Press, 1947).
41. Pipes, op. cit.
42. Kramer, op. cit.
43. Khalid, op. cit. Clearly this is a typo, for al-Sanusiyya was a Sufi and not Wahhabi movement.
44. Tariq Al-Bishri, "Al-Malamih al-'Ama li al-Fikr al-Siyasi al-Islami fi al-Tarikh al-Mu'asir," in Al-Nafisi (ed.), op. cit., 149–175.
45. Muhammad Jabir Al-Ansari, *Takwin al-'Arab al-Siyasi wa Maghza al-Dawla al-Qutriyya: Madhkal ila I'adat Fahm al-Waqi' al-'Arabi* (Beirut: Center for the Studies of Arab Unity, 1995).
46. Al-Bishri, op. cit.
47. Ibid., 153.
48. Ibid., 160–162.
49. Voll, "Wahhabism and Mahdism," op. cit.
50. See Max Weber et al (eds) *From Max Weber* (London: Routledge and Kegan Paul, 1970).
51. Berger, op. cit.; Dobbelaere, op. cit.
52. Eickelman and Piscatori, op. cit.
53. Abd Al-Halim Mahmud, *Al-Ikhwan al-Muslimun: Ahdath Sana'at al-Tarikh* (Cairo: Dar al-Da'wa, 1979).

54. Al-Imam Al-Shahid Hasan Al-Banna, *Min Rasa'il al-Ikhwan al-Muslimin* (Cairo: Dar al-Tiba'at wa al-Nashr al-Islamiyya, 1963), 63.

55. Ibid.

56. Al-Mawdudi, *Al-Islam wa al-Madaniyya al-Haditha*, op. cit.

57. Sayyid Qutb, *Da'wat al-Ikhwan al-Muslimun wa 'Abqariyyat bina' al-Jama'atiha* (Alexandria: Dar al-Qadisiyya, n. d.), 26–31. Compare with Sayyid Qutb, *Ma'alim fi al-Tariq* (Beirut: Al-Itihad al-Islami al-'Alami li al-Munazzamat al-Tulabiyya, 1987).

58. Abdulwahhab El-Affendi, *Al-Thawra wa al-Islah al-Siyasi fi al-Sudan* (London: Muntada Ibn Rushd, 1995).

59. Kepel, op. cit.

60. See Emanuel Sivan, *Radical Islam, Medieval Theology and Modern Politics* (New Haven, CT: Yale University Press, 1985).

61. Hasan Al-Banna, *Mudhakarat al-Da'wa wa al-Da'iyya*, op. cit., 50–54.

62. Al-Bishri, op. cit., 155–158.

63. See Said Amir Arjomand, *The Turban and the Crown: The Islamic Revolution in Iran* (New York, NY: Oxford University Press, 1988).

64. See Abdulwahhab El-Affendi, *Al-Islam wa al-Dawla al-Haditha: Nahwa Ru'ya Jadida* (London: Dar al-Hikma, 2000).

65. See Al-Nafisi (ed.), op.cit.

66. Thomas Luckman, "The structural Conditions of Religious Consciousness in Modern Societies," *Japanese Journal of Religious Studies* vol. 6, no.1/2 (1979): 1–137.

67. Talal Asad (an interview done by Siba Mahmud), "Al-Sulta al-Haditha wa I'adat tashkil al-Taqalid al-Diniyya," *Al-Ijtihad* vol. 12, no. 47/48 (Beirut: 2000): 249–281.

Chapter 2

1. Surat Al-Anfal, verse 63, Qur'an.

2. Surat Al-Baqarah, verse 253, Qur'an.

3. Surat Al-Hujurat, verse 13, Qur'an.

4. Surat Al-Ma'idah, verse 48, Qur'an.

5. Muhammad Abdu, *Risalat al-Tawhid* (Cairo: Dar al-Manar, 1373 AH), 3–23. Also, Hasan Hanafi, *Min al-'Aqida ila al-Thawra: Muqaddimat Nazariyya* vol. 1 (Cairo: Maktabat Madbuli, 1988), Chapter II, 100–102.

6. Refers to the state of factionalism and divisiveness that plagued the Muslim world after the four Caliphs.

7. Surat Al-Nisa', verse 83, Qur'an.

8. This is the important addition of Nasr Hamid Abu Zayd in the sciences of the Qur'an.

9. See Hasan Hanafi, "Turath al-Sulta wa Turath al-Mu'arada," *Humum al-Fikr wa al-Watan: Al-Turath wa al-'Asr wa al-Nidal al-Watani* vol. 1 (Cairo: Maktabat Madbuli, 1988), 361–372.

10. See Hasan Hanafi, "Al-Din wa al-Thawra al-'Arabiyya," *Al-Din wa al-Thawra fi Misr 1952-1981: Al-Din wa al-Nidal al-Watani* vol. 3 (Cairo: Maktabat Madbuli, 1989), 245–306.

11. *Al-Mithaq: Juzur al-Nidal al-Watani* (Cairo: al-Hay'a al-'Amma li al-Isti'lamat, 1964).

12. See Hasan Hanafi, "Athar al-Imam al-Shahid Sayyid Qutb 'ala al-Harakat al-Diniyya al-Mu'asira," *Al-Din wa al-Thawra fi Misr: al-Harakat al-Islamiyya al-Mu'asira* vol. 5, 167–300.

13. Surat Al-Baqarah, verse 285, Qur'an.

14. See Hasan Hanafi, "Al-Tatawwur al-Dini fi Masr al-Haditha," and "Athar al-'Amil al-Dini 'ala Tawzi' al-Dakhal al-Qawmi fi Misr," in *Al-Din wa al-Thawra fi Misr 1952–1981*, 3–288.

15. See Hasan Hanafi, "Al-Usuliyya al-Islamiyya," in *Al-Din wa al-Thawra fi Misr, 1952-1981* vol. 6, 3–205.

16. Surat Al-Ma'idah, verse 44, Qur'an. The following two verses come from the same chapter, verses 45 and 47.

17. See Hasan Hanafi, "Al-Hakimiyya Tatahadda," in *Humum al-Fikr wa al-Watan: Turath al-'Asr wa al-Hadatha* vol. 1, 429–450.

18. Oppressive Violence, Liberating Violence, and Revolutionary Violence.

19. See Hasan Hanafi, "Madha Ta'ani Shahadat 'La Ilaha illa Allah, wa Anna Muhammadan Rasul Allah?'" *Al-Din wa al-Thawra fi Misr 1952-1981: Al-Yamin wa al-Yasar fi al-Fikr al-Dini* vol. 7, 147–161.
20. Surat Al-Kafirun, verse 6, Qur'an.
21. Hasan Hanafi, *Muqaddima fi 'Ilm al-Istighrab* (Cairo: Al-Dar al-Fanniyya, 1991), 695–710, and also Muhammad 'Abid Al-Jabiri and Hasan Hanafi, *Hiwar al-Mashriq wa al-Maghrib* (Cairo: Maktabat Madbuli, 1993), 34–37.
22. Some of its symbols are Kamil Abu Al-Majd, Yusuf Al-Qaradawi, Khalaf Allah Muhammad Khalaf Allah, the Progressive Islamists in Tunisia, the Islamic Left in Egypt and the reformers in Iran.

Chapter 3

1. For instance, see the book by Steve Wiseman, *The Islamic Bomb*, and the book by K. Ballet, *The Islamic Bomb of Pakistan*. Also, Samuel Huntington, "Clash of Civilizations," *Foreign Affairs* vol. 72, no. 3 (Summer 1993).
2. See, for instance, Gilles Kepel, "Islamism Reconsidered," *Harvard International Review* vol. 22, no. 2 (Summer 2000). See also Hisham Ja'far, "Al-Harakat al-Islamiyya wa ma ba'd al-Siyasa," *Majallat al-Mujtama'* (Kuwait: March 2, 1999).
3. See the many in-depth studies that explored this topic: Laura Guazzone (ed.) *The Islamist Dilemma: The Political Role of Islamist Movements in the Contemporary Arab World* (New York, NY: Ithaca, 1996); John Esposito, *Political Islam: Revolution, Radicalism, or Reform* (Boulder, CO: Lynne Rienner Publishers, 1997); Dale Eickelman and James Piscatori, *Muslim Politics* (Princeton: Princeton University Press, 1996); and Ahmad S. Moussalli, *Moderate and Radical Islamic Fundamentalism: The Quest for Modernity, Legitimacy, and the Islamic State* (Gainsville, FL: University of Florida Press, 1999).
4. Yusuf Al-Qaradawi, *Al-Sahwat al-Islamiyya bayna al-Juhud wa al-Tatarruf* (Qatar: Kitab al-Umma, 1984), 23–26.

5. Salah Al-Sawi, *Al-Tatarruf al-Dini: Al-Ra'y al-Akhar* (Cairo: Al-Afaq al-Dawliyya li al-I'lam, 1984), 15.

6. Al-Qaradawi, op. cit., 39–41.

7. Al-Sawi, op. cit., 10–11.

8. Ibid., 13.

9. See, for instance, Joseph Gusfield (ed.) *Protest, Reform and Revolt: A Reader in Social Movements* (New York, NY: John Wiley and Sons Inc., 1970); John Wilson, *Introduction to Social Movements* (New York, NY: Basic Books, 1973); Paul Wilkinson, *Social Movements* (New York, NY: Praeger Publishers, 1971).

10. Wilkinson, op. cit., 26–27.

11. Ibid., 14.

12. See Salim 'Ali Al-Bihnsawi, *Al-Hukm wa Qadiyyat Takfir al-Muslim* (Cairo: Dar al-Ansar, 1977).

13. Al-Qaradawi, op. cit., 59–62.

14. Hasan Al-Hudaybi, *Du'at la Qudat* (Cairo: 1977).

15. See Nazih Ayyubi, *Al-Dawla al-Markaziyya fi Misr* (Beirut: Center for the Studies of Arab Unity, 1989). See also Ghassan Salame (ed.) *Democracy without Democrats?* (London: I.B. Tauris, 1994).

16. Sayyid Qutb, *Ma'alim fi al-Tariq* (Cairo: Dar al-Shuruq, 1988), 102–103 and 164. See also Ridwan Al-Sayyid, "Harakat al-Islam al-Mu'asira: Ta'amulat fi Bi'atiha al-Idiolojiyya wa al-Siyasa," *Siyasat al-Islam al-Mu'asir: Muraja'at wa Mutaba'at* (Beirut: Dar al-Kitab al-'Arabi, 1997).

17. Sayyid Qutb, op. cit., 97–98. See the important study of Ahmad Moussalli on the thought of Sayyid Qutb, *Al-Usuliyya al-Islamiyya: Dirasa fi al-Khitab al-Idioloji wa al-Siyasi 'inda Sayyid Qutb, Bahth Muqaran li Mabadi' al-Usuliyyin wa al-Islahiyyin* (Beirut: Al-Nashir li al-Tiba'a wa al-Nashr wa al-Tawzi' wa al-I'lan, 1993); and Yvonne Haddad, "Sayyid Qutb: Ideologue of Islamic Revival," in John Esposito (ed.) *Voices of Resurgent Islam* (New York, NY: Oxford University Press, 1982); "The Qur'anic Justification for an Islamic Revolution," *The Middle East Journal* vol. 37, no. 1 (Winter 1983).

18. Sayyid Qutb, op. cit. 165.

Chapter 4

1. On democracy and pluralism in the Arab world, see, *Al-Hayat*, August 4, 1993, 19, and September 25, 1993, 14 and 17. The series ran August 2–6, 1993. See also *Qadaya al-Isbu'*, no. 15, September 10–17, 1993, 1–2. For fundamentalists interested in the same issue, see Rashid Al-Ghannushi on *Al-Hurriyyat al-'Ama fi al-Islam* (Beirut: Center for the Studies of Arab Unity, 1993) and Fahmi Al-Huwaidi, *Al-Islam wa al-Dimocratiyya* (Cairo: Markaz al-'Ahram li al-Tarjama wa al-Nashr, 1993). In 1990, the Beirut Center for Studies of Arab Unity convened a conference in Cairo to discuss democracy in the Arab world. The London-based widely read Arabic newspaper, *Al-Hayat*, serialized in August 1993 a long debate for five days around civil society, pluralism and democracy in Egypt and the Arab world.

2. "Will Democracy Survive in Egypt?" *Reader's Digest* (Canadian Edition, December 1987) vol. 131, no. 788: 149. "The Arab World where Troubles for the US Never End," *US News and World Report* (February 6, 1984), vol. 96: 24. Samuel P. Huntington, "The Clash of Civilizations," *Foreign Affairs* vol. 72, no. 3 (Summer 1993): 22–49.

3. Timothy D. Sisk, *Islam and Democracy* (Washington, DC: United States Peace Institute Press, 1992), vii.

4. *New Perspective Quarterly,* vol. II, no. 2 (Spring 1994): 20–37. The complete titles of the articles are:
   - Kanan Makiya, "From Beirut to Sarajevo: Can Tolerance be Born of Cruelty?"
   - Hahar Ben Jelloun, "Laughing at God in North Africa."
   - Farida Faouzia Charfi, "When Galileo Meets Allah."
   - Tariq Aanuri, "Justice is the Strife."
   - Naguib Mahfouz, "Against Cultural Terrorism."

5. The Editor, *New Perspective Quarterly,* vol. II, no. 2 (Spring 1994): 3.

6. "Media Mongols at the Gate of Baghdad," *New Perspective Quarterly*, vol. 10, no. 3 (Summer 1993): 10.

7. "The Islamic-Confucian Connection," Ibid., 19. See also Huntington, op. cit. For similar attitudes see "Will Democracy Survive in Egypt?"

op. cit. and "The Arab World where Troubles for the US Never End," op. cit.

8. "The Arab World where Troubles for the US Never End," op. cit., 21.

9. Judith Miller, "The Challenge of Radical Islam," *Foreign Affairs* vol. 72, no. 2, (1993): 54–55 and see the complete article, 43–55.

10. Ibid. In the same vein see, Bernard Lewis "Islam and Liberal Democracy," *The Atlantic Monthly* (February 1993): 89–98. This article is also used by Miller to support her argument.

11. Edward Djerejian, "One Man, One Vote, One Time," *New Perspective Quarterly* vol. 10, no. 3 (Summer 1993): 49.

12. Ibid.

13. Ibid.

14. Augustus Norton, "Inclusion Can Deflate Islamic Populism," *New Perspective Quarterly* vol. 10, no. 3 (Summer 1993): 50.

15. Ibid.

16. Ibid., 51. For studies that deal with similar issues and the relationships between political elites, Islamists and the West, see Ghassan Salame, "Islam and the West," *Foreign Policy* no. 90 (Spring 1993): 22–37. See also Dale Eickelman, "Changing Interpretations of Islamic Movements," in William Roff (ed.) *Islam and the Political Economy of Meaning* (London: Croom Helm, 1987), 13–30.

17. William Zartman, "Democracy and Islam: The Cultural Dialectic," Annals of the AAPSS, 524 (November, 1992): 191.

18. John Esposito and James Piscatori, "Democratization and Islam," *Middle East Journal* vol. 45, no. 3 (Summer 1991): 434. Along the same line of argument, see Gudrun Kramer, "Islamist Democracy," *Middle East Report* 183, vol. 23, no. 4, (July-August): 2–8.

19. Gudrun Kramer, "Liberalization and Democracy in the Arab World," *Middle East Report* 174, vol. 22, no. 1 (January–February 1992): 25 and see 22–24.

20. *Al-Hayat*, April 24, 1993, 19. Some of the books that have been resurrected include *Freedom of Thought* by Salame Musa, *Islam and the Fundamentals of Government* by 'Ali 'Abd Al-Razzaq, *the Future of Culture in Egypt* by Taha Hussein, *The Liberation of Woman* by

Qasim Amin, *The Nature of Tyranny* by 'Abd Al-Rahaman Al-Kawakibi and many others, including briefs for modernist political thinkers such as Abdu and Al-Afghani. See also on the war of ideas and political control, Alexander Flores' article "Secularism, Integralism and Political Islam," *Middle East Report* no. 183 (July–August, 1993): 35–38.

21. *Al-Safir*, April 2, 1993, 8.

22. *Al-Hayat*, June 3, 1993, 8. See also Flores, "Secularism," 32–33. See also *Al-Diyar*, July 22, 1994, 14.

23. For details on this issue see *Al-Safir*, June 10, 1993, 1; and *Al-Safir*, June 16, 1993, 1 and 10. For the views of the Mufti of Egypt on violence, see *Al-Wasat*, November 11, 1993, no. 94, 29–21.

24. *Al-Safir*, July 10, 1993, 10. His books include *Al-Imam al-Shafi'i and the Foundation of Moderate Ideology* and *The Concept of Text: A Study in Qur'anic Sciences* .

25. Ibid. For the latest figures, see *Al-Wasat*, July 25, 1994, 4–5. Not all sentences were given by the regular courts—56 of the 58 death sentences were given by martial courts; the other two by the higher courts of national security or emergency court.

26. *Al-Safir*, April 3, 1993, 10. Al-'Awwa, *Fi al-Nizam al-Siyasi li al-Dawla al-Islamiyya* (Cairo: Dar al-Shuruq, 1989), 85–113.

27. *Al-Hayat*, February 4, 1994, 7. See also the five long and diverse articles and dialogues that *Al-Hayat* has serialized in August 2–5 under the title "Civil Society in Egypt and the Arab World." On interest in democracy in the Arab world and the resistance of the governments to such a society, see for instance *Al-Hayat*, August 4, 1993, 19, and September 25, 1993, 14 and 17.

28. *Al-Shu'la*, no. 26, March 1993, 38 and 39–40.

29. *Al-Hayat*, August 3, 1993, 19. See also, *Al-Hayat*, February 3, 1994, 17. On the democratic changes that have been taking place in the Arab world and North Africa, see Lisa Anderson, "Liberalism in Northern Africa," *Current History* vol. 89, no. 546 (April 1990): 145–146, 148 and 174–175. See also on the state of democracy in the Arab world, Hilal Khashan, "The Quagmire of Arab Democracy,"

ASQ vol. 1, no. 1 (Winter 1992) 17–33. Consult also John Esposito, "Political Islam: Beyond the Green Menace," *Current History* vol. 93 (January 1994): 19–24. Al-Jawjari's views are contained in his book *Al-Hizb al-Islami* (Cairo: The Arabic Center for Journalism and Publications, 1993).

30. *Qira'at Siyasiyya* vol. 3, no. 2 (Spring 1993): 197–198. *Qadaya Dawliyya* published the Manifesto in its March issue of 1993.

31. Rifa'at Al-Sa'id, *Hasan al-Banna, Mu'assis Harakat al-Ikhwan al-Muslimin* (Beirut: Dar al-Tali'a, 4th ed., 1986), 93–94, 99–100 and 112–116. Al-Sa'id's leftist account is not favorable, but the facts mentioned in it minus the author's analysis still serve to show that the Brotherhood has not officially sanctioned or employed violence. On the active involvement of Al-Banna and his organization in civil society and their cooperation with other civil segments, see, for instance, Ishaq Musa Al-Husseini, *Moslem Brethren* (Beirut: Khayat's College Book, 1956), Richard Mitchell, *The Society of Muslim Brothers* (London: Oxford University Press, 1964) and Charles Adams, *Islam and Modernism in Egypt* (New York, NY: Russell and Russell, 1986). See also the views of 'Umar Al-Tilmisani in Rif'at Sayyid Ahmad, *Al-Nabiy al-Musallah: Al-Rafidun* (London: Riad al-Rayyis Books Ltd., 1991), 199–200. On Al-Banna's ideology, see Ahmad Moussalli, "Hasan al-Banna's Islamist Discourse on Constitutional Rule and Islamic State," *Journal of Islamic Studies* vol. 4, no. 2 (1993): 161–174.

32. Al-Sa'id, *Hasan al-Banna*, op. cit., 101–107, 112, 117 & 122-124.

33. Ibid., 129, 132–39 and 169–179.

34. Hasan Al-Banna, *Majmu'at Rasa'il al-Shahid Hasan al-Banna* (Beirut: Dar al-Qur'an al-Karim, 1984), hereafter cited as *Rasa'il al-Imam*, 48 and 56–60; Al-Banna, *Majmu'at* op. cit., 14, 169, 309, 331–322 and 335–337; Al-Banna, *Kalimat Khalida* (Beirut: n.p, 1972), 45.

35. Henry Munson, *Islam and Revolution in the Middle East* (New Haven, CT: Yale University Press, 1988), 78–79. See also Dilip Hiro, *The Rise of Islamic Fundamentalism* (New York, NY: Routledge, 1989), 69–72.

36. Hasan Al-Banna, *Din wa-Siyasa* (Beirut: Maktabat Huttin, 1970), 40–45; and Al-Banna, *Majmu'at Rasa'il al-Shahid Hasan al-Banna* (Beirut: Al-Mu'assasa al-Islamiyya, 4th. ed. 1984), hereafter cited as *Majmu'at Rasa'il*, 161–165. On Al-Banna's biography, see, for instance, *Memoirs of Hasan al-Banna Shaheed* translated by M. N. Shaikh (Karachi: International Islamic Publishers, 1981), and Rif'at Al-Sa'id, *Hasan al-Banna, Mu'assis Harakat al-Ikhwan al-Muslimin*.

37. Al-Banna, *Majmu'at Rasa'il*, op. cit.,165; Banna, *Majmu'at Rasa'il al-Imam al-Shahid Hasan al-Banna* (Beirut: Dar al-Qalam, n.d.), hereafter cited as *Majmu'a*, 304 and 343–47; and Al-Banna, *Din wa-Siyasa*, 57-59.

38. Al-Banna, *Majmu'at Rasa'il*, op. cit., 160–161 and 317–318; and Al-Banna, *Al-Imam Yatahadath ila Shabab al-'Alam al-Islami* (Beirut: Dar al-Qalam, 1974), 99; and Al-Banna, *Majmu'a*, op. cit., 99 and 332–337.

39. Al-Banna, *Majmu'at Rasa'il*, op. cit., 95–96, 165–167, 317, 320–323, 325 and 328–330; Al-Banna, *Minbar al-Jum'a* (Alexandria: Dar al-Da'wa, 1978), 78–79 and 136; Al-Banna, *Al-Da'wa* no. 7 (1979), 9. On the centrality of the demand for an Islamic state in the fundamentalist thought, see Bruce Lawrence, *Defenders of God: The Revolt against the Modern Age* (San Francisco: Harper and Row, 1989), 187–226.

40. Al-Banna, *Majmu'at Rasa'il*, op. cit., 96–97, 161–163 and 167–169; and Al-Banna, *Rasa'il al-Imam*, 53.

41. Al-Banna, *Nazarat fi Islah al-Nafs wa al-Mujtama'* (Cairo: Maktabat al-'I'tisam, 1969), 194; Al-Banna, *Minbar al-Jum'a*, op. cit., 24–25, 63, 72 and 347; Al-Banna, *Majmu'at Rasa'il*, op. cit., 317; Al-Banna, *Majmu'a*, op. cit. 63, 72, 101, 104 and 317; Al-Banna, *Rasa'il al-Imam*, 53–55; and Al-Banna, *Al-Imam al-Shahid Yatahadath*, 15–17.

42. Al-Banna, *Al-Salam fi al-Islam* (Beirut: Manshurat al-'Asr al-Hadith, 1971), 27–29. On his acceptance of pluralism, see 'Abd Al-Khabir Mahmud 'Ata, "Al-Haraka al-Islamiyya wa Qadiyat al-Ta'addudiyya," *Al-Majallat al-'Arabiyya li al-'Ulum al-Siyasiyya,* Nos. 5 and 6 (April 1992): 115–116; on Al-Banna's own declaration of accepting equal rights and pluralism, see *Al-Salam fi al-Islam* , op. cit., 37 and passim.

For similar views in Jordan, see Taqiy Al-Din Al-Nabahani, *Al-Takatul al-Hizbi* (Jerusalem: n.p., 2nd ed., 1953), 23–57 and *Nizam al-Hukm* (Jerusalem: Matba'at al-Thiryan, 1952), 56–59.

43. Al-Nabahani, *Al-Takatul al-Hizbi*, op. cit., 23–25.

44. Ibid., 24–57.

45. Al-Nabahani, *Nizam al-Hukm*, op. cit., 56–59.

46. Iyad Barghouty, "Al-Islam bayna al-Sultah wa al-Mu'arada," *Qadaya Fikriyya: Al-Islam al-Siyasi, al-Usus al-Fikriyya wa al-Ahdaf al-'Amalliyya* (Cairo: Dar al-Thaqafah al-Jadidah, 1989), 237–238. For an update of the current status of Islamic parties in Jordan, see "'Itijahat al-Harakah al-Islamiyya fi al-Urdun," *Al-Safir*, August 20, 1993, 13; and "Tanzimat al-Harakat al-Islamiyya: Harakat al-Ikhwan al-Muslimin fi al-'Urdun: Al-Nash'ah wa al-Tatawwur," *Al-Hayat*, Tayyarat Section, August 14, 1993, 3. On the importance of justice as a political doctrine in Islamic political thought, see Charles E. Butterworth, "Political Islam," Annals of the AAPSS, 524 (November, 1992): 26–37.

47. Munir Shafiq, "Awlawiyyat amam al-Ijtihad wa al-Tajdid," *Al-Ijtihad wa Tajdid fi al-Fikr al-Islami al-Mu'asir* (Malta: Center for the Studies of the Muslim World, 1991), 64–65.

48. Sa'id Hawwa, *Al-Madkhal ila Da'wat al-Ikhwan al-Muslimin bi-Munasabat Khamsin 'Aman 'ala Ta'sisiha* (Amman: Dar al-Arqam, 2nd edition, 1979), 13–18. On the Muslim Brotherhood's participation in elections in Syria, see Al-Habib Al-Janhani, "Al-Sahwa al-Islamiyya fi Bilad al-Sham: Mithal Suriyya," *Al-Harakat al-Islamiyya al-Mu'asira fi al-Watan al-'Arabi* (Beirut: Center for the Studies of Arab Unity, 2nd edition 1989), 105–120.

49. Hawwa, *Al-Madkhal*, op. cit., 282.

50. Muhammad S. Al-'Awwa, *Al-Hayat*, August 3, 1993, 19. See also Al-'Awwa, "Al-Ta'adudiyya min Manzur Islami," *Minbar al-Hiwar* vol. 6, no. 20 (Winter 1991): 134–136.

51. Ibid., 19. On the Islamic movement in Egypt, see Muhammad A. Khalafallah's article in *Al-Haraka al-Islamiyya fi al-Watan al-'Arabi*, 37 and *passim*. See also Rislan Sharaf Al-Din, "Al-Din wa al-Ahzab

al-Siyasiyya al-Diniyya," *Al-Din fi al-Mujtama' al-'Arabi* (Beirut: Center for the Studies of Arab Unity, 1990), 180 and *passim*.

52. Al-'Awwa, "Al-Ta'adudiyya al-Siyasiyya min Manzur Islami," 129–132 and *passim*.

53. Ibid., 133–134. For a summary of the historical acceptance of pluralism by the scholars such as Ibn Taymiyya and authoritative exegesis of the Qur'an such as *Tafsir al-Jilalayin*, see 136–152. For an independent source on the views of the scholars who accepted the people's choice as the legitimate means of government, see Abu Bakr Al-Jassas, *Dirash fi Fikratihi: Bab al-Ijtihad*, edited and introduced by Zuhayr Kibi (Beirut: Dar al-Muntakhab, 1993), 29–41; on those who rejected it, such as the majority of Shi'ites, see 75–86. On the relationship between actual politics and the development of religion and *ijtihad*, see Ismail, *Sociolojia*, 139–138.

54. Al-'Awwa, *Fi al-Nizam al-Siyasi*, 77; and Al-'Awwa, "Al-Ta'adudiyya al-Siyasiyya min Manzur Islami," 136–137 and 152–153.

55. Louis Cantouri and Arthur Lowrie, "Islam, Democracy, the State and the West: Summary of a Lecture and Roundtable Discussion with Hasan al-Turabi," *Middle East Policy* vol. 1, no. 3 (1992): 52–54.

56. Hasan Al-Turabi, *Tajdid Usul al-Fiqh* (Jeddah: Al-Dar al-Su'udiyya li al-Nashr wa al-Tawzi', 1984), 10–16; and Hasan Al-Turabi, *Qadaya al-Hurriyya wa al-Wahda, al-Shura wa al-Dimocratiyya, al-Din wa al-Fan* (Jeddah: Al-Dar al-Su'udiyya li al-Nashr wa al-Tawzi', 1987), 17–18.

57. Hasan Al-Turabi, *Tajdid al-Fikr al-Islami* (Jeddah: Al-Dar al-Su'udiyya li al-Nashr wa al-Tawzi', 2nd edition, 1987), 20, 73 and 132–133; Hasan Al-Turabi, "Awlawiyyat al-Tayyar al-Islami," *Minbar al-Sharq*, no. 1 (March 1992): 21–26, 69–72, 81–82, 136–138, 167–169 and 198–199.

58. Al-Turabi, *Qadaya*, 25–27 and 31–33, Al-Turabi, *Tajdid al-Fikr*, 68–80; and Al-Turabi, "Awlawiyyat," 16. On the differences between *shura* and democracy, see Salih Hasan Sami', *Azmat al-Hurriyya al-Siyasiyya fi al-Watan al-'Arabi* (Cairo: Al-Zahra' li al-I'lam al-'Arabi, 1988), 49–61.

59. Al-Turabi, *Qadaya*, 51–57; and Al-Turabi, *Tajdid al-Fikr*, 45, 66–68, 75, 93–97 and 162–163.

60. On Al-Turabi's definition of religion and the need for revolution see *Tajdid al-Fikr*, 200–203 and 106–119; For more on the general and Islamic relationships that make the establishment of society worthwhile, see Al-Turabi, *Al-Iman wa Atharuhu fi Hayat al-Insan* (Jeddah: Al-Dar al-Su'udiyya li al-Nashr wa al-Tawzi', 1984), 181–261; on the social connotations and their fulfillment, see Ibid., 112–121; on the role of science in society, see Ibid., 269–301; and on the importance of society's unity in the general interest, see Ibid., 325–329.

61. Al-Turabi, *Usul al-Fiqh*, op. cit., 27–29.

62. Al-Turabi, *Al-Itijah al-Islami Yuqadim al-Mar'a bayna Ta'alim al-Din wa Taqalid al-Mujtama'* (Jeddah: Al-Dar al-Su'udiyya li al-Nashr wa al-Tawzi': 1984), 6–13 and 42–44. On the essential conditions and requirements for the independence of women, see Ibid., 45–49.

63. Al-Turabi, *Tajdid al-Fikr*, op. cit., 108–109, 164–165, 133–139 and 160–163.

64. Al-Turabi, *Usul al-Fiqh*, op. cit., 18–25 and 32–35.

65. Ibid., 36–37 and 42–45; Al-Turabi, *Tajdid al-Fikr*, op. cit., 26–31, 36–49, 54–63, 76–77, 148–149 and 172–143.

66. Al-Turabi, *Tajdid al-Fikr*, op. cit., 68–71; for a discussion of the forms of *shura*, see Al-Turabi, *Qadaya*, op. cit., 72–77 and 80–81.

67. Al-Turabi, *Qadaya*, 10–19 and 22–28.

68. Ibid., 20–21 and 29–30.

69. Ibid., 34–37 and 44–47.

70. Al-Turabi, *Al-Salat 'Imad al-Din* (Beirut: Dar al-Qalam, 1971), 124–133, 138–147 and 156–158.

71. Al-Ghannushi, *Bayrut al-Masa'*, May 15, 1993, 15; and Al-Ghannushi, "Mustaqbal al-Tayyar al-Islami," *Minbar al-Sharq*, vol.1, no.1 (March 1992): 3–32. For a general discussion of Al-Ghannushi and *Harakat al-Itijah al-Islami*, see 'Abd al-Khabir Mahmud 'Ata, "Qadiyat al-Ta'addudiyya," 116–117.

72. Al-Ghannushi and Al-Turabi, *Al-Harakah al-Islamiyya wa al-Tahdith* (n.p., 1981), 34–35. See also Muhammad 'Abd al-Baqi Al-Hirmasi, "al-Islam al-Ihtijaji fi Tunis," *Al-Harakat al-Islamiyya al-Mu'asira*, 273–286.

73. Al-Ghannushi, "Hiwar," *Qira'at Siyasiyya* vol. 1, no. 4 (Fall 1991): 14–15 and 35–37; and Al-Ghannushi, "Al-Islam wa al-Gharb," *Al-Ghadir*, Nos. 10 and 11 (1990): 36–37. On his and other fundamentalists' acceptance of democracy, see also John Esposito and James Piscatori, "Democratization and Islam," *Middle East Journal* vol. 45, no. 3 (Summer 1991): 426–434 and 437–438. On his political life see Al-Ghannushi, "Hiwar," 5, and 'Abd al-Qadir Al-Zugul, "Al-Istratijia al-Jadida li Harakat al-Itija al-Islami," in *Al-Din fi al-Mujtama'*, 346–348. For the possibilities of liberalization, see also Gudrun Kramer, "Liberalization and democracy in the Arab World," *Middle East Report* (January–February, 1992): 22–25.

74. Rashid al-Ghannushi, "Al-Islam wa al-Gharb," *Al-Ghadir* no. 10 and 11 (December 1990): 37.

75. Muhammad Al-Hashimi Al-Hamidi, "Awlawiyyat Muhimma fi Daftar al-Harakat al-Islamiyya: Nahwa Mithaq Islami li al-'Adl wa al-Shura wa Huquq al-Insan," *Al-Mustaqbal al-Islami* no. 2 (November 1991): 19–21; the quotation is from Ibid., 14–15.

76. See the Program of the Islamic Salvation Front (Al-Barnamaj al-Siyasi li Jabhat al-Inqadh al-Islamiyya), *Minbar al-Sharq* no. 1, March. On the Front and democracy, see Esposito and Piscatori, "Democratization," 437–438. On the possibilities of civil society in Islam, see "Bahth 'an Mujtama' Madani Manshud," *Mustaqbal al-'Alam al-Islami* vol. 1, no. 4 (Fall 1991): 225–237.

77. Ahmad Moussalli, *Radical Islamic Fundamentalism: The Ideological and Political Discourse of Sayyid Qutb* (Beirut: American University of Beirut, 1992), 19–24 and *passim*.

78. Ibid., 24–30. See also Sayyid Qutb, *Nahwa Mujtama' Islami* (Beirut: Dar al-Shuruq, 5th edition, 1982), 11–12, *Al-Mustaqbal li Hadha al-Din* (Cairo: Maktabat Wahba, 1965), 71–90, *Al-Islam wa Mushkilat al-Hadara* (Beirut: Dar al-Shuruq, 8th edition, 1983), 77–78 and 83–87.

79. Moussalli, *Radical Islamic Fundamentalism*, op. cit., 31–39. See Mitchell, *The Society of Muslim Brothers*, op. cit., 103 and 187–189. Badrul Hasan, *Milestones* (Karachi: International Islamic Publishers, 1981), 7–13 and 30–31; Asaf Hussain, *Islamic Movements in Egypt, Pakistan, and Iran* (Great Britain: Mansell Publishing Limited, 1983), 7–11 and 91.

80. Sayyid Qutb, *Hadha al-Din* (Cairo: Maktabat Wahba, 4th. edition, n.d.), 32 and 123; and Sayyid Qutb, *Ma'rakat al-Islam wa al-Ra'simaliyya* (Beirut: Dar al-Shuruq, 4th edition, 1980), 49 and 60.

81. On the necessity of the choice of people, see Qutb, *Ma'alim fi al-Tariq* (Beirut: Dar al-Shuruq, 7th edition, 1980), 50 and 71–77; and Qutb, *Al-'Adala al-Ijtima'iyya fi al-Islam* (Cairo: Dar al-Shuruq, 7th edition 1980), 73 and 107–108, 206–207; Qutb, *Ma'rakat al-Islam wa al-Ra'simaliyya*, 67, 85 and 75; Qutb, *Fiqh al-Da'wa* (Beirut: Mu'assasat al-Risala, 1970), 61.

82. Qutb, *Al-'Adala*, op. cit., 102–105 and 167; Qutb, *Fiqh*, op. cit., 84; Qutb, *Ra'simaliyya*, op. cit., 60.

83. Qutb, *Nahwa Mujtama' Islami* (Beirut: Dar al-Shuruq, 6th edition, 1983), 46–52.

84. Qutb, *Al-'Adala*, op. cit., 37, 107–108, 111 and 157–169; Qutb, *Fi Zilal*, vol. 1, Part 3: 329; Qutb, *Ma'alim*, op. cit., 58–96, 72 and 132; Qutb, *Ra'simaliyya*, op. cit., 66–70; Qutb, *Tafsir Ayat al-Riba* (Beirut: Dar al-Shuruq, 1970), 84; and Qutb, *Nahwa Mujtama'*, op. cit., 46–69.

85. Qutb, *Al-'Adala*, 66–68 and 111; and Qutb, *Al-Salam al-'Alami wa al-Islam* (Beirut: Dar al-Shuruq, 7th edition, 1983), 102–118.

86. Qutb, *Fi al-Tarikh, Fikra wa Minhaj* (Cairo: Dar al-Shuruq, 1974), 23–36 and 76; Qutb, *Al-'Adala*, op. cit., 35, 59, 73–80, 86, 113 and 119; and Qutb, *Fi Zilal*, vol. 2: 689. For his view on women and the structure of the family, see Qutb, *Fi Zilal*, vol. 1, Part 1: 235, Part 2: 234, Part 4: 587; Qutb, *Al-'Adala*, op. cit., 60–65.

87. Qutb, *Hadha al-Din*, op. cit., 11 and 91; Qutb, *Ma'alim*, op. cit., 64–67 and 162–163; Qutb, *Al-'Adala*, op. cit., 107 and 198; Qutb, *Nahwa Mujtama'*, op. cit., 62, 92–99, 102–120, 123 and 134; and Qutb, *Al-Salam*, op. cit., 161–165.

88. Qutb, *Ma'alim*, op. cit., 11–15 and 22; Qutb, *Al-'Adala*, op. cit., 197; Qutb, *Hadha al-Din*, op. cit., 11, 29–30 and 65–57; Qutb, *Fiqh*, op. cit., 15–32 and 88–89. See also, Qutb, *Al-Salam*, op. cit., 118–120; and Qutb, *Nahwa Mujtama'*, op. cit., 137–143; and Qutb, *Al-Islam wa Mushkilat al-Hadara*, op. cit., 189–193. On the proper political system according to Qutb, see *Al-Salam*, op. cit., 122–143.

89. Qutb, *Al-Islam wa Mushkilat al-Hadara*, op. cit., 96–107; and Qutb, *Nahwa Mujtama'*, op. cit., 150–152 and *passim*. On the characteristics of the two parties and the West, see Qutb, *Hadha al-Din*, op. cit., 84–87; Qutb, *Al-Islam wa Mushkilat al-Hadara*, op. cit., 7–9; Qutb, *Al-Ra'simaliyya*, op. cit., 58; and Qutb, *Ma'alim*, op. cit., 59 and 89.

90. On these issues and his life, see Muhammad T. Barakat, *Sayyid Qutb: Khulasat Hayatih, Minhajuhuh fi al-Haraka wa al-Naqd al-Muwajah ilayh* (Beirut: Dar al-Da'wa, n.d.), 19; Salah A. Khalidi, *Sayyid Qutb, al-Shahid al-Hay* (Amman: Dar al-Firqan, 1983), 147–149; Qutb, "Limadha A'damuni?" *Al-Muslimun*, no. 4, 6–9; Moussalli, *Radical Islamic Fundamentalism*, op. cit., chapter 1.

91. On the prison experience see Rif'at al-Sa'id's article in *Qadaya Fikriyya: al-Islam al-Siyasi: Al-Usus al-Fikriyya wa al-Ahdaf*, 15 and *passim*. See also Moussalli, *Radical Islamic Fundamentalism*, op. cit., 34–36. On a first-hand and sympathetic account of the torture that Shukri, Qutb and others were subjected to, as well as the movement itself see, Muhammad Mahfuz, *Alladhina Zulimu* (London: Riad al-Rayyis Books Ltd., 1988), 7–141. On Shukri's thought as put forward in his trial, see Rif'at Sayyid Ahmad, Second Document in *Al-Nabiy al-Musallah: Al-Rafidun*, 53–57.

92. Salih Sirriyya, Second Document, "Risalat al-Iman," *Al-Rafidun* (1973), 31–32.

93. Ibid., 42–44 and 48; and Mahfuz, *Alladhina Zulimu*, op. cit., 83, 120–123, 222, 233 and 242.

94. 'Abud Al-Zumar, Third Document, in *Al-Rafidun*, 113–121; and Mahfuz, *Alladhina Zulimu*, op. cit., 226, 254, 267–268, 271 and 273.

95. Fifth Document, *Al-Rafidun*, 150 and 160–164; and 'Abd Al-Khabir, "Qadiyyat al-Ta'aduddiya," op. cit., 118–120. See also Sa'id, *Qadaya*

Fikkriyya, op. cit., 30–31. Sixth Document, *Al-Rafidun*, op. cit., 165, 169 and 173–174. On the organization itself, see Rif'at Sayyid Ahmad, *Al-Nabiy al-Musallah: Al-Tha'irun* (London: Riad al-Rayyis Books Ltd., 1991), 185–186.

96. "Wathiqat I'lan al-Harb 'ala Majlis al-Sha'b," *Al-Tha'irun*, 187–189. For a description of how this organization views each political party and the political system in Egypt, see Ibid., 193–197.

97. "Wathiqat Muhakamat al-Nizam al-Misri," *Al-Tha'irun*, 273–275 and 290–291 where the different types of rulers are specified. For similar views see "Wathiqat al-'Ihya' al-Islami," in Kamal Al-Sa'id Habib, *Jama'at al-Jihad al-Islami*, 199–229. On Tanzim al-Jihad and its splits and offshoots, which are numerous, see Mahfuz, *Alladhina Zulimu*, op. cit., 213–283.

98. *Al-Safir*, September 25, 1993, 10 and *Al-Diyar*, September 25, 1993, 14.

Chapter 6

1. Olivier Roy, *The Failure of Political Islam* (Cambridge, MA: Harvard University Press, 1994); James Walsh, "The Sword of Islam," *Time International* (June 15, 1992): 18–22; Graham Fuller, "Islamic Fundamentalism," *The Washington Post*, January 19, 1992.

2. Bassam Tibi, *The Challenge of Fundamentalism: Political Islam and the New World Disorder* (Berkeley and Los Angeles, CA: University of California Press, 1988), 111–154; Martin E. Marty and R. Scott Appleby (eds) *Fundamentalisms Observed* (Chicago, IL: University of Chicago Press, 1991), 127–151.

3. John L. Esposito, *The Islamic Threat: Myth and Reality?* (New York, NY: Oxford University Press, 1991), 127–151.

4. Compare with Ridwan Al-Sayyid, *Siyasat al-Islam al-Mu'asir, Muraj'at wa Mutaba'at*, 157–204. Ahmad S. Moussalli (ed.) *Islamic Fundamentalism: Myths and Realities* (Reading: Ithaca Press, 1998); Fred Halliday, *Islam and the Myth of Confrontation* (London: I.B. Tauris, 1995).

5. For the development between the two world wars, compare John Keegan, *The First World War* (Santa Monica, CA: Rand Corporation, 2000), 350–436; Giovanni Arrighi, *The Long Twentieth Century* (Chicago, IL: University of Chicago Press, 1994), 211–248. On the Islamic world during the beginning of the twentieth century, Lothrop Steward, *Hadir al-'Alam al-Islami*, translation by 'Ajaj Nuwayhid and commentary by Al-Amir Shakib Arsalan (Egypt: Al-Matba'at al-Salafiyya, 1925), 287–321; and on the makeup of the Middle East, see David Frumakin, *Salam ma Ba'dahu Salam: Wiladat al-Sharq al-Awsat 1914-1922*, translated by As'ad Ilias (Beirut: Dar Riad al-Rayyis, 1992); and on the conditions of the caliphate and the state until the abolition of the caliphate, see Wajih Kawtharani, *Al-Dawla wa al-Khilafa fi al-Khitab al-'Arabi ibbana al-Thawra al-Kamaliyya* (Beirut: Dar al-Tali'a, 1996).

6. On the Islamic reform and its changes, see Fahmi Jid'an, *Usus al-Taqaddum 'inda Mufakkiri al-Islam fi al-Qarn al-Tasi' 'Ashar* (Beirut: Al-Mu'assasa al-'Arabiyya li al-Dirasat wa al-Nashir, 1981); David Commins, *Al-Islah al-Islami*, translated by Muhammad Majid Al-Radi (Damascus: Dar al-Hasad, 1999); Ridwan Al-Sayyid, *Siyasat*, 157–204, 323–336; Ridwan Al-Sayyid, "Al-Tafakkur al-Islami fi al-Masihiyya fi al-'Usur al-Haditha," *Al-Masihiyya wa al-Islam, Maraya Mutaqabila* (Lebanon: Jami'at al-Balamand, 1997), 31–36.

7. Compare with Charles Smith, "The Crisis of Orientalism, The Shift of Egyptian Intellectuals to Islamic Subjects in the 1930s," *International Journal of Middle Eastern Studies* vol. 4 (1973): 382–410.

8. On Sayyid Qutb's relations with Al-Mawdudi, compare with Yousef Chueiri, *Islamic Fundamentalism* (Boston: Twayne, 1990), 93–119. Muhammad Ahmad Khallafallah, "Al-Sahwa al-Islamiyya fi Misr," *Al-Harakat al-Islamiyya fi al-Watan al-'Arabi* (Beirut: Markaz Dirasat al-Wihda al-'Arabiyya, 1987), 37–98. Faysal Darraj wa Jamal Barut (eds) *Al-Ahzab wa al-Harakat wa al-Jama'at al-Islamiyya* vol. 2 (Damascus: Al-Markaz al-'Arabi li al-Dirasat al-Isratijiyya, 1999), 7–14. The most important statements of Al-Mawdudi can be found in his *Nahnu wa al-Hadara al-Gharbiyya* (Cairo: Dar al-Fikr al-'Arab,

1955), which includes an article about the suicide of the Western civilization, published in 1941. See also Al-Nadwi, *Madha Khasir al-'Alam bi Inhitat al-Muslimin* and *Al-Sira' bayna al-Fikra al-Islamiyya wa al-Fikra al-Gharbiyya* that were published early in the 1950s in Cairo. Sayyid Qutb introduced the former. On Al-Mawdudi, see Muhammad 'Amara, *Abu al-A'la al-Mawdudi wa al-Sahwa al-Islamiyya* (Beirut: Dar al-Kalima, 1986). On the Muslim Brotherhood and its extensions, see Richard Mitchell, *The Society of Muslim Brothers,* which was published in 1969 and translated in Cairo in 1977, and covers the first phase only (1928–1955).

9. 'Abd Al-Qadir Al-'Awda, *Al-Tashri' al-Jina'i al-Islami Muqaranan bi al-Qanun al-Wad'i* (1947), and *Al-Islam wa Awda'una al-Qanuniyya* (1949) and *Al-Islam wa Awda'una al-Siyassiyya* (1950).

10. Al-Sayyid, *Siyasat al-Islam*, op. cit.,184–204.

11. Abu Al-A'la Al-Mawdudi, *Risalat al-Arkan al-Arba'a*, 4th edition (Kuwait: Dar al-Qalam, 1971). Sayyid Qutb read this book in English in the early 1950s and considered it to be one of the most important writings in the modern period. Compare with Al-Mawdudi, *Minhaj al-Inqilab al-Islami*, 3rd edition (Tripoli: Dar al-Sahwa, 1981).

12. Ahmad Moussalli, *Al-Usuliyya al-Islamiyya: Dirasa fi al-Khitab al-Idioloji wa al-Siyasi 'inda Sayyid Qutb* (Beirut: al-Nashir li al-Tiba'a wa al-Tawzi' wa al-'Ilan, 1993), 143–234.

13. See Ahmad Moussalli, *Al-Khitab al-Islami al-Usuli: Nazariyyat al-Ma'rifa wa al-Dawla wa al-Mujtam'* (Beirut: al-Nashir li al-Tiba'a wa al-Tawzi' wa al-'Ilan, 1993), 71–80. Muhammad Hafiz Diab, *Sayyid Qutb: al-Khitab wa al-Idiologia* (Beirut: Dar al-Tali'a, 1988). A study was also published in 1965 by Qutb's brother, Muhammad Qutb, entitled *Jahiliyyat al-Qarn al-'Ishrin* (Cairo: Maktabat Wahba, 1965).

14. See Malcolm Kerr, *The Arab Cold War, 1958–1968* (Berkeley, CA: University of California Press, 1971).

15. These books were published in 1949, 1949, and 1951 respectively. However, Al-Siba'i's book was published in 1959. On this trend, see Muhammad Jamal Barut, *Yathrib al-Haditha: Al-Harakat al-Islamiyya*

al-Rahina (Beirut: Dar Riad al-Rayyis, 1994), 95–124, Diab, *Sayyid Qutb*, 100–103.

16. For the trend that opposes capitalism and its transformation, Hamid Enayat, *Al-Fikr al-Siyasi al-Islami al-Mu'asir*, translated by Ibrahim Al-Dusuqi Basha (Cairo: Dar al-Zahra' li al-Nashr, 1988), 274–300; and on Al-Sayyid Muhammad Baqr Al-Sadr and Hizb al-Da'wa, see Shibli Al-Mallat, *Tajdid al-Fiqh al-Islami, Muhammad Baqr al-Sadr bayna al-Najaf wa Shi'it al-'Alam* (Beirut: Dar al-Nahar, 1997). See also Al-*Ahzab wa al-Harakat* vol. 2, 303–351. However, up till now, there is no study on the thinking of Muhammad Al-Ghazali, but his biography was published in 1988 by Muhammad 'Amara by the International Institute of Islamic thought in Virginia in the United States.

17. Yusuf Al-Qaradawi, *Al-Hal al-Islami: Fariyda wa Darura* (Cairo: Dar al-Shuruq, 1974). Also, he has other work concerning the Islamic solution.

18. On *jihad*, see the thinking of Hasan Al-Banna and Sayyid Qutb and radical Islamic movements, see Ahmad Moussalli, *Al-Usuliyya al-Islamiyya*, 121–155, 202–215. On contemporary Islamic radicalism, see Rif'at Sayyid Ahmad, *Tanzimat al-Ghadab al-Islami fi al-Sab'iniyat* (Egypt: 1989). Sayyid Ahmad published Egyptian Jihadist Islamist texts in two volumes by Dar Riad al-Rayyis in Beirut 1991.

19. On the Muslim Brotherhood in Syria until the death of Al-Siba'i, see G. Reissner, *Die Muslim Bruder in Syrien* (Freiburg: Schwarz Verlan, 1973). Also, see Hanna Batatu, "Syrian Muslim Brethren," in F. Halliday and H. Alawi (eds) *State and Ideology in the Middle East* (London: 1988), 168–220; Nazih Ayyubi, *Political Islam: Religion and Politics in the Arab World* (New York, NY: Routledge, 1991), 87–98. See as well *Al-Ahzab wa al-Harakat* vol.1, 255–323.

20. Compare with Gudrun Kramer, "Al-Islamiyyun wa al-Hadith 'an al-Dimoqratiyya," *Al-Ijtihad* vol. 5, no. 21 (Beirut: 1993):101–121. Fahmi Al-Huwaydi, "Al-Islam wa al-Dimoqratiyya," *Al-Mustaqbal al-'Arabi* vol. 12, no. 166 (Beirut: 1992): 11–32, and his book *Al-Islam wa al-Dimoqratiyya* (1994). *Al-Harakat al-Islamiyya wa al-Dimoqratiyya*

(Beirut: Center for the Arab Unity Studies, 1999) and Haydar Ibrahim 'Ali, *Al-Tayyarat al-Islamiyya wa Qadiyyat al-Dimoqratiyya* (Beirut: Center for the Arab Unity Studies, 1996).

21. See A. E. Mayer, *Islam and Human Rights: Traditions and Politics* (Boulder, CO: Westview Press, 2nd edition, 1991), and also Ridwan Al-Sayyid "Mas'alat Huquq al-Insan fi al-Fikr al-Islami al-Mu'asir," *Al-Abhath* vol. 46 (Beirut: 1998): 3–35.

22. Compare with Sana Abed-Kotob, "The Accommodationists Speak: Goals and Strategies of the Muslim Brotherhood of Egypt," *International Journal of Middle Eastern Studies* vol. 27, no. 2 (1995): 321–339.

23. See John Voll, *Continuity and Change in the Modern World* (Syracuse, NY: Syracuse University Press, 1994), Esposito and Voll, *Islam and Democracy*.

24. Compare with Ridwan Al-Sayyid, "Al-Islamiyyun wa al-'Awlama, al-'Alam fi Mir'at al-Hawiyya," *Al-Din wa al-'Awlama wa al-Ta'addudiyya* (Lebanon: Jami'at al-Balamand, 2000); Muhammad Arkun, "Al-Islam al-Mu'asir amam Turathihi wa al-'Awlama," *Qadaya fi Naqd al-'Aql al-Dini* (Beirut: Dar al-Tali'a, 1998), 153–198. On the impact of the Second Gulf War and the new world order on the Islamists, see James Piscatori (ed.) *Islamic Fundamentalism and the Gulf Crisis* (Chicago, IL: University of Chicago Press, 1991).

25. Shireen Hunter, *The Future of Islam and the West, Clash of Civilizations or Peaceful Coexistence* (Reading: Ithaca Press, 1998) and also "Muhadarat fi Hiwar al-Hadarat," Conference on "How to enter the year of civilization?" (Damascus: Iranian Cultural Center, 2000).

26. For a comparison of Hamas and Islamic *Jihad* in Palestine, see the study of Ziad Abu Umr (1994). See also *Al-Ahzab wa al-Harakat* vol. 1, 371–437 and vol. 2, 215–281, B. Milton-Edwards, *Islamic Politics in Palestine* (1999) and compare with *Al-Harakat al-Islamiyya fi Muwajahat al-Taswiyya* (Beirut: Markaz al-Dirasat al-Istratijiyya wa al-Buhuth al-Tawthiq, 1995).

27. Jean Lecca, "Al-Taharruk nahwa al-Dimoqratiyya fi al-Watan al-'Arabi," in Ghassan Salama (ed.) Conference papers on "Dimocratiyya min Dun Dimoqratiyyin: Siyasat al-Infitah fi al-'Alam al-Arabi/al-Islami" (Beirut: Center for the Arab Unity Studies, 1995), 360–388. Ahmad Shaki Al-Sabihi, *Mustaqbal al-Mujtama' fi al-Watan al-'Arabi* (Beirut: Markaz Dirasat al-Wihda al-'Arabiyya, 2001), 98–102.

28. Compare with Ridwan Al-Sayyid and 'Abd Al-Ilah Bilqaziz, *Azmat al-Fikr al-Siyasi al-'Arabi* (Damascus and Beirut: Dar al-Fikr al-Mu'asir, 2000). On this problem, see Fred Haliday, *Al-Umma wa al-Din fi al-Sharq al-Awsat*, translated by 'Abd Al-Ilah Al-Nu'aymi (Beirut: Dar al-Saqi, 1995), 183 and *passim*.

29. Muhammad Mahdi Shams Al-Din, *Fi al-Ijtima' al-Siyasi al-Islami* (Beirut: al-Mu'assasa Al-Jami'iyya, 1995), 168–242.

30. Muhammad Rida Muharram, *Tahdith al-'Aql al-Siyasi al-Islami* (Cairo: Dar Sina li al-Nashr, 1986). See Ridawn Al-Sayyid and Bilqaziz, *Azmat al-Fikr al-Siyasi al-'Arabi*, 11–14. Haydar Ibrahim 'Ali, *Azmat al-Islam al-Siyasi* (Cairo: al-Markaz al-Sudani lil Buhuth, 1991). Muhammad 'Amara, *Azmat al-Fikr al-Hadith* (Cairo: Dar al-Shuruq, 1998).

31. Compare with Al-Shatibi, *Al-Muwafaqat fi Usul al-Ahkam*, edited by Abd Allah Darraz (Egypt: Matba'at al-Taqaddum Al-'Ilmiyya, n.d.), 11–12. See also 'Abd Al-Majid Al-Saghir, *Al-Fikr al-Usuli wa Ishkaliyat al-Sulta al-'Ilmiyya fi al-Islam, Qira'a fi Nash'at 'Ilm al-Usul wa Maqasid al-Shari'a* (Beirut: Dar al-Muntakhab al-'Arabi, 1994). For the employment of this issue in contemporary Islamic thought, see Ridwan Al-Sayyid, *Siyasat al-Islam*, 244–246. In the last few years, eight books on *maqasid al-shari'a*, including three from the International Institute of Islamic thought, were published. Compare with the studies by 'Abd al-Majid Turki and Salah Al-Din Jourshi in Volumes 8 and 9 of *Al-Ijtihad* (1990).

32. On the method of authentication, see Ridwan Al-Sayyid, *Siyasat al-Islam*, 171–183.

33. Compare with Ridwan Al-Sayyid, *Al-Jama'a wa al-Sulta wa al-Dawla* (Beirut: Dar al-Kitab al-'Arab, 1997), on the view of the caliphate and the structure of the state, see 21–85.

34. Wajih Kawtharani, *Mukhtarat Siyasiyya min Majallat al-Manar* (Beirut: Dar al-Tali'a, 1980), 97.

35. Armando Salvatore, *Islam and the Political Discourse of Modernity* (Reading: Ithaca Press, 1997).

36. On worldviews in Islamic thought, see R.L. Euben, *Enemy in the Mirror, Islamic Fundamentalism and the Limit of Modern Rationalism* (Princeton, NJ: Princeton University Press, 1999), 154–165; Armando Salvatore, "Discursive Contentions in Islamic Terms: Fundamentalism versus Liberalism?" in Moussalli, *Myths and Reality*, 75–102.

37. Wahba Al-Zuhayli, *Haq al-Hurriya fi al-'Alam* (Damascus and Beirut: Dar al-Fikr al-Mu'asir, 2000), 211. Zuhayli, a well-known jurist, published an encyclopedia of jurisprudence, *Al-Fiqh al-Islami wa Adillatih*. In the early 1960s, he published his famous book, *Athar al-Harb fi al-Fiqh al-Islami*, and argued for the right of citizenship.

38. The document was published in the *Nahar* newspaper on May 8, 2001, 18. Compare with a shorter and less ambitious document published by al-Jama'a al-Islamiyya in *Al-Safir* newspaper, Beirut, April 25, 2001, 5. On the documents of the Egyptian Wasat party see Su'ud Al-Mawla, *Min Hasan al-Banna ila Hizb al-Wasat* (Beirut: Markaz al-Bayan Al-Thaqafi, 2000), 162, 214.

BIBLIOGRAPHY

'Ali, Haydar Ibrahim. "Al-Usus al-Ijtima'iyya li al-Zahira al-Diniyya: Mulahazat fi 'Ilm al-Ijtima'," in 'Abd Al-Baqi Al-Hirmasi et al, *Al-Din fi al-Mujtama' al-'Arabi* (Beirut: Center for the Studies of Arab Unity, 1990).

'Ali, Haydar Ibrahim. *Al-Tayyarat al-Islamiyya wa Qadiyyat al-Dimoqratiyya* (Beirut: Markaz Dirasat al-Wihda al-'Arabiyya, 1996).

'Amara, Muhammad. *Abu al-A'la al-Mawdudi wa al-Sahwa al-Islamiyya* (Beirut: Dar al-Kalima, 1986).

'Amara, Muhammad. *Al-A'mal al-Kamila li Jamal al-Din al-Afghani* (Cairo: Dar al-Kitab al-'Arabi, 1968).

'Amara, Muhammad. *Azmat al-Fikr al-Hadith* (Cairo: Dar al-Shuruq, 1998).

'Ata, 'Abd al-Khabir Mahmud. "Al-Haraka al-Islamiyya wa Qadiyat al-Ta'addudiyya." In *Al-Majallat al-'Arabiyya li al-'Ulum al-Siyasiyya* no. 5–6 (April 1992).

"'Itijahat al-Harakah al-Islamiyya fi al-Urdun." *Al-Safir*, August 20, 1993.

"Al-Barnamaj al-Siyasi li Jabhat al-Inqadh al-Islamiyya." *Minbar al-Sharq* no. 1 (March 1991).

"Bahth 'an Mujtama' Madani Manshud." *Mustaqbal al-'Alam al-Islami* vol. 1, no. 4 (Fall, 1991).

"Muhadarat fi Hiwar al-Hadarat." Conference on "How to Enter the Year of Civilization?" (Damascus: Iranian Cultural Center, 2000)

"Tanzimat al-Harakat al-Islamiyya: Harakat al-Ikhwan al-Muslim fi al-'Urdun: Al-Nash'ah wa al-Tatawwur." *Al-Hayat* Tayyarat Section, August 14, 1993.

"The Arab World where Troubles for the US Never End." *US News and World Report*, February 6, 1984, vol. 96.

Abdu, Muhammad. *Risalat al-Tawhid* (Cairo: Dar al-Manar, 1373 h).

Abed-Kotob, Sana. "The Accommodationists Speak: Goals and Strategies of the Muslim Brotherhood of Egypt." *International Journal of Middle East Studies* vol.27, no. 2 (1995).

Adams, Charles. "Maududi and the Islamic State." In John Esposito (ed.) *Voices of Resurgent Islam* (Oxford: Oxford University Press, 1983).

Adams, Charles. *Islam and Modernism in Egypt* (New York, NY: Russell and Russell, 1986).

Ahmad, Rif'at Sayyid. *Al-Nabiy al-Musallah: Al-Tha'irun* (London: Riad al-Rayyis Books Ltd., 1991).

Ahmad, Rif'at Sayyid. *Al-Nabiy al-Musallah: Al-Rafidun* (London: Riad al-Rayyis Books Ltd., 1991).

Ahmad, Rif'at Sayyid. *Tanzimat al-Ghadab al-Islami fi al-Sab'iniyat* (Egypt: 1989).

Al-'Awwa, Muhammad. *Al-Hayat*, August 3, 1993.

Al-'Azmeh, Aziz. *Al-'Ilmaniyya min Manzur Mukhtalif* (Beirut: Center for the Studies of Arab Unity, 1992).

Al-Ansari, Muhammad Jabir. *Takwin al-'Arab al-Siyasi wa Maghza al-Dawla al-Qutriyya: Madhkal ila I'adat Fahm al-Waqi' al-'Arabi* (Beirut: Center for the Studies of Arab Unity, 1995).

Al-Azm, Sadiq Jalal. "Is Islam Secularizable?" In Elizabeth Ozdalga and Sune Persson (eds) *Civil Society, Democracy and the Muslim World* (Istanbul: Swedish Research Institute in Istanbul, 1997).

Al-Banna, Hasan. *Kalimat Khalida* (Beirut: n.p., 1972), 45.

Al-Banna, Hasan. *Majmu'at Rasa'il al-Shahid Hasan al-Banna* (Beirut: Dar al-Qur'an al-Karim, 1984).

Al-Banna, Hasan. *Al-Imam Yatahadath ila Shabab al-'Alam al-Islami* (Beirut: Dar al-Qalam, 1974).

Al-Banna, Hasan. *Al-Salam fi al-Islam* (Beirut: Manshurat al-'Asr al-Hadith, 1971).

Al-Banna, Hasan. *Din wa-Siyasa* (Beirut: Maktabat Huttin, 1970).

Al-Banna, Hasan. *Majmu'at Rasa'il al-Imam al-Shahid Hasan al-Banna* (Beirut: Dar al-Qalam, n.d.).

Al-Banna, Hasan. *Majmu'at Rasa'il al-Shahid Hasan al-Banna* (Beirut: Al-Mu'assasa al-Islamiyya, 4th. ed. 1984).

Al-Banna, Hasan. *Min Rasa'il al-Ikhwan al-Muslimin* (Cairo: Dar al-Tiba'at wa al-Nashr al-Islamiyya, 1963).

Al-Banna, Hasan. *Minbar al-Jum'a* (Alexandria: Dar al-Da'wa, 1978).

Al-Banna, Hasan. *Mudhakarrat al-Da'wa wa al-Da'iyya* (Cairo: al-Maktab al-Islami, 1983).

Al-Banna, Hasan. *Nazarat fi Islah al-Nafs wa al-Mujtama'* (Cairo: Maktabat al-I'tisam, 1969).

Al-Bihnsawi, Salim 'Ali. *Al-Hukm wa Qadiyyat Takfir al-Muslim* (Cairo: Dar al-Ansar, 1977).

Al-Din, Muhammad Mahdi Shams. *Fi al-Ijtima' al-Siyasi al-Islami* (Beirut: al-Mu'assasa al-Jami'iyya, 1995).

Al-Din, Rislan Sharaf. "Al-Din wa al-Ahzab al-Siyasiyya al-Diniyya." *Al-Din fi al-Mujtama' al-'Arabi* (Beirut: Center for the Studies of Arab Unity, 1990).

Al-Ghannushi, Rashid and Hasan al-Turabi. *Al-Harakah al-Islamiyya wa al-Tahdith* (n.p., 1981).

Al-Ghannushi, Rashid. *Bayrut al-Masa'*, May 15, 1993.

Al-Ghannushi, Rashid. "Al-Islam wa al-Gharb." *Al-Ghadir* no. 10–11 (December 1990).

Al-Ghannushi, Rashid. "Hiwar." *Qira'at Siyasiyya* vol. 1, no. 4 (Fall 1991).

Al-Ghannushi, Rashid. "Mustaqbal al-Tayyar al-Islami." *Minbar al-Sharq* vol. 1, no. 1 (March 1992).

Al-Ghannushi, Rashid. *Al-Hurriyyat al-'Ama fi al-Islam* (Beirut: Center for the Studies of Arab Unity, 1993).

Al-Hamidi, Muhammad al-Hashimi. "Awlawiyyat Muhimma fi Daftar al-Harakat al-Islamiyya: Nahwa Mithaq Islami li al-'Adl wa al-Shura wa Huquq al-Insan." *Al-Mustaqbal al-Islami* no. 2 (November 1991).

Al-Harakat al-Islamiyya fi Muwajahat al-Taswiya (Beirut: Markaz al-Dirasat al-Istratijiyya wa al-Buhuth al-Tawthiq, 1995).

Al-Hudaybi, Hasan. *Du'at la Qudat* (Cairo: 1977).

Al-Husseini, Ishaq Musa. *Moslem Brethren* (Beirut: Khayat's College Book, 1956).

Al-Huwaydi, Fahmi. "Al-Islam wa al-Dimocratiyya" *Al-Mustaqbal al-'Arabi* vol. 12, no. 166 (Beirut: 1992)

Al-Huwaydi, Fahmi. *Al-Harakat al-Islamiyya wa al-Dimoqratiyya* (Beirut: Markaz Dirasat al-Wihda al-"Arabiyya, 1999).

Al-Huwaydi, Fahmi. *Al-Islam wa al-Dimocratiyya* (Cairo: Markaz al-'Ahram li al-Tarjama wa al-Nashr, 1993).

Al-Jabiri Muhammad 'Abid, and Hasan Hanafi. *Hiwar al-Mashriq wa al-Maghrib* (Cairo: Maktabat Madbuli, 1993).

Al-Janhani, Al-Habib. "Al-Sahwa al-Islamiyya fi Bilad al-Sham: Mithal Suriyya." *Al-Harakat al-Islamiyya al-Mu'asira fi al-Watan al-'Arabi* (Beirut: Center for the Studies of Arab Unity, 2nd. ed. 1989).

Al-Jassas, Abu Bakr. *Dirash fi Fikratihi: Bab al-Ijtihad.* Edited and introduced by Zuhayr Kibi (Beirut: Dar al-Muntakhab, 1993).

Al-Jawjari, 'Adil. *Al-Hizb al-Islami* (Cairo: The Arabic Center for Journalism and Publications, 1993).

Al-Kinz, 'Ali. "Al-Islam wa al-Hawiyya: Mulahazat li al-Bahth." In Al-Hirmasi, *Al-Din*, 102.

Al-Mallat, Shibli. *Tajdid al-Fiqh al-Islami, Muhammad Baqr al-Sadr bayna al-Najaf wa Shi'it al-'Alam* (Beirut: Dar al-Nahar, 1997).

Al-Mawdudi, Abu Al-A'la. *Minhaj al-Inqilab al-Islami* (Tripoli: Dar al-Sahwa, 3rd ed. 1981).

Al-Mawdudi, Abu Al-A'la. *Al-Islam and al-Madina al-Haditha* (Cairo: Dar al-Ansar, 1978).

Al-Mawdudi, Abu Al-A'la. *Islamic Law and Constitution* (Lahore: Islamic Publications, 1969).

Al-Mawdudi, Abu Al-A'la. *Nahnu wa al-Hadara al-Gharbiyya* (Cairo: Dar al-Fikr al-'Arab, 1955).

Al-Mawdudi, Abu Al-A'la. *Risalat al-Arkan al-Arba'a* (Kuwait: Dar al-Qalam, 4th ed., 1971).

Al-Mawla, Su'ud. *Min Hasan al-Banna ila Hizb al-Wasat* (Beirut: Markaz al-Bayan al-Thaqafi, 2000).

Al-Mithaq: Juzur al-Nidal al-Watani (Cairo: al-Hay'a al-'Amma li al-Isti'lamat, 1964).

Al-Nabahani, Taqiy Al-Din. *Al-Takatul al-Hizbi* (Jerusalem: n.p., 2nd ed., 1953).

Al-Nabahani, Taqiy Al-Din. *Nizam al-Hukm* (Jerusalem: Matba'at al-Thiryan, 1952).

Al-Qaradawi, Yusuf. *Al-Hal al-Islami: Fariyda wa Darura* (Cairo: Dar al-Shuruq, 1974).

Al-Qaradawi, Yusuf. *Al-Sahwat al-Islamiyya bayna al-Juhud wa al-Tatarruf* (Qatar: Kitab al-Umma, 1984).

Al-Sabihi, Ahmad Shaki. *Mustaqbal al-Mujtama' fi al-Watan al-'Arabi* (Beirut: Center for Arab Unity Studies, 2001).

Al-Saghir, 'Abd al-Majid. *Al-Fikr al-Usuli wa Ishkaliyat al-Sulta al-'Ilmiyya fi al-Islam, Qira'a fi Nash'at 'Ilm al-Usul wa Maqasid al-Shari'a* (Beirut: Dar al-Muntakhab al-'Arabi, 1994).

Al-Sawi, Salah. *Al-Tatarruf al-Dini: Al-Ra'y al-Akhar* (Cairo: Al-Afaq al-Dawliyya li al-I'lam, 1984).

Al-Sayyid, Ridwan and 'Abd al-Ilah Bilqaziz. *Azmat al-Fikr al-Siyasi al-'Arabi* (Damascus and Beirut: Dar al-Fikr al-Mu'asir, 2000).

Al-Sayyid, Ridwan. "Al-Islamiyyun wa al-'Awlama, al-'Alam fi Mir'at al-Hawiyya." *Al-Din wa al-'Awlama wa al-Ta'addudiyya* (Lebanon: Jami'at al-Balamand, 2000).

Al-Sayyid, Ridwan. "Al-Tafakkur al-Islami fi al-Masihiyya fi al-'Usur al-Haditha." *Al-Masihiyya wa al-Islam, Maraya Mutaqabila* (Lebanon: Jami'at al-Balamand, 1997).

Al-Sayyid, Ridwan. "Harakat al-Islam al-Mu'asira: Ta'amulat fi Bi'atiha al-Idiolojiyya wa al-Siyasa." *Siyasat al-Islam al-Mu'asir: Muraja'at wa Mutaba'at* (Beirut: Dar al-Kitab al-'Arabi, 1997).

Al-Sayyid, Ridwan. "Mas'alat Huquq al-Insan fi al-Fikr al-Islami al-Mu'asir," *Al-Abhath* vol. 46 (Beirut: 1998).

Al-Sayyid, Ridwan. *Al-Jama'a wa al-Sulta wa al-Dawla* (Beirut: Dar al-Kitab al-'Arab, 1997).

Al-Shatibi. *Al-Muwafaqat fi Usul al-Ahkam*. Edited by 'Abd Allah Darraz (Egypt: Matba'at al-Taqaddum al-'Ilmiyya, n.d.).

Al-Ta'adudiyya min Manzur Islami. *Fi al-Nizam al-Siyasi li al-Dawla al-Islamiyya* (Cairo: Dar al-Shuruq, 1989).

Al-Ta'adudiyya min Manzur Islami. *Minbar al-Hiwar* vol. 6, no. 20 (Winter 1991).

Al-Turabi, Hasan. *Al-Itijah al-Islami Yuqadim al-Mar'a bayna Ta'alim al-Din wa Taqalid al-Mujtama'* (Jedah: Al-Dar al-Su'udiyya li al-Nashr wa al-Tawzi': 1984).

Al-Turabi, Hasan. *Tajdid Usul al-Fiqh* (Jedah: Al-Dar al-Su'udiyya li al-Nashr wa al-Tawzi', 1984).

Al-Turabi, Hasan. "Awlawiyyat al-Tayyar al-Islami." *Minbar al-Sharq* no. 1 (March 1992).

Al-Turabi, Hasan. "Islam, Democracy, the State and the West: Summary of a Lecture and Roundtable Discussion with Hasan al-Turabi." Prepared by Louis Cantouri and Arthur Lowrie. *Middle East Policy* vol. 1, no. 3 (1992).

Al-Turabi, Hasan. *Al-Iman wa Atharuhu fi Hayat al-Insan* (Jedah: Al-Dar al-Su'udiyya li al-Nashr wa al-Tawzi', 1984).

Al-Turabi, Hasan. *Al-Salat 'Imad al-Din* (Beirut: Dar al-Qalam, 1971).

Al-Turabi, Hasan. *Qadaya al-Hurriyya wa al-Wahda, al-Shura wa al-Dimocratiyya, al-Din wa al-Fan* (Jedah: Al-Dar al-Su'udiyya li al-Nashr wa al-Tawzi', 1987).

Al-Turabi, Hasan. *Tajdid al-Fikr al-Islami* (Jedah: Al-Dar al-Su'udiyya li al-Nashr wa al-Tawzi', 2nd ed. 1987).

Al-Zugul, 'Abd al-Qadir. "Al-Istratijia al-Jadida li Harakat al-Itija al-Islami." In *Al-Din fi al-Mujtama'* (Beirut: Center for the Arab Unity Studies, 1990).

Al-Zuhayli, Wahba. *Haq al-Hurriya fi al-'Alam* (Damascus and Beirut: Dar al-Fikr al-Mu'asir, 2000).

Anderson, Lisa. "Liberalism in Northern Africa." *Current History* vol. 89, no. 546 (April 1990).

Arjomand, Said Amir. *The Turban and the Crown: The Islamic Revolution in Iran* (New York: Oxford University Press, 1988).

Arkun, Muhammad. "Al-Islam al-Mu'asir amam Turathihi wa al-'Awlama." In *Qadaya fi Naqd al-'Aql al-Dini* (Beirut: Dar al-Tali 'a, 1998).

Arrighi, Giovanni. *The Long Twentieth Century* (Chicago, IL: University of Chicago Press, 1994).

Arsalan, Shakib. *Limadha Ta'akhar al-Muslimun wa Taqaddama Khayruhum?* Edited by Sheikh Hasan Tamim (Beirut: Dar al-Maktabat al-Hayat, 1975).

Asad, Talal. "Al-Sulta al-Haditha wa I'adat tashkil al-Taqalid al-Diniyya," an interview done by Siba Mahmud. *Al-Ijtihad* vol. 12, no. 47-48 (Beirut: 2000).

Ayyubi, Nazih. *Al-Dawla al-Markaziyya fi Misr* (Beirut: Center for the Studies of Arab Unity, 1989).

Ayyubi, Nazih. *Political Islam: Religion and Politics in the Arab World* (New York, NY: Routledge, 1991).

Badrul, Hasan. *Milestones* (Karachi: International Islamic Publishers, 1981).

Barakat, Muhammad T. *Sayyid Qutb: Khulasat Hayatih, Minhajuhuh fi al-Haraka wa al-Naqd al-Muwajah ilayh* (Beirut: Dar al-Da'wa, n.d.).

Barghouty, Iyad. "Al-Islam bayna al-Sultah wa al-Mu'arada," in *Qadaya Fikriyya: Al-Islam al-Siyasi, al-Usus al-Fikriyya wa al-Ahdaf al-'Amaliyya* (Cairo: Dar al-Thaqafah al-Jadidah, 1989).

Barut, Muhammad Jamal. *Yathrib al-Haditha: al-Harakat al-Islamiyya al-Rahina* (Beirut: Dar Riad al-Rayyis, 1994).

Batatu, Hanna. "Syrian Muslim Brethren." In F. Halliday and H. Alawi (eds) *State and Ideology in the Middle East* (London: 1988).

Berger, Peter L. *The Sacred Canopy: Elements of a Sociological Theory of Religion* (Garden City, NY: Doubleday and Company, 1967).

Binder, Leonard. *Islamic Liberalism: A Critique of Development Ideologies* (Chicago, IL: University of Chicago Press, 1972).

Bruce, Steve. *Religion in the Modern World: From Cathedrals to Cults* (Oxford: Oxford University Press, 1996).

Butterworth, Charles E. *Political Islam. ANNALS*, AAPSS, 524 (November, 1992).

Chueiri, Yousef. *Islamic Fundamentalism* (Boston: Twayne, 1990).

Commins, David. *Al-Islah al-Islami*. Translated by Muhammad Majid al-Radi (Damascus: Dar al-Hasad, 1999).

Darraj, Faysal and Jamal Barut (eds) *Al-Ahzab wa al-Harakat wa al-Jama'at al-Islamiyya* vol. 2 (Damascus: Al-Markaz al-'Arabi li al-Dirasat al-Isratijiyya, 1999).

Diab, Muhammad Hafiz. *Sayyid Qutb: al-Khitab wa al-Idiologia* (Beirut: Dar al-Tali'a, 1988).

Didier, Hugue. "Al-Islam wa al-Muqaddas." *Mawaqif* no. 65 (Beirut: Fall 1991).

[233]

Dobbelaere, Karel. "Secularization: A Multi-Dimensional Concept." *Current Sociology* vol. 29, no. 2 (Summer 1981).

Eickelman, Dale and James Piscatori. *Muslim Politics* (Princeton, NJ: Princeton University Press, 1996).

Eickelman, Dale. "Changing Interpretations of Islamic Movements." William Roff (ed.) *Islam and the Political Economy of Meaning* (London: Croom Helm, 1987).

El-Affendi, Abdulwahhab (ed.) *Rethinking Islam and Modernity: Essays in Honor of Fathi Osman* (Leicester: Islamic Foundation, 2001).

El-Affendi, Abdulwahhab. "Studying My Movement: Social Science without Cynicism." *International Journal of Middle Eastern Studies* 23 (1991).

El-Affendi, Abdulwahhab. "The Long March from Lahore to Khartoum: Beyond the Muslim Reformation." *BRISMES Bulletin* vol. 17, no. 2 (1990).

El-Affendi, Abdulwahhab. *Al-Islam wa al-Dawla al-Haditha: Nahwa Ru'ya Jadida* (London: Dar al-Hikma, 2000).

El-Affendi, Abdulwahhab. *Al-Thawra wa al-Islah al-Siyasi fi al-Sudan* (London: Muntada Ibn Rushd, 1995).

El-Affendi, Abdulwahhab. *Turabi's Revolution: Islam and Power in Sudan* (London: Grey Seal Books, 1991).

Enayat, Hamid. *Al-Fikr al-Siyasi al-Islami al-Mu'asir*. Translated by Ibrahim al-Dusuqi Basha (Cairo: Dar al-Zahra' li al-Nashr, 1988).

Esposito, John, and James Piscatori. "Democratization and Islam." *Middle East Journal* vol. 45, no. 3 (Summer 1991).

Esposito, John. "Political islam: Beyond the Green Menace." *Current History* vol. 93 (January 1994).

Esposito, John. *Political Islam: Revolution, Radicalism, or Reform* (Boulder, CO: Lynne Rienner Publishers, 1997).

Esposito, John. *The Islamic Threat: Myth and Reality?* (New York, NY: Oxford University Press, 1991).

Euben, R.L. *Enemy in the Mirror, Islamic Fundamentalism and the Limit of Modern Rationalism* (Princeton, NJ: Princeton University Press, 1999).

Fenn, Richard K. "The Process of Secularization: A Post-Parsonian View." *Journal for the Scientific Study of Religion* vol. 9, no. 2 (Summer 1970).

Flores, Alexander. "Secularism, Integralism and Political Islam." *Middle East Report* no. 183 (July-August 1993).

Frumakin, David. *Salam ma Ba'dahu Salam: Wiladat al-Sharq al-Awsat 1914-1922*. Translated by As'ad Ilias (Beirut: Dar Riad al-Rayyis, 1992).

Fuller, Graham. "Islamic Fundamentalism." *Washington Post*, January 19, 1992.

Gellner, Earnest. "Fundamentalism as a Comprehensive System: Soviet Marxism and Islamic Fundamentalism." In Martin Marty and Scott Appleby (eds) *Fundamentalisms Observed* (Chicago, IL: Chicago University Press, 1995).

Gellner, Earnest. *Conditions of Liberty: Civil Society and its Rivals* (London: Penguin Books, 1994).

Gibb, H.A.R. *Modern Trends in Islam* (New York, NY: Octagon Press, 1947).

Guazzone, Laura (ed.) *The Islamist Dilemma: The Political Role of Islamist Movements in the Contemporary Arab World* (New York, NY: Ithaca, 1996).

Gusfield, Joseph (ed.) *Protest, Reform and Revolt: A Reader in Social Movements* (New York, NY: John Wiley and Sons Inc., 1970).

Haddad, Yvonne. "Sayyid Qutb: Ideologue of Islamic Revival." In John Esposito (ed.) *Voices of Resurgent Islam* (New York, NY: Oxford University Press, 1982).

Haddad, Yvonne. "The Qur'anic Justification for an Islamic Revolution." *Middle East Journal* vol. 37, no. 1 (Winter 1983).

Halliday, Fred. *Al-Umma wa al-Din fi al-Sharq al-Awsat*. Translated by 'Abd al-Ilah al-Nu'aymi (Beirut: Dar al-Saqi, 1995).

Halliday, Fred. *Islam and the Myth of Confrontation* (London: I.B. Tauris, 1995).

Hanafi, Hasan. "Al-Din wa al-Thawra al-'Arabiyya." *Al-Din wa al-Thawra fi Misr 1952-1981: Al-Din wa al-Nidal al-Watani* vol. 3 (Cairo: Maktabat Madbuli, 1989).

Hanafi, Hasan. "Turath al-Sulta wa Turath al-Mu'arada." *Humum al-Fikr wa al-Watan: Al-Turath wa al-'Asr wa al-Nidal al-Watani* vol. 1 (Cairo: Maktabat Madbuli, 1988).

Hanafi, Hasan. *Min al-'Aqida ila al-Thawra: Muqaddimat Nazariyya* vol. 1 (Cairo: Maktabat Madhbuli, 1988).

Hanafi, Hasan. *Muqaddima fi 'Ilm al-Istighrab* (Cairo: Al-Dar al-Fanniyya, 1991).

Hawwa, Sa'id. *Al-Madkhal ila Da'wat al-Ikhwan al-Muslimin bi-Munasabat Khamsin 'Aman 'ala Ta'sisiha* (Amman: Dar al-Arqam, 2nd ed., 1979).

Hiro, Dilip. *The Rise of Islamic Fundamentalism* (New York, NY: Routledge, 1989).

Hunter, Shireen. *The Future of Islam and the West, Clash of Civilizations or Peaceful Coexistence* (Reading: Ithaca Press, 1998).

Huntington, Samuel. "Clash of Civilizations." *Foreign Affairs* vol. 72, no. 3 (Summer 1993).

Hussain, Asaf. *Islamic Movements in Egypt, Pakistan, and Iran* (Great Britain: Mansell Publishing Limited, 1983).

Ja'far, Hisham. "Al-Harakat al-Islamiyya wa ma ba'da al-Siyasa." *Majallat al-Mujtama'*, March 2, 1999.

Jid'an, Fahmi. *Usus al-Taqaddum 'inda Mufakkiri al-Islam fi al-Qarn al-Tasi' 'Ashar* (Beirut: Al-Mu'assasa al-'Arabiyya li al-Dirasat wa al-Nashir, 1981).

Jourshi, Salah Al-Din. "Al-Haraka al-Islamiyya Mustaqbaluha Rahin al-Taghiyrat al-Jazriyya." In 'Abd Allah Al-Nafisi (ed.) *Al-Harakat al-Islamiyya: Ru'uah Mustaqbaliyya, Awraq fi al-Naqd al-Dhati* (Cairo: Maktabat Madbuli, 1989).

Kawtharani, Wajih. *Al-Dawla wa al-Khilafa fi al-Khitab al-'Arabi ibbana al-Thawra al-Kamaliyya* (Beirut: Dar al-Tali'a, 1996).

Kawtharani, Wajih. *Mukhtarat Siyasiyya min Majallat al-Manar* (Beirut: Dar al-Tali'a, 1980).

Keddie, Nikki. *An Islamic Response to Imperialism: Political and Religious Writings of Sayyid Jamal Al-Din Al-Afghani* (Berkeley: University of California Press, 1968).

Keegan, John. *The First World War* (Santa Monica, CA: Rand Corporation, 2000).

Kepel, Gilles. "Islamism Reconsidered." *Harvard International Review* vol. 22, no. 2 (Summer 2000).

[236]

Kepel, Gilles. *The Prophet and the Pharaoh: Muslim Extremism in Egypt* (London: Alsaqi Books, 1985).

Kerr, Malcolm. *Islamic Reform: the Political and Legal Theories of Muhammad Abduh and Rashid Rida* (Berkeley, CA: University of California Press, 1966).

Kerr, Malcolm. *The Arab Cold War, 1958-1968* (Berkeley, CA: University of California Press, 1971).

Khalid, Detleve, "The Phenomenon of Re-Islamization." *Aussenpolitik* no. 29 (1978).

Khalidi, Salah A. *Sayyid Qutb, al-Shahid al-Hay* (Amman: Dar al-Firqan, 1983).

Khallafallah, Muhammad Ahmad. "Al-Sahwa al-Islamiyya fi Misr." *Al-Harakat al-Islamiyya fi al-Watan al-'Arabi* (Beirut: Markaz Dirasat al-Wihda al-'Arabiyya, 1987).

Khashan, Hilal. "The Quagmire of Arab Democracy." *Arab Studies Quarterly* vol. 1, no. 1 (Winter 1992).

Kramer, Gudrun "Al-Islamiyyun wa al-Hadith 'an al-Dimoqratiyya. " *Al-Ijtihad* vol. 5, no. 21 (Beirut: 1993).

Kramer, Gudrun. "Islamist Democracy." *Middle East Report* Issue 183, vol. 23, no. 4 (July-August1993).

Kramer, Gudrun. "Liberalization and Democracy in the Arab World." *Middle East Report* Issue 174, vol. 22, no. 1 (January-February 1992).

Kramer, Martin. "Fundamentalism at Large: The Drive for Power." *Middle East Quarterly* vol. 3, no. 2 (June 1996).

Lapidus, Ira M. "The Separation of State and Religion in the Development of Early Islamic Society." *International Journal of Middle Eastern Studies* vol. 6, no. 4 (1975).

Lawrence, Bruce. *Defenders of God: The Revolt against the Modern Age* (San Francisco, CA: Harper and Row, 1989).

Lecca, Jean. "Al-Taharruk nahwa al-Dimoqratiyya fi al-Watan al-'Arabi." In Ghassan Salama (ed.) *Dimocratiyya min Dun Dimoqratiyyin: Siyasat al-Infitah fi al-'Alam al-Arabi/al-Islami* (Beirut: Center for the Arab Unity Studies, 1995).

Lewis, Bernard. "Islam and Liberal Democracy." *The Atlantic Monthly* (February 1993).

[237]

Lothrop, Steward. *Hadir al-'Alam al-Islami.* Translation by 'Ajaj Nuwayhid and commentary by Al-Amir Shakib Arsalan (Egypt: Al-Matba'at al-Salafiyya, 1925).

Luckman, Thomas. "The Structural Conditions of Religious Consciousness in Modern Societies." *Japanese Journal of Religious Studies* vol. 6, no.1/2 (1979).

Mahfuz, Muhammad. *Alladhina Zulimu* (London: Riad al-Rayyis Books Ltd., 1988).

Mahmud, Abd Al-Halim. *Al-Ikhwan al-Muslimun: Ahdath Sana'at al-Tarikh* (Cairo: Dar al-Da'wa, 1979).

Marty, Martin E. and R. Scott Appleby (eds) *Fundamentalisms Observed* (Chicago, IL: University of Chicago Press, 1991).

Mayer, A. E. *Islam and Human Rights: Traditions and Politics* (Boulder, CO: Westview Press, 2nd ed., 1991).

Memoirs of Hasan al-Banna Shaheed. Translated by M. N. Shaikh (Karachi: International Islamic Publishers, 1981).

Miller, Judith. "The Challenge of Radical Islam." *Foreign Affairs* vol. 72, no. 2, 1993.

Mitchell, Richard. *The Society of Muslim Brothers* (London: Oxford University Press, 1964).

Moussali, Ahmad S. "Hasan al-Banna's Islamist Discourse on Constitutional Rule and Islamic State." Journal of Islamic Studies vol. 4. no. 2 (1993).

Moussalli, Ahmad S. (ed.) *Islamic Fundamentalism: Myths and Realities* (Reading: Ithaca Press, 1998).

Moussalli, Ahmad S. *Al-Khitab al-Islami al-Usuli: Nazariyyat al-Ma'rifa wa al-Dawla wa al-Mujtama'* (Beirut: al-Nashir li al-Tiba'a wa al-Tawzi' wa al-'Ilan, 1993).

Moussalli, Ahmad S. *Al-Usuliyya al-Islamiyya: Dirasa fi al-Khitab al-Idioloji wa al-Siyasi 'inda Sayyid Qutb, Bahth Muqaran li Mabadi' al-Usuliyyin wa al-Islahiyyin* (Beirut: Al-Nashir li al-Tiba'a wa al-Nashr wa al-Tawzi' wa al-I'lan, 1993).

Moussalli, Ahmad S. *Moderate and Radical Islamic Fundamentalism: The Quest for Modernity, Legitimacy, and the Islamic State* (Gainsville, FL: University Press of Florida, 1999).

Moussalli, Ahmad S. *Radical Islamic Fundamentalism: The Ideological and Political Discourse of Sayyid Qutb* (Beirut: American University of Beirut, 1992).

Muharram, Muhammad Rida. *Tahdith al-'Aql al-Siyasi al-Islami* (Cairo: Dar Sina li al-Nashr, 1986).

Munson, Henry. *Islam and Revolution in the Middle East* (New Haven, CT: Yale University Press, 1988).

Pipes, Daniel. *In the Path of God: Islam and Political Power* (New York, NY: Basic Books, 1983).

Piscatori, James (ed.) *Islamic Fundamentalism and the Gulf Crisis* (Chicago, IL: University of Chicago Press, 1991).

Qutb, Muhammad. *Jahiliyyat al-Qarn al-'Ishrin* (Cairo: Maktabat Wahba, 1965).

Qutb, Sayyid. *Da'wat al-Ikhwan al-Muslimun wa 'Abqariyat bina' Jama'atiha* (Alexandria: Dar al-Qadisiyya, n. d.).

Qutb, Sayyid. *Fi al-Tarikh, Fikra wa Minhaj* (Cairo: Dar al-Shuruq, 1974).

Qutb, Sayyid. *Fiqh al-Da'wa* (Beirut: Mu'assasat al-Risala, 1970).

Qutb, Sayyid. *Hadha al-Din* (Cairo: Maktabat Wahbah, 4th ed., n.d.).

Qutb, Sayyid. *Tafsir Ayat al-Riba* (Beirut: Dar al-Shuruq, 1970).

Qutb, Sayyid. *Al-'Adala al-Ijtima'iyya fi al-Islam* (Cairo: Dar al-Shuruq, 7th ed. 1980).

Qutb, Sayyid. *Al-Islam wa Mushkilat al-Hadara* (Beirut: Dar al-Shuruq 8th ed. 1983).

Qutb, Sayyid. *Al-Mustaqbal li Hadha al-Din* (Cairo: Maktabat Wahba, 1965).

Qutb, Sayyid. *Ma'alim fi al-Tariq* (Beirut: Al-Itihad al-Islami al-'Alami li al-Muhazamat al-Tulabiyya, 1987).

Qutb, Sayyid. *Ma'alim fi al-Tariq* (Beirut: Dar al-Shuruq, 7th ed. 1980).

Qutb, Sayyid. *Marakat al-Islam wa al-Ra'simaliyya* (Beirut: Dar al-Shuruq, 4th ed. 1980).

Qutb, Sayyid. *Nahwa Mujtama' Islami* (Beirut: Dar al-Shuruq, 5th ed. 1982).

Reissner, G. *Die Muslim Bruder in Syrien* (Freiburg: Schwarz Verlan, 1973).

Roff, William (ed.) *Islam and the Political Economy of Meaning* (London: Croom Helm, 1987).

Roy, Olivier. *The Failure of Political Islam* (Cambridge, MA: Harvard University Press, 1994).

Said, Edward. *Orientalism* (London: Routledge and Kegan Paul, 1978).

Salame, Ghassan (ed.) "Islam and the West." *Foreign Policy* no. 90 (Spring 1993).

Salame, Ghassan (ed.) *Democracy without Democrats?* (London: I.B. Tauris, 1994).

Salvatore, Armando. "Discursive Contentions in Islamic Terms: Fundamentalism versus Liberalism?" In Moussalli, *Myths and Reality*.

Salvatore, Armando. *Islam and the Political Discourse of Modernity* (Reading: Ithaca Press, 1997).

Sami', Salih Hasan. *Azmat al-Hurriyya al-Siyasiyya fi al-Watan al-'Arabi* (Cairo: Al-Zahra' li al-I'lam al-'Arabi, 1988).

Sardar, Zia, *Orientalism* (Buckingham: Open University, 1999).

Shafiq, Munir. "Awlawiyyat amam al-Ijtihad wa al-Tajdid." *Al-Ijtihad wa Tajdid fi al-Fikr al-Islami al-Mu'asir* (Malta: Center for the Studies of the Muslim World, 1991).

Sisk, Timothy D. *Islam and Democracy* (Washington, DC: United States Peace Institute Press, 1992).

Sivan, Emanuel. *Radical Islam, Medieval Theology and Modern Politics* (New Haven, CT: Yale University Press, 1985).

Smith, Charles. "The Crisis of Orientalism, The Shift of Egyptian Intellectuals to Islamic Subjects in the 1930s." *International Journal of Middle East Studies* vol. 4 (1973).

Tessler, Mark. "The Origins of Popular Support for Islamist Movements." In John Entelis (ed.) *Islam, Democracy, and the State in North Africa* (Bloomington, IN: Indiana University Press, 1997).

Tibi, Bassam. *The Challenge of Fundamentalism: Political Islam and the New World Disorder* (Berkeley and Los Angeles, CA: University of California Press, 1988).

Turner, Bryan. *Orientalism, Postmodernism and Globalization* (London: Routledge, 1994).

Voll, John. "Wahhabism and Mahdism: Alternative Syles of Islamic Renewal." *Arab Studies Quarterly* vol. 4 (1982).

Voll, John. *Continuity and Change in the Modern World* (Syracuse, NY: Syracuse University Press, 1994).

Walsh, James. "The Sword of Islam." *Time International* (June 15, 1992).

Weber, Max et al (eds) *From Max Weber* (London: Routledge and Kegan Paul, 1970).

Wilkinson, Paul. *Social Movements* (New York, NY: Praeger Publishers, 1971).

Will Democracy Survive in Egypt? *Reader's Digest* vol. 131, no. 788 (Canadian Edition, December 1987).

Wilson, Bryan. "Aspects of Secularization in the West." *Japanese Journal of Religious Studies* vol. 3, no. 3/4 (1976).

Wilson, John. *Introduction to Social Movements* (New York, NY: Basic Books, 1973).

Zartman, William. "Democracy and Islam: The Cultural Dialectic." *ANNALS*, AAPSS 524 (November, 1992).

INDEX

A

Abdu, Muhammad 18, 19, 20, 30, 67
  and "Islamic awakening" 95
  moderate views of 90, 124–125
  national party program 59
  opposes revolution 62
  politics vs education 34
Abraham, Prophet 54
Afghan Arabs 156, 185
Afghanistan
  assisted by West 156, 182
  Islamic rule in 45, 73, 75, 171
  war in 182
Africa 90
Ahmad, Akbar S. 118
Al-Afghani, Jamal Al-Din 16, 62, 95
  anti-colonialism of 30, 58–59
  calls for Arab unity 59
  development of political Islam 58–59
  Islam and the state 34
  and "Islamic awakening" 95
  and modern Islamic movements 18, 19–20, 50
  opposition to radicalism 123
  politics vs education 34
  and scientific progress 16
  United States experience 145
Al-Aqsa Mosque 62, 88
Al-'Awwa, Muhammad S. 137–138
Al-Azhar 36, 125, 130
Al-Azhar, Sheikh 124
Al-Banna, Hasan 20, 31, 178, 179
  acceptance of all religions 134
  acceptance of pluralism/democracy 134
  assassination 63, 67, 72, 75, 131, 145
  call for political inclusion 117, 129–130, 132

  and collapse of Caliphate 36–37
  denunciation of Egyptian politics 132
  and Egyptian nationhood 33
  Islam and the state 34, 133
  and Muslim Brotherhood 31, 32, 62–63
Al-Bishri, Tariq 29–30, 35, 187
Al-Dalhawiyya 30, 36
Al-Dhahabi, Sheikh 70
Al-Din, Nasr, Shah of Persia 19–20
Al-Fasi, 'Allal 59
Al-Ghannushi, Rashid 142–144, 195
Al-Ghazali, Abu Hamid 24, 90, 181
Al-Hamidi, Muhammad Al-Hashim 144
Al-Haq, Sheikh Jad 124–125
Al-Haq, Zia 44
Al-Hizb al-Jumhuri (Sudan) 8
Al-Hudaybi, Hasan 182
Al-Ikhwan al-Muslimun 131, 146
Al-Inqadh, Jabhat 144
Al-Jama 'al-Islamiyya al-Jihadiyya 152
Al-Mahdiyya movement 30, 61
Al-Mawdudi, Abu Al-A'la 21–22, 32–33, 41
  and Caliphate movement 36–37
  criticism of West 176
  and isolation of Islamic groups 34, 35
  and *jahiliyya* 35
  and Qur'anic vice-regency 178–179
Al-Mubarak, Muhammad 181–182
Al-Nabahani, Taqiy Al-Din
  persecution of 136
  on political parties 134–135
Al-Nahda 40, 132
Al-Nasir, Jamal 'Abd 43, 69